THE PRINCIPLES AND PRACTICE OF HAIRDRESSING

LEO PALLADINO, B.A., M.I.T.

*Head of Department of Social and Scientific Studies,
Gloucestershire College of Arts and Technology*

Second Edition

MACMILLAN

First edition 1972
Reprinted 1974 (with corrections), 1977 (twice), 1978, 1980
1981
Second edition 1983
Reprinted 1983, 1984 (twice), 1985, 1986

Published by
Higher and Further Education Division
MACMILLAN PUBLISHERS LTD
Houndmills, Basingstoke, Hampshire RG21 2XS
and London
Companies and representatives
throughout the world

Printed in Hong Kong

ISBN 0-333-34903-2

Contents

epidermis and layers, the dermis, papillary and reticular layers. Subcutaneous tissue. 10. The scalp and epicranial aponeurosis. 11. The skull — bones of the head and face. 12. Hair growth — replacement, growing stages, activation. Influencing factors — health and diet, components of diet, age and sex, hormones, endocrine ductless glands. Heredity, climate and seasons, physical conditions. Disease. 13. Hair shape formation.
Revision tests and vocabulary.

8. Electrolysis, epilation and depilatories. 9. Science of hair care. 10. Aesthetics and hair care. 11. Hair care and postiche.
Revision tests and vocabulary.

Preface to the First Edition

This book is intended to be used by all engaged in hairdressing, particularly by students and apprentices taking qualifying examinations. It is of special use to those studying courses offered by the City and Guilds of London Institute, and the Hairdressing Council. I hope that all students will find the text of interest and that the book will provide a systematic guide to the course from the first simple introduction to the craft up to advanced standards of proficiency.

The book is an integrated one, relating other subjects, particularly hairdressing science, and art, to the techniques and skills of hairdressing. Each chapter may be read separately in any order; the first part in each chapter gives an introduction to the subject, and parts 2 and 3 build on the basic fundamentals so as to introduce the more advanced work.

Several chapters may more profitably be read in conjunction with one another. For example, Chapters 3, 5, 6 and 7 deal with temporary and permanent curling or waving. Chapters 8, 9 and 10 deal with cutting, dressing or hairstyling, and are intended to complement one another. Chapters 12, 13 and 14 deal with the structure of hair and skin, its care and the recognition of common skin diseases, and are best read together. The other chapters stand independently, particularly those on shampooing and colouring, though they remain of course essential parts of the whole.

The final chapter, 15, is intended as a guide to the work as a whole and is an endeavour to represent visually the relationship between each of the main topics. This, it is thought, will be of value to the student and to the lecturer working in a controlled college course, and it will also greatly benefit those others who may use the book in a self-teaching situation. Every attempt has been made to present the most suitable methods in hairdressing techniques, and a number of variants have been included, bearing in mind the limitations imposed by the final length of the book.

I should like to take this opportunity of acknowledging with sincere thanks all those who have been responsible for the production of the book; in particular I wish to record my gratitude to my wife who has read and re-read the script at every stage, and to my family for their forebearance during the period in which it was written. I have to thank Stanley Thornes, of the Macmillan Press, for his continued help .and encouragement; Douglas Bartrick for his help with the photography and illustration classification; Janice Herriman for reading and checking the science content; Sue Simpson, of Oxford Illustrators, for her help and work on the line drawings; H. K. Heppell, Principal of Gloucester Technical College, for reading and commenting on a large part of the script; to those who taught me my craft, and all those friends and colleagues in hairdressing, education and related organizations for their great help and encouragement.

LEO PALLADINO

January 1972

Preface to the Second Edition

Since the first edition was published in 1972, the changes in hairdressing that have taken place confirm what was featured in the original edition: namely, that a knowledge and understanding of the basic principles and techniques enable most students to adapt to the inevitable changes that come about through time.

The popularity with blow styling continues. The amount of styling with hot brushes has really come to the fore, particularly for home use. This has emphasized still more the importance of good hair cutting and shaping. Systems of perming and conditioning, too, have improved and the effects of better-looking hair and style are most acceptable.

The emphasis that was placed on the relation of practical hairdressing to science, art and wigmaking is still vitally necessary for the aspiring young professional hairdresser.

In this edition illustrations have been changed in some areas to help clarify the points being made, and a new appendix has been added to give the now frequently used European percentage strengths of hydrogen peroxide. The ordering of the text of Chapter 15 has been altered so as to stress much more strongly the importance of related subjects to practical techniques.

It is my hope that this edition will continue to cater for the needs of the prospective and practising student of hairdressing.

September 1982   LEO PALLADINO

Acknowledgements

The Leonardo da Vinci original in the Royal Library, Windsor Castle, which appears in this book as Fig. 4.11, is reproduced by gracious permission of Her Majesty the Queen.

The author and publishers gratefully acknowledge the assistance given by the following in providing other illustrative material for this book: The Institute of Dermatology, University of London; Messrs Wella (Gt. Britain) Ltd; Messrs Teeda Ltd, London; Messrs Cavendish House Ltd, Cheltenham; Messrs Serventi Ltd, London; Messrs Walker Crosweller Ltd, Cheltenham.

L. P.

Chapter One

Introduction

1. Hairdressing, the practice of working with growing hair, consists of cleaning or shampooing, curling or waving, cutting, colouring, bleaching and decolouring, styling and dressing, and care and conditioning. The hairdresser is faced with a host of techniques, and the principles underlying them must be mastered before they can be used effectively. To this end related subjects are included in the training of young hairdressers.

2. The aim of good hairdressing is to apply artistic skill and knowledge to the enhancement of the client's appearance, in a way which yields satisfaction to both parties. This involves knowledge and understanding of people, an appreciation of art, beauty or aesthetics, and the effects of social contact.

Knowledge of hair structure and the systems of the human body proves an invaluable aid when application of techniques and procedures is made. Since nearly all the materials used may in one way or another affect the body, a study of related science, including basic chemistry, anatomy and physiology, hygiene and possible effects on the body, should be made.

Communication, by spoken and by written word, is a vital tool of the hairdresser. Without the facility to listen, understand and express oneself clearly, e.g. addressing clients correctly or writing a businesslike letter, the management of business or career is heavily handicapped.

Boardwork, i.e. the working of hair after it is separated from the head, and postiche, i.e. the dressed hair piece, are now rewarding and popular aspects of hairdressing. Throughout the working life of a hairdresser a knowledge of postiche, its making and dressing, can prove invaluable.

3. The hairdresser, whilst benefiting from the application of knowledge of other subjects, must always base his work on a thorough understanding and competence in the techniques of the craft. There is a vast heritage of hairdressing work and knowledge which lies behind the modern hairdresser, and which the successful have not ignored.

In the past the barber surgeons, as hairdressers were then known, not only cut hair but performed minor surgical procedures and extracted teeth; others specialized in dressings of hair including fantasy postiche, and further specialization in work on men or women produced the ladies' and men's hairdressers. Nowadays there is a tendency for hairdressing to become unisexual both in the salons and styles of work carried out.

Today the variety of styles and fashions, multiplicity of methods, the integration afforded with other crafts, businesses, subjects and interests and the personalities and individuals involved, offers the young hairdresser a lifetime of enjoyment, achievement and satisfaction, if true professional standards of craftsmanship are attained.

4. Methods of training. Several routes to professional qualification are open to would-be hairdressers.

On leaving school one may become an apprentice for a period of three years in a well-conducted salon. During this time the salon training should be augmented by attendance at a technical college or college of further education where a course of study, leading to recognized examinations and qualifications, may be followed. These courses taken at a technical college may require release from the salon on one day a week; or alternatively block release, which covers several weeks of full-time attendance in which all the necessary work is done in preparation for the examinations, and in which total attendance is roughly the same as would be achieved by day release.

An accepted alternative to apprenticeship is the two-year full-time training course, usually at a college of further education. Here the training period is conducted in properly equipped salons where all the work in theory and practice is carried out. Usually the college courses work in conjunction with the local and national hairdressing requirements, and a day-release scheme from college to an outside salon may be operated. After completing examinations at the end of two years the full-time student is accepted as equal in status to the three-year-trained apprentice, whom he or she may then join in the hairdressing craft.

There are schools, run on a commercial basis, where one may learn hairdressing. This presents an easy, and probably the most convenient, means of entry to the craft for the adult, mature student. These private schools require students to study for periods of three to six months, or longer if necessary, after which, with school examinations passed, they enter the craft. Some schools are well known for their good results and are generally accepted.

Apart from the initial training periods, further experience may profitably be gained by attendance at a variety of manufacturers' schools, where the student hairdresser is trained in the correct use of their products. This is very useful and enables the student to acquire a varied and interesting range of experience of different methods and products.

Recognized courses and examinations. Courses of study may differ in detail from each other, but they are planned with similar ends in view by members of the craft and teachers who have studied carefully the requirements which need to be fulfilled by the competent hairdresser.

The examinations accepted generally in Great Britain are those of the City and Guilds of London Institute, the Hairdressing Council, and the Incorporated Guild of Wigmakers, Perfumers and Hairdressers. Most of these are available at technical colleges and colleges of further education throughout the country.

Prior to the more general provision of courses in Local Education Authority colleges, a body known as the Academy Directorate regulated courses and examinations at private academies, and for many years provided the only avenue to recognized qualifications. This body still makes a valued contribution to the training of hairdressers by continuing its traditionally accepted work.

Further information may be acquired of courses and examinations by writing to the organizations listed as follows:

City and Guilds of London Institute,
76 Portland Place, London, W.1

Hairdressing Council, 39 Grafton Way, London, W.1

The Incorporated Guild of Hairdressers,
33 Great Queen Street, London, W.1

The Academy Directorate of Great Britain,
2 Skinner Street, Gillingham, Kent

and to local colleges of further education, private hairdressing schools and manufacturers of hairdressing products.

5. The course of study and training is important and it is necessary, at the end of it, that the hairdresser should know what to do, how to do it safely and satisfactorily, and to achieve the results required. Knowing in theory without being able to achieve it in practice is not good enough, e.g. understanding colour without application does not help, and knowing the chemistry of processes will not enable them to be practically applied. An all-round

knowledge in practice and theory is required, on which further skills may be built.

In the beginning the young hairdresser is faced with many small points which later are recognized to be fundamentally important.

Among these are the standards of *hygiene,* appearance and deportment. Bad personal hygiene can result in ill-health and, in one who has close daily contact with others in the salon, can be most unpleasant; therefore it is in the interest of every hairdresser to be clean and fresh at all times. Many prospective clients will be influenced by first impressions, and an unkempt dirty appearance will neither encourage them to attend the salon nor allow hairdressing, no matter how good, to be carried out.

Deportment, the way one stands, walks and conducts oneself, is equally important, and adopting the correct postures when working will enable the various techniques to be carried out with the minimum of effort and fatigue.

Attitude. Personal attitudes towards the many people encountered daily in the salon are reflected in the way one feels, thinks and acts towards them, i.e. client, employer, manager and teacher. This in turn will affect their attitudes and how much is returned in custom, time and training. One must learn to live with people; to listen and not do too much talking until one has learnt to speak constructively; to be pleasant and courteous, but never obsequious. One should try to be helpful, respectful and friendly.

It requires patience and time to achieve the right relationships with colleagues, clients and others, but the effort is found to be rewarding in that work is enjoyed besides being well done.

Attitude to fashion and dress needs to be such that good taste is displayed by wearing suitable clothes, colours and make-up, which will attract respect and admiration, whilst avoiding extremes or theatrical effects in one's appearance.

Punctuality is always important, since most business in the salon is based on an appointment system which makes good use of time. A client cannot be attended to if she leaves because the assistant has failed to arrive on time. Always try to be early for appointments, lectures or interviews.

The client should be promptly welcomed, and politely attended throughout her stay in the salon. She must never be allowed to feel that she is a nuisance or in the way, since this engenders dissatisfaction, leading to loss of patronage.

The appointment book should be carefully treated and all insertions neatly and correctly entered, preferably with pencil so that erasures or changes may be easily made. This helps to prevent mistakes and enables the client's name to be readily recognized. Record systems are designed to record past hairdressing, which enables it to be accurately repeated if required, e.g. a colour record card should give the type, number and colour, full details of work done and the results achieved. If appointments, and details of work, are not accurately and carefully recorded, the systems are rendered useless and this results in the client being inconvenienced, often to the detriment of the salon and all concerned.

The telephone, although a vital aid in the salon, is often neglected. When it rings, a client is at the other end of the line who deserves the same prompt attention as a client arriving in person. Always answer clearly, giving the name of the salon and its number. Make a habit of immediately recording the message or information given.

6. Salon training. After the first few weeks in a salon, when the junior has become familiar with the storage places of materials and equipment, and used to attending to people, a start may be made in learning the use of tools. Preliminary exercises to cultivate the co-ordination of hands, eyes, tools and hair are practised, using practice hair and blocks to simulate heads and, as skill is developed, a start may be made upon simple procedures with live models.

This will present a new set of problems; each head has its own peculiarities, and a great deal more care and judgement needs to be exercised. If the preparatory work has been thorough and the methods and techniques understood, then success will soon follow.

During training the work must of necessity be slow, so that sufficient time may be given to perfecting techniques; greater speed of working can be developed when correct working methods are thoroughly understood. Problems will be encountered which can be overcome with patient practice and careful guidance.

One of the biggest problems met with is the wide variety of techniques and methods, and the way they may be individually applied. To the young student this is confusing, and it helps to concentrate and learn one technique at a time, without attempting too much at once. Generally, there are several methods of achieving a desired end result. If the desired result is achieved, the method is correct; if it is not, then the method was faulty or was wrongly applied. It is only after good results have been achieved that a young hairdresser can understand and compare different methods.

7. Hairdressing courses and examinations will entail reading, discussion, note-taking and note-making. Throughout the course practical methods of work will be discussed and it is usual for the main points and outlines to be clearly noted for later study. Further notes may be compiled and added, such as experience of a particular technique, methods used, time taken, results achieved and mistakes and corrections listed. These will be useful at later stages for revising work done or checking some forgotten detail; they may serve as a guide to another junior hairdresser. Some examination bodies require a written record of course work which is assessed as evidence of progress, and for this purpose an individual set of notes, neatly compiled, is better than a set identical with those of others in the class.

If work is done regularly, on time, so that it does not pile up, there will be time for revision or for looking up points not fully understood in the days before the examinations. This applies to practical work as well as to theory, and it results in the student being competent in the material of the course, which is the only satisfactory preparation for any examination.

After passing the basic examination a more advanced one may be the next step; since this is usually an extension of basic work done, the notebooks and all work previously compiled will be found valuable.

8. The principles and practice of hairdressing. It is not possible to become a hairdresser solely by reading a book; nevertheless the chapters which follow will serve as a guide to the young trainee and to the practising hairdresser preparing for craft examinations. Each chapter deals with an aspect of hairdressing together with related subjects, and although each may be read and studied separately, many of them are to some extent dependent on others.

The chapters on cutting, styling and dressing are closely interdependent and, as in practical work, one cannot be taken in isolation.

Hair structure and diseases of the skin and hair have been treated separately since they arise in many parts of the work, and treatment of diseases has been specifically excluded for the obvious reason that it lies outside the province of the hairdresser.

If the following words contribute to the professional thinking and practice of hairdressing, and to the success of young future hairdressers, the efforts and hopes of all involved in compiling them will have been fulfilled.

Reception and Client Preparation

1. Reception of the client precedes any practical hairdressing and sets the tone between client and hairdresser in the provision of services that may follow. It begins with the client's first contact with the salon, proprietor, manager or assistant, and however made, the client must always be received politely, efficiently and correctly.

It will include a pleasant greeting, the making of appointments, answering questions, possibly giving advice, and generally offering information to meet the client's needs. Details of methods of work used in the salon, type of products used, and the cost of different services may be required. Requests for certain types of hair style, postiche, beauty services and accessories may be made.

The client may be received directly, in person, at the reception area or indirectly on the telephone; or she may make initial requests by writing to the salon. (Fig. 2.1).

2. The receptionist is in attendance at the entrance of many salons, to deal with all inquiries. A client may then be introduced to an assistant who will deal directly with her needs. In other salons the assistants are responsible for receiving clients at the reception area. Whether a trained receptionist is in attendance or not, the hairdressing assistant eventually receives the client. (Fig. 2.2).

3. The client is the essential part of the hairdressing business. Without clients there would be no salons, and no need for hairdressing staff. The client attends a salon for the services she may purchase, and the way they are carried out. This includes quality of work, pleasant surroundings, hygienic conditions, and well-mannered and efficient staff.

In the course of time and training, skills that make for good-quality craftsmanship may be acquired. The atmosphere in the salon can only be pleasant if every member of the staff exercises goodwill and forbearance in her dealings with her colleagues as well as with the client. Dissension, bickering, jealousy or bad temper must be avoided or controlled, so that the salon always has an atmosphere of harmony. The client should never be aware of friction between staff or be the subject of it.

Fig. 2.1   Reception area

4. Hygienic conditions must at all times be maintained by the staff. Each assistant must clear away all soiled towels, gowns and hair, etc., after attending each client, or see that the person responsible for this particular job does it properly, if a reasonable state is to be maintained. Much of the normal tidying of some salons is the job of the apprentice or junior. Cleaners are often employed to carry out the larger items of floor cleaning and polishing. When major items occur, e.g. drains become blocked, heating, water or ventilating systems break down, it is the staff's responsibility to inform the manager or employer immediately, to prevent damage and unhygienic conditions.

5. Conduct in the salon, particularly when it is

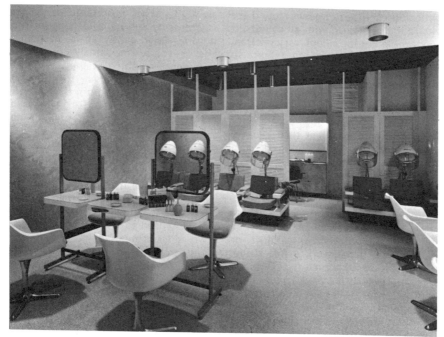

Fig. 2.2   The salon

very busy, often becomes strained. It is necessary to be well mannered and pleasant to all clients at all times. Hurrying rarely achieves anything but shoddy work and dissatisfaction. Continually rushing work causes skills and techniques to be lost. This results in repetition of set, shape or style and loss of clients and prestige. Steady, efficient, thoughtful working, without wasting time, maintains quality of workmanship, clientele and pleasant surroundings.

6. **Attending the client**, after reception, requires further inquiry as to the services to be carried out. These are important and should be made unhurriedly, sincerely and directly to the client.

The client's answers often need careful consideration, particularly when the requests are almost, or completely, impossible. She may frame her words in such a way that she conveys the wrong meaning. She may request a hair style for the wrong reasons or something quite unsuitable. It is the assistant's duty to interpret clients' requests and this should never be left entirely to an apprentice. A junior should not express surprise or her opinion at what may well be an unusual request. She should convey what is said to the assistant, who should make further inquiry.

If the client is to receive attention, make her comfortable and commence the preparation. Any delay should be explained; never allow the client to sit and wait not knowing if or when she is to be attended. It is not always possible to work exactly to time, particularly when earlier clients are unavoidably late.

A late client may have to be kept waiting, or another appointment made, but if the position is explained she will invariably fit in with what is suggested. If she is ignored, or blamed for upsetting the system, this may add to her embarrassment and cause her to leave without further exchange.

7. **Preparation of the client** is necessary for the hairdressing services requested. Having decided what treatment is needed, assemble all tools and materials to be used, together with whatever protective covering is needed for the client. This will enable the hairdresser to avoid unnecessary running about.

Protective coverings, e.g. gowns, wraps or 'cloths', should be used to cover all clothes fully. The client may have a special date or appointment to keep and will want to look her best. If clothes are spoilt, inconvenience may be caused which often results in annoyance, dissatisfaction and a resolution never to attend the salon again.

The protective gown should be carefully and gently positioned on the client. There is no need to throw the gown with flourishes as though it were a bull-baiting cape. This can be dangerous, particularly if another assistant is working nearby. Do not allow the gown to open at the neck as hairdressing progresses. Secure the gown firmly, but not too tightly, in position with the fasteners. Some gowns are designed 'coat fashion' with the ties at the front, others are 'smock fashion' with ties at the back.

Varieties of wraps, gowns or capes are made for different processes. Black or dark tinting gowns are suitably made for hair colouring which will absorb the materials spilt on to them. It is unsightly to place a white or light-coloured towel or gown around the client that looks as if it is stained with all colours. It may be clean and sterile but it can look very unclean. Cutting gowns are usually of a smooth texture to prevent hairs clinging, and plastic materials are often used for cutting, bleaching or colouring. Some of these have edges which soon become soiled and unsightly.

Protective aids, apart from gowns, are, for example, small linen towels, absorbent tissues, hand, face or larger towels, cotton wool and neck strip tissues. These are placed about the neckline or shoulders to prevent water and other liquids running on to the client, or are conveniently placed for use after shampooing or other service.

Towels should not be tucked into necklines of dresses or liquids will be soaked up which will wet the dress. Position towels to prevent discomfort or damage to the client. For most work a soft tissue, linen or Turkish towel is placed around the client and covered by a gown. Neck strips may be used for cutting to prevent loose cut hairs falling into clothes and collars, causing irritation and discomfort.

Coverings for salon chairs, if used, should be in position to prevent surface staining. Despite all that may be done it is possible for materials to drip on to clothes; always check to see the chair is clean, and use materials carefully without dripping or splashing.

Stained clothes should be noted by the manager who should consider what action is to be taken. Usually the client is asked to bring the stained clothes back so that they may be cleaned. Alternatively, the client may be asked to have the clothes cleaned and send the bill to the salon for payment. It is necessary to inform the cleaner of the chemicals used that caused the stain so that the garments may be correctly treated.

8. Preparing the client for hairdressing. (a) Place a neck strip or tissue towel over the collar or shoulders. (b) Place a protective wrap or gown gently in position and secure at the neck, back or front. (c) For shampooing, place a Turkish-type towel on the gown over the shoulders. If cutting first, place cotton wool, a neck strip or a cutting cape in place of the towel. (d) Make sure all clothes are covered and the client is comfortable. (e) Remember to check that the chair is clean; and that absorbent materials act like sponges and should not be tucked into necklines. (f) Place towels over the chair backs, particularly if they are high, to prevent materials falling between the client and the chair.

9. Preparation of the client's hair requires it to be free from backcombing and tangles. Thorough preparation will break or loosen lacquer coating the hair and will remove dust, dirt, scale and other loose material from the hair and scalp. This enables the hair to be easily combed, brushed and generally worked. Unless this is done it becomes difficult for the assistant and uncomfortable for the client.

Preparing the hair. (a) Loosen the hair with the fingers teasing gently apart, particularly if long. (b) Use a coarse or widely spaced comb or rake. Commence combing at the nape, at the hair points, and gradually work closer to the scalp and higher up the head. (c) Proceed from the neck and bottom sides to the top and front. (d) Remove all tangles and backcombing but do not pull the hair, scratch the skin or break the comb. When loosened and disentangled it is ready for brushing. (e) Brush the hair smoothly and firmly, supporting the head carefully to prevent jerking. Commence brushing at the ends of the hair in the neck, gradually working closer to the scalp and further up the head. (f) When all the hair is flowing, brush in different directions, from forehead to nape, front sides back to the neck, lower sides around to the far side of the neck, and, finally, in the opposite way.

10. Combs and combing. The best combs to use are the professional ones specially made for hairdressers, e.g. the hard vulcanized rubber, vulcanite or ebonite comb. They may be made from many materials, e.g. tortoiseshell, ivory, wood, metal, bone, horn, rubber and various types of plastic. They should be non-inflammable, well balanced, pliable, unaffected by hairdressing chemicals, and easy to clean. All combs should be unbroken, and free of sharp edges or mould lines. A badly made comb may break the hair and damage the scalp. This could result in infection and disease. A broken comb harbours germs in the cracks, not easily removed by cleaning, which may be passed to others.

Some combs are made of materials which cause the hair to fly away; this makes it difficult to control the hair, because the combing action produces static electricity (static or frictional electricity are the terms given to electricity of stationary charges). This is produced by rubbing together unlike bodies, e.g. glass and silk, or a plastic comb on hair. The effect of this is to make the hair stand away from the head, or 'fly' as soon as it is touched by hand or an unsuitable comb.

Use of the comb. Combs used for preparing the hair should have wide-spaced teeth and be held firmly in the centre, well supported by the middle fingers on one side and the thumb and little finger on the other. Held this way, the comb is easily used without placing too much stress or strain on it. Do not allow the fingertips to slide down to the teeth points or the combing action is restricted. (Fig. 2.3).

The comb should be used upright, not flattened so that the back drags the hair, and in a raking action without pulling or tugging. If the combing action is started at the hair points, tangles are soon removed. If started at the roots, further tangling and knotting will result. The scalp end of long hair particularly should be supported to lessen pulling. (Figs. 2.4 & 2.5).

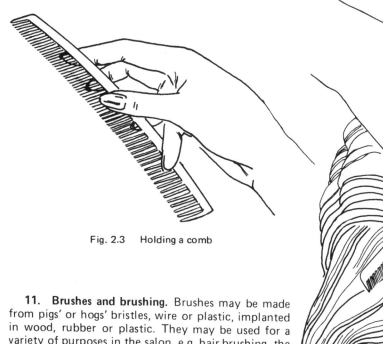

Fig. 2.3 Holding a comb

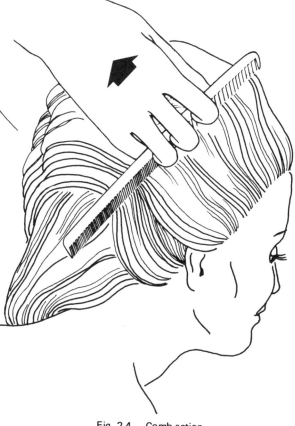

Fig. 2.4 Comb action

11. Brushes and brushing. Brushes may be made from pigs' or hogs' bristles, wire or plastic, implanted in wood, rubber or plastic. They may be used for a variety of purposes in the salon, e.g. hair brushing, the application of materials or clearing loose hairs from the skin. The type to use for hair brushing depends on what is to be achieved and the texture of hair to be brushed. For the preparation of hair prior to other work, a firm-tufted brush which penetrates and easily disentangles is required. The brush should be well balanced and comfortable to hold. The short, nylon-tufted brush is commonly used for general brushing and dressing. Nylon tufts are hard, and if used incorrectly or too frequently the hair becomes damaged; this limits their use.

The natural bristle-tufted brush, preferably with short bristles, enables the hair to be penetrated, gripped and placed, and is popularly used. Since hair and natural bristle are similar materials, the brushing action wears both surfaces equally. The hardness of nylon tufts results in most of the wear being on the hair. The natural, bristle brush is kindest to the hair. This consideration is important to the client who uses her own personal brush more frequently than that used by the hairdresser on her. Clients may brush their hair several times in one day. A hairdresser uses the same brush on the same client at most several times a week.

Generally, if the hair is thick and coarse, a short stiff natural bristle, or a nylon-tufted brush, is suitable for the hairdresser's use in the salon. If the hair is soft and thin, a softer longer bristle may be kinder. Apart from loosening dirt and scale, etc., the brushing action stimulates and distributes natural oil, and this is best achieved with a soft-bristle brush. For dressing and styling hair a variety of mixed bristle and

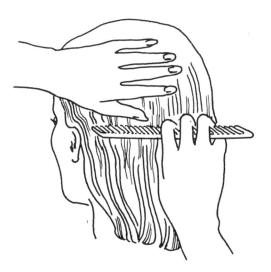

Fig. 2.5 Position of hands, head and comb

nylon or plastic brushes may be used. Personal choice of a brush is finally determined by its weight, length, size and how comfortable it is in use. (Fig. 2.6).

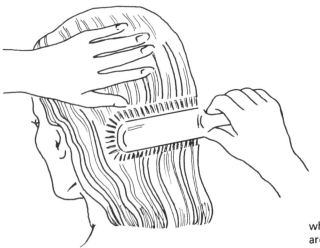

Fig. 2.6   Hands and brushing

Use of the brush. The brush should be correctly applied, i.e. in a smoothing, stroking action, and never scrubbed hard or harshly over the hair and scalp. The brush should be turned with a rolling wrist action, and, as with combing, the head should be supported. The hair may be brushed with one hand holding the brush and the head supported with the other. Two brushes may be used in a rolling action, one following the other. Alternatively, a comb and brush may be used together, one in each hand, first stroking and supporting the hair and the head. (Figs. 2.7 & 2.8).

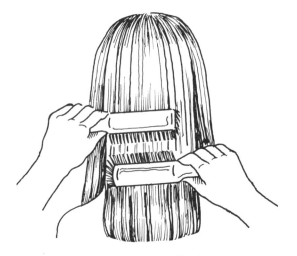

Fig. 2.7   Using two brushes

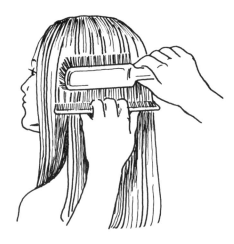

Fig. 2.8   Use of brush and comb

Precaution. If the skin or scalp is torn or scratched when using any type of comb or brush, cleanse the area with clean water, and apply a suitable antiseptic to prevent possible infection. Only tools in good order, which will not cause damage, should be used, and always gently and correctly.

12.   Cleaning combs and brushes should be done as soon as possible after use. They should not be used on another person before cleaning and sterilizing. All loose material should be cleared from combs and brushes which should then be thoroughly washed, placed in disinfectant and dried, or placed in a suitable sterilizer after drying. Tools in disinfectant fluid should be rinsed before using on a client; many disinfectants cause skin irritation and discomfort. Some sterilizing cabinets are made to sterilize and store tools, others are made for sterilizing only. Metal tools should not remain in this type of sterilizer too long or the chemicals may spoil the metal. Manufacturers' instructions should be checked before using sterilizing cabinets. (Fig. 2.9).

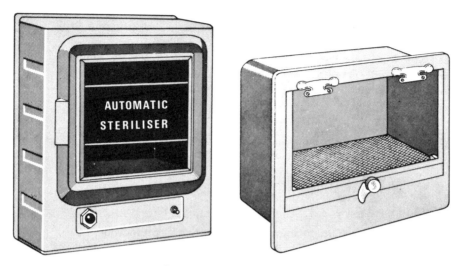

Fig. 2.9   Sterilizing cabinets

Revision test 1

Q. 1   Describe how a client should be received in the salon.
Q. 2   How does personal and general hygiene affect the client?
Q. 3   What does 'preparing the client for hairdressing' mean?
Q. 4   Why is it necessary to 'prepare the client's hair'?
Q. 5   What is a comb? Describe its use.
Q. 6   Describe the differences between bristle and nylon brushes, and give examples when either may be used.
Q. 7   How should combs and brushes be cleaned?
Q. 8   Why is the client important?
Q. 9   Describe the brushing action and what it does.
Q.10   Briefly describe each of the following terms:
(a) Sterilizer. (b) Hair teasing. (c) Protective aids. (d) Combing action. (e) Receptionist.

Revision test 2

Complete the following sentences:

1   Three properties of a professional comb are:
(a)................., (b)................., (c).................
2   Hygienic conditions in the salon are the responsibility of all the ....
3   The salon should always be .... and the staff well mannered and ....
4   The client and her clothes should at all times be ....
5   The following may be used to prevent materials spoiling clothes:
(a)................., (b)................., (c)................., (d).................
6   Combing and brushing loosens knots and .... and helps to loosen ...., ... and ....
7   When combing or brushing the .... should be supported.
8   The hair surface is worn more when .... brushes are used than when .... brushes are used.
9   Combs and brushes should always be .... and ....
10   After cleaning in disinfectant liquids, combs should be thoroughly .... and .... before use.
11   The hair should not be .... or .... or the head .... when combed.

Revision test 3

Complete the following sentences with the word or words listed below.

Pliable. Balanced. Sterilizer. Rake. Protect. Stimulates. Dirt. Infection. Disease. Rinsed.

1   Gowns and towels are used to .... clients' clothes.
2   Liquid disinfectants should be .... from combs before use.
3   Professional combs should be .... and ....
4   A broken comb may cause .... and ....
5   Another name for a comb is a ....
6   Brushing .... the scalp and loosens .... or dust.
7   After cleaning, combs and brushes may be stored in a suitable ....

Vocabulary

Absorbent	Having the ability to absorb or to soak up, e.g. cotton wool.
Accessories	Things that accompany, aid or contribute.
Backcombing	Combing hair back towards the roots.
Bristles	The short hairs of an animal.
Client	A customer or patron of a shop or salon.
Clientele	Group of customers or clients, a following.
Craftsman	A man well trained and skilful in his work.
Disentangle	To free of knots or tangles.
Disinfectant	A substance that kills germs.
Efficiently	Achieving desired results with minimum of effort.
Function	Action or purpose.
Lacquer	Solution to hold dressed hair in position.
Manager	One who conducts, directs or manages.
Neck strip	Absorbent tissue or paper used round neck.
Nylon	A synthetic, man-made fibre.
Politely	Courteously, showing consideration for the welfare of others.
Postiche	False added hair; a hair piece or wig.
Prestige	Good reputation, or high standing, due to past actions.
Proprietor	The owner.
Protective coverings	Gowns, wraps, capes, towels, etc.
Rake	Name given to a comb with widely spaced teeth.
Reception	Area where clients are received. The receiving of clients.
Receptionist	One trained in the methods of reception.
Requests	Things or services asked for.
Salon	French word for reception room for fashionable ladies.
Sterile	Free of living germs.
Sterilized	Made free of living germs.
Sterilizing cabinet	Cabinet used for sterilizing tools.
Tint cape	Usually a dark plastic or rubber covering.
Ventilating	Promoting a free circulation of air.

Reception and Client Preparation

13. Décor and reception. The building of a clientele will, to some extent, be dependent on the appearance of the salon and reception area. This will strongly influence the first impressions gained by the clients. If the layout and design are tastefully arranged, and maintained in a clean and tidy state, clients will be encouraged to return for further services. No matter how good the design or layout, a dirty or slovenly salon can only be repulsive to clients. (Fig. 2.10).

The same may be said of the general appearance and personal hygiene of the staff, particularly in respect of body freshness; fingernails should be clean and, if varnished, unchipped; hair, skin and overalls should obviously be clean. Client numbers can be drastically reduced even though good hairdressing is carried out, if due regard is not paid to the client's health and well-being. It is better for all concerned if good hairdressing can be given in pleasant, hygienic conditions.

14. Display of the salon's services is a means of attracting prospective clients. The aesthetic arrangements of the shop window and reception areas should present an attractive, uncluttered appearance of goods and services offered. Display may consist of a variety of hair styles using different media, e.g. photographs, sketches, diagrams, drawings or various types of 'head'. A range of products may be displayed, or one product emphasized.

The use of colour, and the way it is displayed with other material, is important. A single dressed head, backed by a carefully draped coloured material, may be effective and pleasing. 'Before' and 'after' effects of hairstyling, using heads or sketches, may be of interest to clients. Displays consisting of the suitability of hair arrangements, using different types and shapes of face, can be effective. There are endless ways of displaying the services offered by the salon.

Other facilities, e.g. beauty, cosmetic, manicure or other specialist services, if offered by the salon, may

Fig. 2.10   Reception area

be displayed in a similar way to hairdressing. Packing too much into a small area should be avoided. A little displayed, and often changed, is usually more interesting.

Display depends on appreciation of 'what looks right', and the fundamentals of artistic arrangement. It is not suggested that the hairdresser becomes a display artist as part of his work, but it is surprising how much of the hairdresser's experience can be applied to attractive display. Alternatively commercial firms may be contracted, on a weekly or monthly basis, to take care of all the salon's display.

15. Advertising through newspapers, magazines, cinema, and television may be useful to present before large numbers of people the services offered. Letterheads, appointment cards, display and price lists, shows, lectures and demonstrations are other means of display and advertising where aesthetic appreciation may be applied. Good hairdressing, and the favourable comments of the client when she leaves the salon, are the best form of good advertising.

The way different products, for sale to clients, are used in the salon is often overlooked. Surprising results may be achieved if the staff display good suitable hair styles, cosmetics or postiche, and are good examples to the client. The display of unsuitable dress and hair styles, and unkempt, badly coloured or bleached hair, is neither pleasing nor encouraging and does not help to sell the varied services.

16. Aesthetics and hair preparation are related when one considers the design, shape and colour of the tools, materials and equipment used. The choice of wraps, gowns and towels, in both material and colour, has a part to play. To some, certain colours have a harsh, jarring effect, while other colour combinations produce soothing effects. Brilliant strong colours may clash badly, and pastel shades may look insipid. Certain fabric textures put some clients' 'teeth on edge', but others may be soothed by them. Music, if used in the salon, can produce desirable and undesirable effects on a client's mood, and the way she may respond to hairdressing services. It is necessary to cultivate appreciation to be able to choose what may produce the most pleasing effect. This in turn helps to create an atmosphere of client appreciation, and readiness to attend the salon for its standards and qualities.

17. Science and reception. The cleanliness of the reception area and salon must of course go beyond appearances. The hygienic state of the salon affects all who use it, and by-laws and regulations governing standards of hygiene are laid down by local authorities, government departments and craft organizations, for the well-being of all concerned. Compliance with these rules is the responsibility of those who work in the salon. The working conditions and the number of different people using the salon will create a situation where bacteria and other micro-organisms can multiply. Clothing, working surfaces, tools, materials, equipment, and most items used in the salon are a possible means of harbouring germs. The risks of passing harmful bacteria on to clients are high under such conditions, unless measures are taken to prevent them. Fortunately, many of the chemicals used are bactericidal or antiseptic and will kill or inhibit the growth of many micro-organisms.

18. Bacteria and fungi. Bacteria are commonly found in the air, sometimes in drinking water and in food. Many types of bacteria do not cause disease and are termed *non-pathogenic.* These are present, under normal conditions, in the digestive system of the body where they help in the digestion of certain food materials. Other non-pathogenic bacteria are present in the soil and help to produce various chemicals required by plants. Other types of bacteria will cause disease; these are called pathogenic bacteria, of which there are different forms.

Pathogenic bacteria are usually named after the manner in which they are seen to group themselves when viewed under a microscope, or after their shape.

Cocci (sing. coccus) are round-shaped bacteria usually found singly or in groups. Streptococci appear in stringlike formations, and staphylococci in groups or bunches. These bacteria cause sore throats and pus-forming diseases, e.g. boils, impetigo and sycosis. Diplococci are paired cocci and are responsible for diseases of the lungs, e.g. pneumonia. Cocci, under normal conditions, may be present on the skin surface, the normal resistance of which prevents infection. If the skin is torn or cut then the cocci can enter the body and cause infection.

Bacilli (sing. bacillus) are rod-shaped organisms causing such diseases as, e.g. tuberculosis, influenza, diphtheria and typhoid.

Spirilla (sing. spirillum) are rigid, spiral rod-shaped bacteria, few of which are pathogenic. (Fig. 2.11).

Fungi (sing. fungus) are plant organisms which may be *saprophytic*, i.e. the type that lives on dead and decaying matter, or *parasitic*, i.e. the type that lives on living matter, and both are found in diseases of the body. Fungi form several groups, e.g. moulds, rusts, yeasts and mildews. Tinea capitis, or ringworm of the scalp, is caused by a fungal infection of the scalp and hair. Athlete's foot, or ringworm of the foot, is a fungal infection. Many scaly scalp conditions are aggravated, and possibly caused, by fungal infections.

19. Sterilization and antisepsis are methods of killing or inhibiting bacteria and fungi growth to prevent the spread of disease. Hospital surgical instruments are sterilized so that no living bacteria are allowed to contaminate patients, but after sterilizing they are kept in sterile containers to prevent more

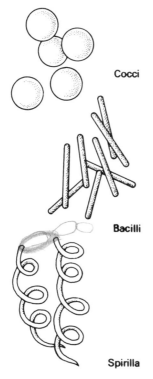

Cocci

Bacilli

Spirilla

Fig. 2.11   Bacteria

bacteria reaching them. The salon's tools, once they are sterilized, should at least be covered before using them on a client.

Methods of sterilization consist of the use of moist heat, e.g. *steaming* and *boiling*, and dry heat, e.g. *baking*, which kills most common bacteria if the temperature is high, e.g. 100—150°C. for 5—20 minutes. Boiling water is a common sterilization method particularly useful for salon linen. This method should not be used on salon tools since the edges are likely to be made less sharp unless wrapped in gauze, for example. Steaming is convenient for producing hot sterile towels for face and scalp treatments, and the steam urn, a feature of many men's salons, may be used. Since it takes time to sterilize a towel completely in a steamer urn, freshly laundered towels should be used. The steam-under-pressure method of sterilization is popular in hospitals and laboratories, in the form of an *autoclave*, which works something like a pressure-cooker. Burning destroys all bacteria but is only useful for waste materials.

Ultra-violet light is used for sterilizing tools that cannot be heated, and its disinfecting action kills some, but not all, bacteria. It is commonly used in many salons where it is produced in a cabinet which is convenient for storing clean tools. All implements placed in an ultra-violet-light cabinet should be turned so that the light is able to reach all surfaces; the light cannot kill organisms unless it is directed on to them.

The formaldehyde vaporizing cabinet is a convenient means of killing bacteria and fungi on implements used in the salon. Formaldehyde is available in solid or liquid form, which, on heating, vaporizes to form formaldehyde gas. It is useful for disinfecting non-metal tools, combs, nets, brushes, etc. Metal tools become corroded if left too long in formaldehyde.

Disinfectants, germicides, bactericides and fungicides are chemicals, in solutions or solid form, that kill micro-organisms, bacteria and fungi. Some are effective with one or more types of organism, while other disinfectants are effective when used on specific organisms. Some of the first disinfectants discovered, e.g. phenol, or carbolic acid and the cresols, both coal-tar derivatives, are still used. Chlorine and iodine are old, but still commonly used, disinfectants. Modern compounds of phenol, cresol, chlorine and iodine are particularly useful. Hexachlorophene is a modern disinfectant useful for incorporating in soap.

The quaternary ammonium compounds form a large group of effective disinfectants. Cetrimide is an example which is used in some setting lotions and hairdressing products. These disinfectants are becoming popular and more used, since they are effective against the organisms found in the salon. Formalin, i.e. formaldehyde in solution, is another popular disinfectant.

General sterilizing in the salon may best be carried out for non-metal tools, rollers, combs, etc., in vaporizing cabinets. Metal tools should be placed in an ultra-violet-light cabinet, after being cleansed with ethyl alcohol, which removes grease and acts as a disinfectant. A quaternary ammonium compound, of the correct strength, is a useful liquid disinfectant in which combs may be placed. There are numerous products suitable for use in laundry and washing equipment for sterilizing towels, gowns, etc., and floors, toilets and working surfaces.

The correct dilutions of liquid disinfectants must be made. Some are corrosive and caustic, and all are to be used with care. Always wash and clean surfaces before sterilizing to remove dirt and grease which may lessen the effectiveness of the disinfectant. Rinse all combs and tools thoroughly after immersion in liquid disinfectants. Most disinfectants may be diluted to make *antiseptics* which inhibit bacteria growth, but do not kill them, e.g. hydrogen peroxide and tincture of iodine.

20. Boardwork and hair preparation require a different set of brushes and disentanglers. All hair, whether 'cut hair', as cut from the head, or 'combings', i.e. hair collected from several combings, is usually first passed through a hackle. A hackle consists of a number of steel prongs embedded in an oblong wooden base, which is fixed to a bench or table, with the prong points uppermost. The prongs are closer together at the front, and as the hair passes through points first, as when combing growing hair, the tangles are removed and the hair smoothed. Hackling and disentangling in boardwork is similar to combing in hairdressing.

It is dangerous to leave the hackle uncovered when not in use, and it should always be stored on shelves level with the waist so that it cannot be stepped on or fall from a height when being removed.

Hair tangle occurs when the surface of one hair interlocks with another, or when the length of hair intertwines or knots itself round other hairs. When preparing 'hair combings' for postiche the hair should be 'turned', i.e. positioned as it would be on the scalp, a boardwork preparation process. If left unturned the hair soon tangles and becomes unmanageable. (Fig. 2.12).

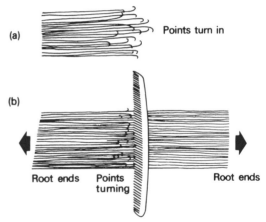

Fig. 2.13   Hair turnings

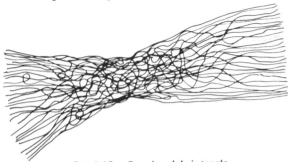

Fig. 2.12   Boardwork hair tangle

Turning the hair so that its surface cell edges are in the same direction (see 'Hair cuticle', page 161) minimizes tangling. A method of turning consists of moving small bundles of hair across the surface of hot soapy water. A felting movement with the thumb and forefinger helps the ends of the hair to turn towards the root, leaving the root ends unturned. The bundles are dried, the turned hair backcombed, and separated by drawing off the root ends and placing them in neat piles, with all the hair points at one end and the root ends at the other. The new bundles of turned hair are tied and stored until required for use. (Fig. 2.13).

Drawing brushes, mats or cards are used to hold the hair when being used for weft work, i.e. interweaving hair on to silks or threads, and knotted work, i.e. knotting hairs on to foundation net or gauze. Drawing brushes consist of bristles implanted in oblong wooden bases, used one on top of the other, for holding lengths of hair being worked. Drawing cards or mats consist of small bent metal-pronged wire teeth embedded in rubber or leather bases, and used in pairs similar to drawing brushes, to hold the hair.

Small postiche combs are used to attach a piece of postiche to the hair on the scalp. They are sewn to the underside and allow the piece to be firmly

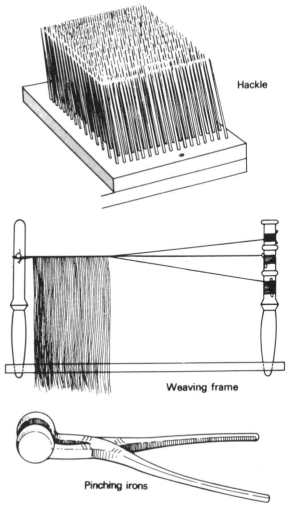

Fig. 2.14   Boardwork tools

positioned on the head. Combs and brushes used for postiche dressing are similar to those used in the salon but often smaller. Special care must be taken in using these when dressing postiche. It is easy to catch and tear foundations which could involve expensive repairing. Make sure that the correct combing methods are used, i.e. start from the hair points and gradually work to the root ends. When the foundation base is reached the comb should be angled so that the comb points do not embed themselves in the weft, knots or foundation base.

Revision test 1

Q. 1 Personal and general hygiene are important in the salon. List and describe the points concerned.
Q. 2 Describe a method of preparing a client and her hair. Give reasons and list six precautions to be taken.
Q. 3 Name and describe three different organisms causing disease and the diseases produced.
Q. 4 How is hair prepared for use in making postiche?
Q. 5 What materials are used for making combs and brushes? What are the differences and what determines choice?
Q. 6 What is sterilization and antisepsis? Give examples and list the reasons for the use of each.
Q. 7 What is hair tangle? Use sketches and diagrams to illustrate answers.
Q. 8 How may the client be affected by the various aspects of the salon and reception area?
Q. 9 Name five tools used to disentangle, smooth or hold hair. State the precautions to be taken with each.
Q.10 Briefly describe each of the following terms:
(a) Turning. (b) Hygiene. (c) Static electricity. (d) Bacteria. (e) Rake.

Revision test 2

Complete the following sentences:

1 Combing and brushing should not be allowed to .... or .... the hair.
2 When brushing or combing, electricity called .... or .... may be produced which causes the hair to ....
3 Combs may be made from ...., ... or ....
4 Metal tools should be sterilized by removing dirt and grease with .... and placing in a .... or a sterilizing cabinet.
5 A reliable means of sterilizing is the vaporizing cabinet which involves the use of .... gas.
6 Four organisms which cause infection are ...., ..., ... and ....
7 Four different types of bristle used in brushes are ...., ..., ... and ....
8 If the skin is torn or scratched it should be .... and a suitable .... applied.
9 Three substances that will kill bacteria are ...., ... and ....
10 A substance which in Ibits the growth of bacteria is called an ....

Revision test 3

Complete the following sentences with the word or words listed below:

Hydrogen peroxide. Rake. Tincture of iodine. Antiseptic. Disinfectant. Hackle. Ultra-violet light. Pathogenic. Non-pathogenic. Formaldehyde gas.

1 Formaldehyde in solution is called formalin and may be used as a ....
2 Sterilizing cabinets are used to disinfect, and .... and .... may be used in them.
3 The names of two tools used for disentangling hair are .... and ....
4 Disease-causing organisms are called .... and those which do not cause disease are called ....
5 Two examples of antiseptics are .... and ....
6 An .... is a substance which inhibits the growth of bacteria.

Vocabulary

Aesthetics	The science or theory of the beautiful.
Antisepsis	The prevention of sepsis.
Antiseptic	A substance that inhibits bacterial growth.
Bacteria	Round or rod-shaped organisms.
Card	A tool used to hold hair being worked in boardwork, similar to a hackle.
Cocci	Round-shaped disease-producing bacteria.
Combings	Boardwork term given to hair collected from the comb after many combings.
Diplococci	Bacteria found in pairs.
Disinfectants	Substances that kill and inhibit the growth of micro-organisms.
Germicides	
Bactericides	
Fungicides	
Formaldehyde	A gas vapour given off when formalin is heated.
Foundation	The base or net on which hair is knotted or weft is sewn.
Fungi	Vegetable or plant organisms.
Hackle	Boardwork term used for a tool or process of disentangling hair.
Micro-organism	A very small living body.
Non-pathogenic bacteria	Organisms that do not cause disease.
Parasite	Organism that lives off another living body.
Pathogenic	Disease-causing.
Postiche	A finished, dressed piece of boardwork.
Quaternary ammonium compounds	Effective disinfectants, often abbreviated to 'quats'.
Saprophyte	Organism that lives off dead or decaying materials.
Sepsis	Poisoning due to pathogenic bacteria or putrefying organisms.
Staphylococci	Bacteria found in groups or bunches.
Streptococci	Bacteria found in strips or stringlike formations.
Turning	Boardwork term for the process of lining up the roots and points of the hair.
Weft	Boardwork term given to the result of weaving hair on silks, threads or strings.

Curls and Curling

1. Curl. A curl is a series of circular or spiral turns in a strip of hair which is used to produce a variety of S-shaped movements. The curl is usually set in wet hair and dressed out when dry.

2. Curls for setting. Various types of curl are used in setting and many individual hairdressers have their own methods of formation. Although the method and manner of curling varies, which tends to confuse, there remain clearly definable basic types of curl. (Fig. 3.1).

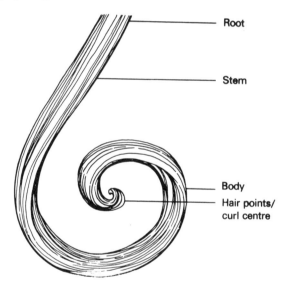

Fig. 3.1   Curl parts

The wet hair is so positioned that the final dressing is determined by its placing. Basically the hair should not be set in one position and then dressed in another. For practical setting the hair is placed where it is intended that it be dressed. As the dressing loosens, the hair falls back to its original set position. Force dressing, i.e. making the hair lie in a direction other than that intended, should not be relied on or the dressing becomes too difficult for the client to manage. At advanced stages of hairdressing force dressing is used to produce special and different effects. It should not be used to hide or excuse

mistakes made in the pli, i.e. set.

The use of good curl requires a degree of professionalism, not easily copied, which produces effects sought after by many clients. Curls in a pli produce an individual shape which often fits the contours better than all-roller setting methods. However, repetition of similar types of curl and methods of curling results in limited effects without variety. Knowledge of curl effects and techniques is essential to the future hair stylist, and can only be acquired by careful practice. Control of the hair, hands, tools and client movements becomes less difficult with experience.

3. Rules for curls. As with other techniques, curl formation may be guided if a set of basic rules is followed which apply to most curls irrespective of method.

(a)   The hair must be carefully positioned and cleanly combed.

(b)   Only neat and tidy sections should be taken. The size will depend on the length, texture, condition of hair and effects required. (Fig. 3.2).

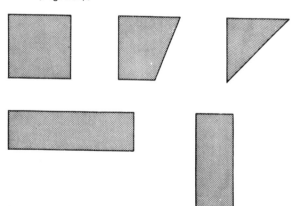

Fig. 3.2   Sections for curls

(c)   The direction of the curl stem or base will determine the direction of the hair section. (Fig. 3.3).

(d)   The direction of the curl body will determine the direction of the wave movement. (Fig. 3.4).

(e) The curl should be formed, without twisting, by carefully rounding each loop or turn of the hair.
(f) The curl should be placed in or on the curl base without buckling or distortion.
(g) Secure the curl, with pins or clips, without disturbing the curl stem or body and without hindering the formation of the following curls. (Fig. 3.5).
(h) Curl arrangements must not be disturbed by the placing of nets, cotton wool or ear protectors.

4. Curling requires the use of the hands and the fingers together with simple tools, e.g. tail comb, pins and clips, etc., and, depending on the type and manner of curling, a variety of curl formers.

The tips of the fingers are used with the hands

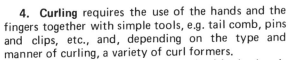

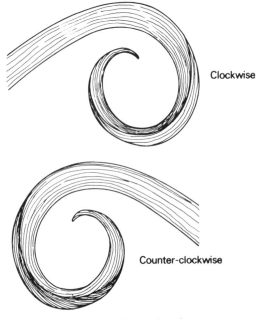

Clockwise

Counter-clockwise

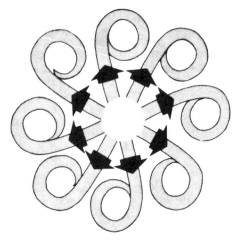

Fig. 3.3   Curl stem directions

Fig. 3.4   Curl body direction

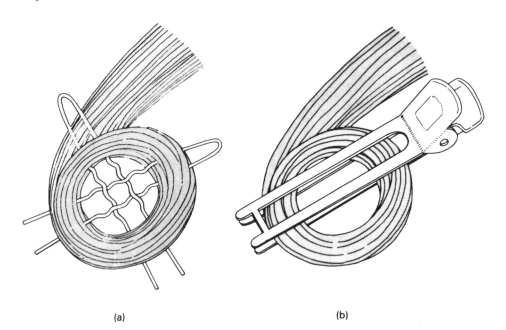

(a)

(b)

Fig. 3.5   Securing curls: (a) pins; (b) clips

directed away from the head so that the set is not disturbed. The tail comb is used to divide and section the hair and to position each strand on the fingers. The curl is then formed by the fingers or the curler on which the hair is placed. Clips or hair pins securely hold the wound curls in position for drying, and crêpe hair, cotton wool or curl end-papers are used to simplify the curling by firmly holding the curl points. Rollers of different shapes and sizes are commonly used to produce curl shapes, but other formers, e.g. curling wheels or root-tensioning curlers, may be used. (Fig. 3.6).

Nets are used to cover the hair to prevent disturbance when drying, and cotton wool or paper ear covers help to protect the skin while the hair is set and dried in position.

Setting lotions are used to help to bind the hair together; this assists control, curl and wave formation, and has the effect of producing a longer-lasting set.

5. Types of curl. Different curls are used for the effects they produce. Most of these are variations of two basic types, i.e. the open or loose and the closed or tight types of curl. These may be formed and placed flat to the head, lifted at various angles, or standing directly up from the head.

The barrelspring curl is the name given to the open or loose type of curl. (It is shaped similarly to a barrelspring, i.e. a type of spring used in hand haircutting clippers.) The centre of the barrelspring curl is open and the effect produced is loose and casual; a name commonly used is the 'casual curl'. Barrelspring, open and loose, describes the manner in which the curl is formed, the way it looks, and the kind of effect produced. The curl is formed so that each loop of the hair is made the same as the previous one. On completion the curl body is placed on the base with the curl points on the underside or topside of the curl. The hair points are best placed beneath the curl if a slight fullness of base is required and above the curl if flatness is the aim. The open barrelspring curl will produce an even wave shape throughout the length of each hair section, and if correctly formed and positioned is used for reverse curl wave shapes. (Fig. 3.7).

The clockspring curl is the closed and tight type of curl. It is formed by each loop of the curl being made smaller than the previous one so that the points form a small closed circle in the curl centre. It is called a clockspring curl because its appearance is similar to a coiled spring in a clock. It is called a closed curl because the points fill the centre, and a tight curl because the result produced is a firm springy effect.

When the clockspring curl is dressed an uneven wave is produced throughout the hair length. The wave formed is larger near the curl base and smaller at the curl points, which limits its uses in fashionable styling. It is particularly useful on lank greasy hair or hair that does not hold a set well, and mainly in the neck sections of some styles. (Fig. 3.8).

6. Methods of curling often affect the result required and a special curl effect may determine the curling method. If a manner of curling produces a wrong curl effect then the method is incorrect. The correct effect is the main consideration and there are invariably several ways or methods of achieving it.

The curl effect is determined by the size of the curl, the tension applied to the hair, and the type of

Fig. 3.6   Hands — curling position

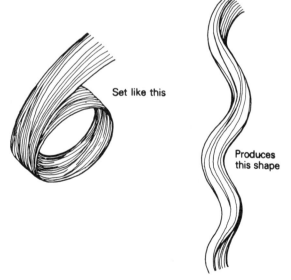

Fig. 3.7   Barrelspring curl, set and dressed

Set like this

Produces
this shape

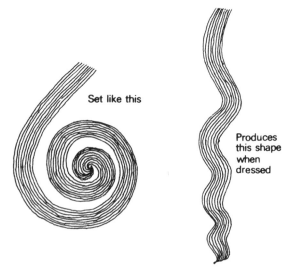

Set like this

Produces this shape when dressed

Fig. 3.8   Clockspring curl, set and dressed

loops formed should be made larger or smaller and placed in or on the previously formed loops, depending on the type of curl required.

Curling method 2. Another method of curling is as follows:
(a)   Hold the section of hair in one hand with the thumb and forefinger, thumb on top, 25—50 mm from the scalp.
(b)   With the thumb and forefinger of the other hand thumb uppermost, grasp the hair approximately 25—50 mm away from the opposite hand.
(c)   With a half turn, by the hand nearest the hair points, place the hair in a loop.
(d)   Transfer the loop formed to the tips of the thumb and forefinger of the other hand.
(e)   Continue to form the point end of the hair in a series of loops, transferring each to the other hand, until all the length is coiled.
(f)   The placing and last loops are formed by turning, with both hands, the coiled length in to the base.
(g)   The curl should be carefully secured with clips or pins. If hair pins are used, place one through the curl stem and body, and another through the curl body, crossing and interlocking at the serrated parts of the pins. Clips are best placed in line with the curl stem, which minimizes marking, and will not hinder curls formed or to be formed.

The roller curl is a curl formed by winding the hair on to metal or plastic shaped rollers. The curl formed is similar to several barrelspring curls standing up from the head. Various sizes of rollers may be used to produce small or large curl or wave shapes. The roller lifts the hair from the head so that high and full shapes may be dressed, and is popularly used in modern setting patterns.

A method of rollering:
(a)   A section of hair, no longer or wider than the size of the roller used, should be cleanly combed straight out from the head.
(b)   The points of the hair section should be placed on the centre of the roller. Both hands are used to maintain the hair angle and retain points in position.
(c)   The roller is turned, locking the hair points against the body of the roller, and both roller and hair wound evenly down to the head. The hair should not be pulled from side to side when winding down.
(d)   The wound roller is placed centrally on the base from which the hair was sectioned.
(e)   The roller is secured by passing a pin through to prevent it unwinding or loosening.

Good curl and wave shape may be produced if the rollers are correctly used; they are, however, often abused and effects result which are the opposite of

curl used in addition to the curling method. If all loops of the curl are formed equally, even waves result. If the loops become smaller towards the points then uneven waves are produced.

Curling method 1. This may be done either tight or loose, big or small, with even or uneven wave, and is as follows:
(a)   A neat section of hair is divided (the size will depend on the type of curl and effect required) and cleanly combed through.
(b)   Hold the hair in the direction in which it is to lie after drying.
(c)   Hold the hair, at mid-length, in one hand with the thumb and forefinger, thumb uppermost.
(d)   With the other hand, using thumb and forefinger with the thumb underneath, hold the hair a little way down from the points and turn the hand to form the first coil or loop. This movement is a wrist action, the hand turning almost completely round at the wrist.
(e)   On completion of the turn and first loop, transfer the looped hair to the finger and thumb of the other hand where it should be firmly held.
(f)   A series of loops are formed in a similar way until the base is reached. The last loop or two are formed by turning the curl body into the base.
(g)   The rounded side of the curl body should be placed in the rounded curl base.
(h)   The curl is secured without spoiling and the supporting hand remains still so that the curl or base is not disturbed.

This curling method may be varied or adapted to form both barrelspring and clockspring curls. The

those intended. It is important that the wound roller is placed centrally on its base; if 'dropped', i.e. placed below the base, the hair becomes dragged, and flatness rather than height is achieved. The hair should not be dragged from either side of the roller or set too far apart, or untidy and badly blended movements are produced. Roller pins pressing in or marking the head should be avoided by passing through the roller in front or behind. The longer the hair the larger the roller that may be used. Too large rollers used on too short hair produce weak and loose movements, even if they are able to stay in the hair. (Fig. 3.9 A & B).

7. Common curling faults:

(a) Lifting the curl base when a flat effect is intended.

(b) Taking too large a section of hair, particularly when it is too short.

(c) Combing the hair in one direction and forming the curl stem in another.

(d) Not rounding the curl body, and buckling the base when positioning the curl.

(e) Bending the curl points back, which causes the ends to hook out, commonly called 'fish-hooks'.

(f) Twisting the hair, causing it to spring in the wrong direction.

(g) Distorting the curl base when securing and not placing the clip in far enough. This allows the curl to slip and the clip to be caught in the setting net.

(h) Lining or marking the hair by clipping across the stem; this applies particularly to bleached or poor-condition hair.

(i) Taking uneven sections which causes curls to be out of line, thereby producing uneven shapes.

(j) Allowing tools or hands to catch on formed curls, and not using the fingertips or carefully lining up each curl loop, which produces untidy, uneven effects.

8. Curl bases and sections of various shapes are used for curling, e.g. oblong, square and triangular. These are determined by curl type and the direction in which the hair is to be placed. Barrelspring curls require slightly oblong bases. Roller curls require wider oblong bases and clockspring curls require a square base. Triangular bases are used with part stand-up type of curls. Oblong and square bases are most commonly used.

Curl practice of two basic types of curl is to be encouraged before attempting to set. Competently placing flat, smooth, round, neat and tidy curls in varying positions will speed the completion of a good set.

There are two directions in which a flat curl may be formed, clockwise and counter-clockwise. The clockwise curl is formed in the direction taken by the hands of a clock. The counter-clockwise curl moves in the opposite direction. Roller and stand-up curls are formed, basically, with their stems directed up from the head. Read the curl rules often when practising (see page 17) and refer to them when the curls are finished, before drying. If the rules are used in this way, mistakes may be noted and corrected and good thinking habits established.

Curl exercises. (a) Commencing at the top, centre part of the head, form a complete circle of barrelspring curls. Form the curl stems long enough for the circle to be completed. Then form an outer ring of curls, close to the first, but moving in the opposite direction. (Fig. 3.10).

(b) Form two straight rows of barrelspring curls, one row clockwise, the other counter-clockwise, across the back of the head or practice block. When dried and simply brushed through, well-formed waves

Correct

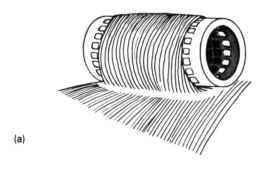

(a)

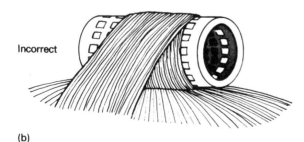

Incorrect

(b)

Fig. 3.9   Rollers: (a) correct; (b) incorrect

are easily produced. This exercise may be applied in various ways for styling. (Fig. 3.11).

9. The clockface method of curl description is useful for recording a pli on paper, or for simply referring to them. The curl in this system has its stem numbered according to the direction in which it is placed, and the curl body described as moving clockwise or counter-clockwise, e.g. a curl with its stem directed at three o'clock, moving clockwise, is referred to as a 3C curl. (Fig. 3.12).

A pli, using the clockface method, may be described as follows: Across the top front of the head form two rows of 6C curls (stems at six o'clock, bodies clockwise), to form a forward movement or fringe. The right side of the head may be set with six 7CC curls (curl stems directed to seven o'clock, bodies moving counter-clockwise), to form a soft movement back from the face rounding on to the cheek. The left side may be set with six 5C curls (stems directed to five o'clock, curl bodies moving clockwise), to form a similar movement to the right side. On top of the head, behind the fringe curls, rollers or stand-up type curls may be used to lift and give height to the hair. One roller may be set forward to give fullness to the top of the fringe, and three rollers set back to produce fullness at the top. Beneath these rollers, at the top back of the head, a row of part standing-up curls may be formed, using 5C curls, with a flatter row of 7CC curls beneath, followed by another row of 5C curls, finally finishing with two or more rows of 7CC curls. (Fig. 3.13).

Fig. 3.11   Two rows of reverse curls

Fig. 3.12   Different curl directions

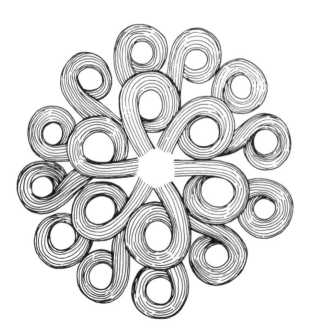

Fig. 3.10   Circle of curls

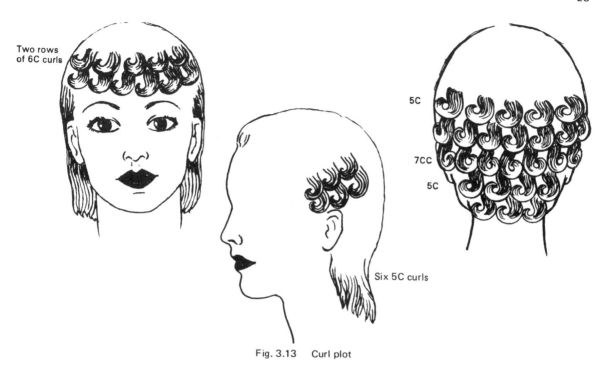

Two rows
of 6C curls

5C

7CC

5C

Six 5C curls

Fig. 3.13   Curl plot

Revision test 1

Q. 1   What is a curl, as used in hairdressing?
Q. 2   Name the main parts of a curl.
Q. 3   Name and describe three different types of curl.
Q. 4   List six rules for curling.
Q. 5   Describe two types of curl former.
Q. 6   List the tools and aids used in curling.
Q. 7   Describe a method of curling.
Q. 8   List six common curling faults.
Q. 9   What is meant by 'force dressing'?
Q.10   Why are curls used in setting?

Revision test 2

Complete the following sentences:

1   The names of three temporary type curls are ...., ... and ....
2   The main parts of the curl are ...., ..., ... and ....
3   Unevenly wound curls produce .... wave shapes, and evenly wound curls produce .... wave shapes.
4   Hair should be set in the .... it is to be dressed.
5   Direction of the hair section is determined by the .... and wave direction by the ....
6   The following curls are used to produce lift and height: ...., ... and ....
7   A system of curl description is called ....
8   Curl size is determined by the hair ...., ... and ....
9   Three curling aids are ...., ... and ....
10   A five o'clock counter-clockwise curl is abbreviated to .... A 7C curl is ....

Revision test 3

Complete the following sentences with the word or words listed below:

Barrelspring. Clockspring. Curl stem. Curl body. Hair pins. Counter-clockwise. Clockwise. Clip. Twisting. Crêpe hair.

1   An open, loose, casual curl is called a .... curl.
2   A closed, tight curl is called a .... curl.
3   Direction of the hair is determined by the ....
4   Wave direction is determined by the ....
5   The word .... is abbreviated to C.
6   The word .... is abbreviated to CC.
7   Pin curls were originally secured with ....
8   Marks on the curl or hair may be caused by badly placed ....
9   When curling, ... the hair is a common fault.
10   A curling aid, which helps to secure curl points, is ....

Vocabulary

Barrelspring curl	A curl formed like a barrelspring.
Bigoudi	Curlers or sticks used to form curls.
Casual curl	An open, loose, even curl.
Clockspring curl	A curl formed like a clockspring.
Clockwise curl	Curl moving clockwise, abbreviated to C.
Counter-clockwise curl	Moving counter-clockwise, abbreviated to CC.
Crêpe hair	A curling aid to secure hair points.
Curl	A curved, rounded section of hair.
Curl base	The scalp end of hair section or curl.
Curl body	Circles of hair forming bulk of curl.
Curl-former	Any shape on which curl is formed.
Curl mark	Mark or line caused by clipping across stem.
Curl paper	Paper used to secure ends or curl points.
Curl section	Amount and size of area formed by hair.
Curl stem	Base or root hair of section or curl.
Dry curl	A curl formed dry or the dried wet curl.
Fish-hook	Bent-back hair points of badly formed curls.
Hair pins	Fine or invisible pins used to secure curls.
Natural movement	The way hair lies naturally.
Pin curl	Name given to curl secured with pins.
Pli	Name given to curled or set hair.
Reverse curls	Alternating rows of casual curls, C and CC.
Roller curl	Barrelspring-type curls formed on rollers.
Spiral curl	Curl formed from root ends of the hair.
Stand-up curl	Curl with stem directed up from head.
Tail comb	Comb with tail used for sectioning and lifting.
Temporary curl	A curl which loosens in moisture or water.
Tension	The stretch placed on hair when curled.
Wave	Shape produced by dressed or loosened curl.
Wet curl	Hair curled when wet.

Chapter Three — Part Two

Curls and Curling

10. Setting is the use of a variety of curls to achieve good hair shapes. The average set requires two or three different types of curl. There should always be enough of one type to complete a shape or movement.

Curl combinations, the shapes and movements produced, and the curling methods used, must be considered when designing the pli. The final shape will depend on this. Some sections of the hair may need to be lifted, partly or fully. Other style effects require flat, curled, loose or tight, straight or waved hair, in different parts of the head. The basic curls, and variations, are used to produce the required effects.

Curl variations of the barrelspring type are: the roller-type curl, the stand-up or cascade curl, the part-lifted curl, the barrel curl and the reverse curl. These variations will differ slightly from the barrelspring curl, since most are formed with the curl points on the inside and with smaller-diameter centres. The barrelspring curl is varied to produce tight, small, large or loose effects by altering the size of the curl.

The roller, stand-up or cascade, and the barrel-type curls are formed similarly. All have their base stems directed up from the head and produce height and fullness to the sections. The roller curl produces the effects of several cascade curls in one area but without the individual shape and movement produced by separate cascade curls. The main difference between these curls is the amount of tension used and their size.

The cascade or stand-up curl is formed on an oblong base, longer than its width, with an open centre and lifted base. The effect produced is a high, soft, casual, loose shape. Its advantage is the individuality of movement and direction produced. (Fig. 3.14).

The barrel curl is formed on a smaller base than that used by a roller. Its variation of stem direction produces interesting shapes. The curl is shaped from the points, or held in the centre and the points placed on to its base. A clip retains the lifted base and curl position. Barrel curls are wider than cascade and narrower than roller curls. (Fig. 3.15).

The part stand-up curl is a particularly useful type; its angle of stem may be varied between that produced by the cascade and the flat barrelspring curls. The clip secures the stem angle. This curl is used where varied curl lift is required and movements graduate from height to flatness. (Fig. 3.16).

The reverse curl is a term given to any curl used in an alternating manner, i.e. one row of curls clockwise, the next placed counter-clockwise, to produce wave shapes and movements. (Fig. 3.17).

Other curl variations include the following:

The root-tensioned curl, known as a French curl, is formed by wrapping the hair ribbon-like around the finger with the base tensed and firmly held. A lifted base with softly waved lengths are the effects of this curl which allows varied directions to be dressed. Several curl formers have been made to produce root-tension curl effects. (Fig. 3.18).

Fig. 3.14   Cascade or stand-up curl

Fig. 3.15   Barrel curl

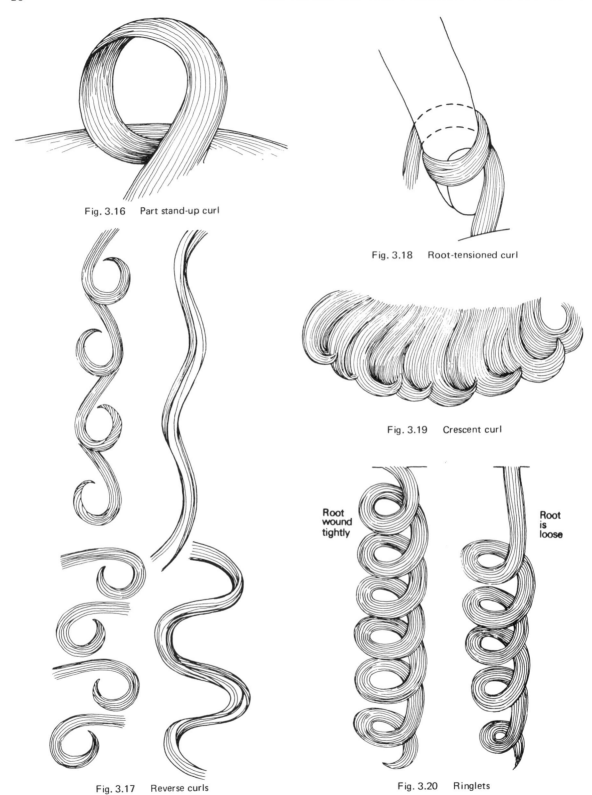

Fig. 3.16   Part stand-up curl

Fig. 3.18   Root-tensioned curl

Fig. 3.19   Crescent curl

Fig. 3.17   Reverse curls

Root
wound
tightly

Root
is
loose

Fig. 3.20   Ringlets

The half-curl or crescent curl is used to produce flat kiss-curl effects on the hairline, wispy shapes at the sides, and flicking ducktail shapes at the back and nape. It is formed by combing the stem direction cleanly, with a large open centre, and securing at the points, without fish-hooking. (Fig. 3.19).

The ringlet curl is an old type but a particularly pleasing shape. It is a feature of many modern dressings and formed in several ways. If formed from the points it will hang loosely since most of the tension is placed at the point end. It may be formed from the roots by spirally winding the hair on thin rollers or long thin curlers. The ends may be secured with crêpe hair, end-papers or string. (Fig. 3.20).

Curling ringlets with heated irons was popular and is still widely used today. Forming ringlets from the roots or points, by rolling the irons until all the hair is wrapped around them, produces pleasing spiral formations. (Fig. 3.21).

Fig. 3.21   Ringlet formation using irons

Curl gadgets of different types and varied shapes of curlers have been devised and used, to produce different curls and effects. Most of them vary the curling method rather than the curl produced. Curl platforms, which raised curl stems and held a wound roller, and circular curl formers or wheels which wound from points or roots, enjoyed a measure of popularity. Some of these are useful but do not replace techniques produced by fingers and simple tools.

11. The steam set is a method of placing dry hair in pli, steaming, and then dressing in the normal way. The hair is first washed and dried. A net should be used to prevent the hair from touching the fan blade of the dryer.

After drying, the hair is then set in the same way as if it were wet. It is more difficult to control and place but it becomes easier with practice. The set hair is then placed in a steamer for three minutes. This allows the hair to become damp and mould to the shapes formed. The set is placed under the dryer again, but only for five minutes. The hair is then ready for dressing.

The steam set enables a quick shape to be produced with shiny and easy-to-dress hair. The normal drying time is considerably reduced and the time taken for complete set and dressing is halved. A head of long hair may be set and dressed in thirty minutes.

12. Heated roller setting is similar to curling with heated irons (see Chapters 6 and 7). The hair is rolled or curled and positioned with heated rollers. The hair is softened by heat and takes the shape in which it is formed or moulded. Applied to the hair after washing and drying, or to dry hair if not too greasy, it becomes a useful and quick setting method.

13. Pli. The term 'pli' derives from the French words *mis-en-pli,* i.e. to put in set or position. It is commonly used in place of the word 'set'. Wet pli or first pli refers to wet hair in position after setting, and dry pli to the set after being dried and dressed. Strictly speaking, the dry pli is the second pli, i.e. a term used to describe placing the hair in set again from a dressed state. A second pli is often used, in competitive hairdressing, to correct a faulty first pli, or to improve the first dressing. (Fig. 3.22).

Fig. 3.22   Pli — first and second

14. Science reference. As the hair is bent or curved in circular shapes which form curls, so the hair is tensioned or stretched. The hair is stretched on the outer side of the curve and compressed on the inner side. Hair is flexible, elastic or 'stretchable' because it is made up of a substance called keratin. Without this physical property there could be little or no hairdressing, since most processes rely on the flexibility of hair. (Fig. 3.23).

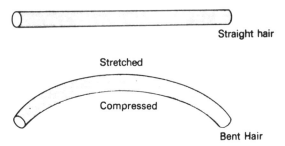

Fig. 3.23   Straight and bent hair

Keratin is a protein made up from a number of chemical combinations or units called polypeptides, which are in turn built of smaller units called amino acids. The polypeptides are likened to long ladder-like chains, with a number of cross-links. Keratin is found in the fingernails, skin and animal epidermal tissue, e.g. horn and feather, and enables hair to be pliable and elastic.

The keratin in the hair is directly acted on in the curling process. When hair is stretched, bent or curved, the keratin linkage system is moved to a new position. When the hair is dried the new shape is retained until acted on by water or moisture, when it reverts to its original natural arrangement.

The hair is able to absorb moisture, and this is termed the hygroscopic property of hair. The amount of moisture in the hair affects its ability to be curled or stretched. Dry hair does not stretch readily or easily. The water content of hair acts as a lubricant and allows the molecular structures of keratin to glide over one another. This allows part of its structure to expand and part of it to contract. When the hair is very dry, as it may be when in poor condition, the surfaces of the keratin molecules grip or seize and do not allow free movement. Water is absorbed in the hair by capillary action, i.e. the spreading of water through minute tube-like spaces between the hair structure, in a similar way to the absorption of ink by blotting paper. (Fig. 3.24).

Drying the hair after washing will evaporate the surface moisture, and normal drying times and temperatures will not unduly affect the hair. Prolonged drying with high temperatures will cause the hair to become dried out, brittle and in poor condition.

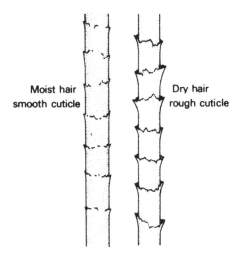

Fig. 3.24   Hair with moisture (cuticle smooth) and hair dry (moisture removed)

Humidity or the moisture content of the atmosphere will affect the duration of the rearranged keratin position or how long a curl will retain its shape. If it is raining or damp the hair absorbs the moisture which causes the keratin structure to revert to its original shape and the curl loosens. Keratin in its normal position is called 'alpha' keratin, and in its stretched state 'beta' keratin. (Fig. 3.25a).

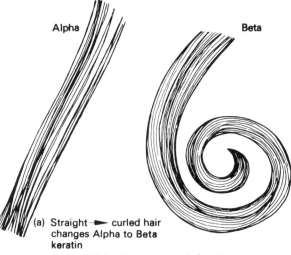

(a) Straight ▶ curled hair changes Alpha to Beta keratin

Fig. 3.25(a)   Keratin — 'alpha' state

The natural curl of hair is due to the shape produced in the formative stage. The keratin arrangement of naturally curly hair is in the = 'alpha' keratin state, and when stretched straight is forced in the 'beta' keratin position. The keratin arrangement in naturally curly and straight hair is 'alpha' and only when forced in a new position does it become 'beta'. (Fig. 3.25b).

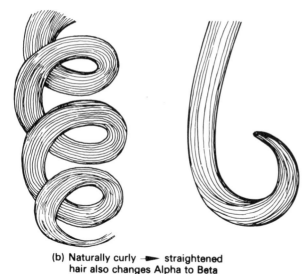

(b) Naturally curly ➤ straightened hair also changes Alpha to Beta keratin

Fig. 3.25(b)   Keratin — 'beta' state

The condition and porosity of hair affects its elasticity or stretchability. If the cuticle, i.e. outside layer of the hair, is open, the moisture content is likely to be low due to normal evaporation, and the amount of stretch restricted. Very dry hair will break easily and if too much tension is applied when curled it may become limp, overstretched and lack spring or bounce.

Curling dry hair with heat is usually best done after washing the hair. Heat softens the hair structure and allows the keratin linkage systems to be moved into a new position, similarly to setting wet hair. This is achieved when blow waving with a hand dryer and curling with heated irons or rollers. It is thought that some of the keratin links are temporarily broken and reform when moisture re-enters the hair.

15. Setting lotions of various types are used to hold hair in position, retain wet curl and wave shapes, and produce a longer-lasting set. This is achieved by slowing down the loosening effects of moisture or lessening the porosity of the hair.

The older types of setting lotion which contained gum, e.g. acacia, karaya and tragacanth, were commonly used for finger waving. These gums form thick lotions which firmly hold and retain shapes formed in the hair. Many have the disadvantage of flaking when dry.

The newer setting lotions are made from quaternary ammonium compounds or plasticizers, e.g. polyvinylpyrolidone, commonly abbreviated to PVP, or polyvinyl acetate. These have the advantage of softening the hair shaft, allowing shapes to be readily formed, preventing the hair from becoming flyaway when dressed, and coating the hair with a fine film of plastic which resists damp and retains the set position longer.

It is important, when using modern lotions, for the hair to be thoroughly towel-dried before application. Too much water left in the hair will dilute the lotion, reduce its effectiveness, or cause flaking on the hair and scalp when it is dry. Flaking is not produced when these lotions are used correctly. Manufacturers add colouring or conditioning agents to some lotions which tone the hair or help to correct an over-greasy or dry hair state. The plasticizing lotions are similar in composition to some types of hair lacquer and most are readily removed by shampooing.

16. Aesthetic reference. The final shape or shapes in which the hair is dressed should be kept in mind during the whole process of setting. The direction each curl stem moves, the way each curl body turns, the combination of curl types and methods of curling, all help to form the lines, curves and patterns which make the final shape. A single line placed by means of a curl stem in a certain direction will have its effect in the finally dressed shape.

The dressing of hair is generally considered to require a measure of artistic appreciation. To set hair in certain positions to achieve an imagined shape requires a great deal more appreciation. Often little artistry is used in the setting foundation, or the set is completely disregarded, relying solely on the ability to dress in the positions required. The basis of good hair shape is set or placed during the setting process, and the ability to dress should be used to enhance. Unless the foundations are well laid, extra dressing will be necessary, more time needed to correct lack of movement, and unpractical, difficult hair shapes result.

Ideally, final dressings should be planned and set for. The look, feel or impression created is important and artistic understanding is necessary for success. To know in which direction this or that curl should be placed, to achieve a certain effect, is a matter of time, practice and experience.

It is in this area of hairdressing particularly that work, exercise and practice in the art room, or on art work, shows the greatest return. It is difficult, in the early days of training, to relate the need for artistry to hairdressing due to the inability to form basic shapes. At a later stage it becomes easier to see where the finer points of art enter the work of the hairdresser, especially in setting and dressing. The effects of the height, depth and width of the curls set can only be appreciated when the ability to form them has been achieved. The line, form and impressions created by them may be fully understood when aesthetic appreciation is achieved.

Some people are able to absorb from everyday happenings impressions which influence their manner and work. Some are able to create originally, seemingly out of thin air, while others have to work hard to produce anything different. The visual arts, e.g. painting, drawing, sculpture, design, architecture, films, ballet, theatre, books, offer a wide range of impressions which usually arouse some reaction which may, directly or indirectly, be applied to hairdressing. A sense of what is liked or disliked, attractive or not, may be cultivated and applied to salon work. Many influences help the young school leaver to develop a sense of good taste in choice of dress and make-up. This is achieved by observation, taking note of others and through the media of advertising. In a similar way, good taste in balance, shape and style may be cultivated through observation of the arts.

Work with various media, e.g. pencil, crayon, paint, helps to create ideas of shape and texture and understanding of colour, shade, line and balance.

It is not suggested that the hairdresser's standard of drawing, painting or sculpture be academically high, or that works of art be produced, but that an aesthetic understanding be cultivated which may be applied to work with hair.

Many natural things, including hair, are used in forms of art and design. The curving lines of wave and curl are reproduced in the flowing and concentric movements of many designs, e.g. fabrics, floor and wall coverings, drapes and curtains, for use in salons and other establishments.

There are many curving lines to be considered in hairdressing and the varied effect one line has on another. The lines of the head, face and neck contours and line of hair growth require thought when placing hair in set. Generally, the effect of a straight line on a curve is to produce a 'hard look'. Curving lines superimposed on square shapes create softness. (Fig. 3.26).

Many varied effects are produced by line and curl patterns on the lines and shapes of the head. Thoughtful application determines effects which produce feelings of pleasure, like, dislike, ugliness and beauty.

Development of artistic appreciation takes time, as does the skill of practical techniques, but it becomes a useful tool of the craft which affects all of one's hairdressing, particularly in the field of fashion styling.

17. The curl in boardwork is a wound or folded piece of weft, i.e. the name given to hair interwoven on silks or threads. It is used as an added hair piece to a dressing or, in similar or contrasting colour, as an addition to hair style or postiche.

There are three types of pin curl, i.e. types of wefted postiche: (a) the pin curl; (b) the pin wave; (c) the pin curl marteau.

(a) *The pin curl* is a small length of weft wound and sewn around a pin wire. The wire becomes the central stem or part of the curl. It is finished with a conical mount or a silk cap, produced by winding sewing silk around the top of the weft and the wire.

Fig. 3.26   Square face shape with hard and soft hairlines

(b) *The pin wave* is similar to a pin curl but the weft is folded, not wound. It is usually sewn without a pin wire and finished with a small loop, by which it may be attached to the dressing.

(c) *The pin curl marteau* contains more weft than a pin curl or wave. It is first folded flat and then attached to a pin wire. It combines both the methods used in forming the pin curl and pin wave.

18. Curling in boardwork involves the use of heated irons of one kind or another. Several methods have been traditionally used to produce temporary curl, e.g. plaiting, crimping and en papillote.

Plaiting is a method of intertwining pieces of hair, either loose hair to be used in postiche or growing from the head. A section of hair is divided in parts, commonly three but up to seventeen, and crossed or intertwined one over or under the other. Soft wave shapes are produced by pinching the plaited hair with heated pinching irons, i.e. flat-ended irons heated and used for hair pinching or pressing, or pressed with a heated flat iron. Plaited hair produces a soft curl or wave useful for adding to postiche or modern dressings. (Fig. 3.27).

Crimping is an old method of lining, marking or frizzing lengths of hair by pressing with heated box or crimping irons, i.e. corrugated-headed irons specially made for the purpose. These are similar to waving irons but with larger shaped metal ends. One head consists of two or more ridges which fit into the hollows of the other head. They are heated and applied to the hair to produce ridges or crimps, but their use is now restricted to historical hair dressings or postiche. (Figs. 3.28 & 3.29).

En papillote, which means 'in paper', is an old method of curling. Small triangular pieces of paper are wrapped around pieces of curled hair and pinched or pressed with heated irons. This may be used on hair to be curled for postiche, or growing from the head. A soft loose curl is produced by this method. (Fig. 3.30).

Fig. 3.29   Crimped hair

Fig. 3.27   Plaited hair

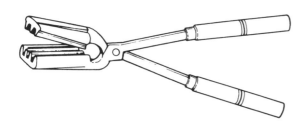

Fig. 3.28   Crimping irons

Fig. 3.30   En papillote

Revision test 1

Q. 1   Describe the differences and uses of two types of curl.
Q. 2   What is a boardwork pin curl? Describe its making.
Q. 3   What is keratin? Describe its function and use.
Q. 4   Name five methods of temporary curling.
Q. 5   How is heat used and applied in curling?
Q. 6   List the differences between roller and other curls.
Q. 7   Describe the curl parts and three rules of curling.
Q. 8   What is the 'clockface system' of curl description?
Q. 9   What are the uses and benefits of curls?
Q.10   Briefly describe each of the following terms:
        (a) En papillote. (b) Mis-en-pli. (c) Croquignole. (d) Root-tensioned. (e) Crescent curl.

Revision test 2

Complete the following sentences:

1   Three variations of a barrelspring curl are:
     (a)...................., (b)...................., (c)....................
2   Winding the hair from points to roots is called ....
3   Three methods of curling hair with heat are called:
     (a)...................., (b)...................., (c)....................
4   Four parts of a hairdressing pin curl are:
     (a)...................., (b)...................., (c)...................., (d)....................
5   The name given to keratin in the 'stretched' state is ...., and in the 'unstretched' state
     ....
6   Four substances used in setting lotions are:
     (a)...................., (b)...................., (c)...................., (d)....................
7   The following curling methods will produce temporary curl:
     (a)...................., (b)...................., (c)....................

Revision test 3

Complete the following sentences with the word or words listed below:

'Alpha' and 'beta' keratin. Hygroscopic. Polypeptides. Amino acids. Chain-link system. Crimping. En papillote.
Croquignole. Spiral.

1   Keratin in a stretched state is called ...., and in an unstretched state ....
2   A substance which absorbs moisture is called ....
3   Keratin is made up of units of .... and ....
4   The chemical structure arrangement in hair is referred to as ....
5   Curling the hair in pieces of paper with heated irons is called ...., and marking or lining the
     hair is called ....
6   Ringlets may be formed by .... winding the hair. .
7   Winding hair from points to roots is called ....

Vocabulary

'Alpha' keratin	The unstretched keratin state.
Amino acid	Units of chemicals which form keratin.
Barrel curl	A wider type of stand-up curl.
'Beta' keratin	The stretched keratin state.
Boardwork pin curl	A wound piece of weft on a pin.
Cascade curl	Stand-up type of barrelspring curl.
Central stem	Centre of a boardwork pin curl or piece.
Chain-link system	Refers to the molecular structure of hair.
Collage	A picture built up of paper or other media.
Conical mount	The finished top of pin curl or marteau.
Crescent curl	The half or kiss curl.
Crimping	Lining, marking or frizzing hair.
Croquignole	Term given to point-to-root winding.
Curled hair	Term given to artificially curled hair.
Curly hair	Term given to naturally curled hair.
En papillote	French term for curling in pieces of paper.
French curl	Usually refers to root-tensioned curl.
Humidity	The moisture content of the atmosphere.
Hygroscopic	The ability to absorb moisture.
Keratin	A chemical protein in hair.
Mis-en-pli	French term for hair in bend or set.
Molecular lubricant	Substance which allows molecule movement.
Part stand-up curl	A curl with stem lifted from head.
Permanent curl	Curl produced by chemical and physical action.
Pin curl marteau	Weft folded and wound around a pin.
Pin wave	A folded piece of weft in boardwork.
Pinching or pressing irons	Irons, heated, to press hair work.
Plaiting	Interlacing of hair.
Polypeptides	Long chain molecules which form keratin.
Reverse curl	Curls placed in alternate rows in different directions.
Second pli	The dressed pli or set.
Steam set	A method of setting dry hair.
Stretchability	Word used for hair stretch or flexibility.

Shampooing and Shampoos

1. Shampoo. The word 'shampoo' is derived from the Hindustani word *champo,* which means to press or rub. Shampooing is the act of pressing or rubbing. To shampoo is to wash, cleanse or remove all dirt, dust, grease or other matter from the surface of the skin and hair by the process of shampooing. This is important for the preparation of the hair for hairdressing techniques and processes, e.g. grease left on the hair may prevent a colouring product or a wave lotion from acting.

The manner in which shampooing is carried out is partly dependent on the equipment and facilities available. There are three common ways of shampooing and each involves the use of a different type of bowl or basin.

2. Types of basin. (*a*) The forward basin, where the client leans forward and over the basin. (*b*) The back-wash basin, where the client leans back on the basin. (*c*) The trough-type basin, where the client may lean backward or forward. The main difference between the use of different basins is the position of the client and operator.

3. The shampooing position in which the client is placed and the position in which the operator stands affect the manner in which the hands are applied and rotated over the client's scalp. The positioning enables the hands to move freely. Too much pressure of the hands or fingers, or incorrectly applied movements during shampooing, may result in discomfort, irritation and possibly headache. (Fig. 4.1).

Apart from cleaning the hair, the method, manner and movements of the shampoo directly affect the mood of the client. If discomfort or irritation has been caused, then on repositioning the client after shampooing, it may be found that she has been put into a bad mood, and may prove difficult to attend or satisfy. These reactions or aroused feelings may occur without the client being directly aware of the cause. Further irritation can be caused by the lightness or harshness of the operator's hands, varying water temperatures, and general carelessness. A correct shampoo application should help to soothe and relax the client, and make the shampoo, and her visit to the salon, more enjoyable.

The action of the hands should be firm but gentle, rotating and smooth. The fingers should be held in a clawed position and the pads of each finger used to feel for the scalp. Do not allow the fingernails to scratch or tear the skin; this can be painful, unpleasant and the cause of infection. Do not allow the fingers to become entangled with the hair, or tug the hair unnecessarily. Lift the hands from the head occasionally, particularly when dealing with long hair. (Fig. 4.2).

The effect of the shampoo, or hand massage movements, on the head is to loosen dirt and dust particles, to spread the shampoo material, and to enable the shampoo and water used to mix with the particles of dirt. Since most dirt on the scalp is of a greasy nature, due to the natural oil of the skin, part of the shampoo will combine with the grease and another part will combine with the water. The shampoo surrounds the dirt, combines with water, and is readily removed by rinsing with more clear water.

4. A method of shampooing. Shampooing follows a generally recognized pattern of procedure. There may be differences due to type of shampoo and equipment used, but the following points will serve as a guide: (*a*) After thoroughly preparing the hair for shampooing, mix and adjust the water flow. (*b*) Mix the water to a comfortable temperature, test on the back of the hand, and check again before applying to the client. Movement of the hose will sometimes vary the water temperature and the sudden shock of hot or cold water can be dangerous. (*c*) Position the client carefully and comfortably over the basin. A clean hygienic strip should be placed between the client and basin to prevent the spread of infection and to cushion the coldness of the basin. (*d*) Wet the client's hair and scalp thoroughly, and do not allow the water to splash on to her clothes. (*e*) Apply the shampoo to the hair by first pouring on to or into the hand, never direct to the hair. If poured direct or continuously too much may be used, causing waste and discomfort due to its sudden coldness. (*f*) Apply the hands and fingers as described and massage firmly, in a rotating, circular movement. Massage the whole head; one spot not covered will become a point of irritation due to

Fig. 4.1   Basin/client/operator positions

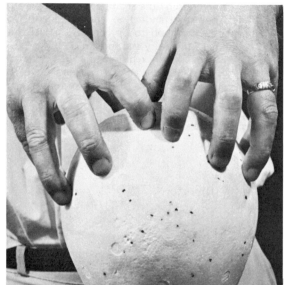

Fig. 4.2   Shampooing — finger action

accrued blood pressure at that spot. (g) Rinse the hair and scalp thoroughly and carefully. (h) Apply more shampoo and massage for the second time. (i) Finally rinse all lather from the hair and skin with clean water. (j) Lift the hair from the eyes and face, and wrap a towel around the head to prevent it falling forward. (k) Reposition the client into an upright position in the chair. Do be gentle when lifting the client's head from over the bowl, particularly after a forward wash. Sudden movements cause the blood to rush to the head and produce giddiness. This applies particularly to the older client, who should be assisted if she is to be moved immediately from the shampoo area. (l) Finally, check the hairline and make sure that all dirt, dust, grease and shampoo has been removed and the hair and scalp are left clean.

The hair should now be ready for combing and preparing for the process to follow. If the client is moved to another position in the salon, do not allow her to do so with wet hair draped over her face. Not only is this dangerous — she could bump into operators working with sharp tools — but it is also most unpleasant.

5.   Shampooing do's and don't's. Remember the following points when carrying out any method of shampooing:

(a)   Do ensure that the protective coverings are in place and that they are not too tight, particularly about the neck.

(b)   Do use only clean sterilized towels and gowns, discard them after use, and do not use on another client without first cleaning and washing. This is common sense and good hygiene, and will prevent the spread of disease.

(c)   When attending the client give complete attention, and never talk 'over' a client.

(d)   If shampoo gets in the client's eyes, gently swill out with cool clean water, and with clean cotton wool or towel wipe from inner corner to outer corner of the eye. A drop of castor oil will ease stinging or discomfort.

(e)   Direct the water flow away from the body when rinsing the hair; this will protect the clothes from a soaking.

(f)   Carefully comb the hair on completion of the shampoo, using the correct method, without pulling or tugging.

(g)   When the client is repositioned for treatments to follow, make sure that the shampoo area has been left clean and tidy, which will appear more pleasant for the next client than a carelessly strewn one.

(h)   Dirty towels should be removed, water taps turned off, shampoo containers returned to correct positions, the bowl rinsed and loose hairs removed. The chair should be left dry and the mirror cleared of any shampoo. It takes just a few minutes to do these things and it is the operator's responsibility to do so, or to see that it is done by those engaged for the purpose. (Figs. 4.3 & 4.4).

(i)   Do not allow the hot water to run continuously; turn it off between washes, or the storage tank will soon empty. This could cause a great deal of unnecessary delay, to say nothing of the cost incurred. More water may be wasted than used, so reduce cost and inconvenience by not allowing it to run to waste.

(j)   On completion of the shampoo, rinse and wash hands before attending to another client. Do not allow shampoo to dry on the hands; this could make them dry and sore.

6. Supply of water required for shampooing needs to be constant. The amount needed for each shampoo will vary between 10—20 litres, depending on its use. The type of water used will vary according to the locality, i.e. it may be soft or hard. Hard water contains chemicals that form a scum deposit when mixed with the chemicals in soap or soap shampoo. The chemicals in hard water are collected from the type of ground or rock that the water passes over on its way to the reservoir.

Water from the clouds in the form of rain falls on different types of rock and land. If some of the chemical salts in the rocks are collected by the water, then hard water may result. Water from rivers and streams, particularly in stony or rocky areas, is likely to be hard. The commonest form of hard water is called 'temporary' hard water, which contains chemicals that can be removed by boiling or by several commercial processes. Water that contains chemicals which cannot be removed by boiling is known as 'permanently' hard water and can only be softened by commercial water-softening processes. Water not softened by boiling or other means forms a scum deposit with soap or soap shampoo. Water which does not form a scum with soap is called soft water e.g. rain and distilled water (see 'Chemicals in water', page 41).

7. Water, plumbing and drainage. Cold water reaches the salon by means of the main supply pipe and is housed near the salon in storage tanks. Receiving and removing the water is achieved by a system of plumbing, a series of pipes that carry water from the mains, through the salon, to the outlet or waste pipes that lead to the drains and sewers. (Fig. 4.5).

An efficient way of removing waste water is necessary. If it is not effectively and efficiently removed from the salon it will stagnate, germ growth or bacteria will be encouraged, and bad odours will result. If bacteria are allowed to form, water becomes

Fig. 4.3   Untidy shampoo area

Fig. 4.4   Tidy shampoo area

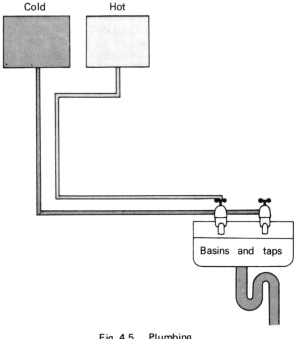

Fig. 4.5   Plumbing

Beneath and between the basin and the main waste pipe there is an S-shaped bend, a waste or water trap. Part of this is detachable to allow a blockage or waste materials, which may have collected in it, to be removed, e.g. a client's ear-ring may be retrieved in this way. The trap is designed so that there is always a water seal in it. This prevents gases and bad smells, arising from the waste and decaying materials in the drains and pipes, from entering the salon. (Fig. 4.7).

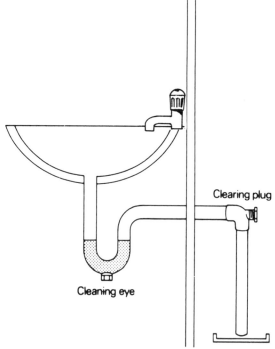

Fig. 4.7   Waste pipe and clearing plug

a disease carrier. In the modern, hygienic salon a free flow of hot and cold water is necessary together with facilities for the efficient removal of the waste.

The flow of water is checked at the tap, the means of control. There are various types of taps, some designed for hot or cold water, and others designed for mixing both. The newer mixing taps or valves are becoming popular since the water can be mixed and then turned off and back on again without altering the preset mixing. This prevents waste of time, hot water and money. (Fig. 4.6).

Fig. 4.6   A modern tap or valve

The hot water system is a means of heating and storing the water taken from the cold water system or the mains, and storing in a separate tank. (Fig. 4.8).

8. **Aesthetics and shampooing.** The appearance of the shampoo area is of importance as regards the effect it has on the client. Apart from the general décor, the hygienic and sanitary arrangements, the display of shampoo containers, with the type and colour of the shampoo, has a pleasing, or otherwise, effect on whoever sits before the display. A clutter of bottles, in varying states of fullness, dry flaking shampoo lifting from bottle necks, unintelligible printed labels half on or off, some with no labels at all, with mixtures of liquids or different shampoos within, are not exactly appealing or designed to please. The client who sees such unsightly arrays will not be favourably impressed with the salon's efficiency or professionalism. In fact, she will doubt whether she is receiving the attention she would wish. (Fig. 4.9).

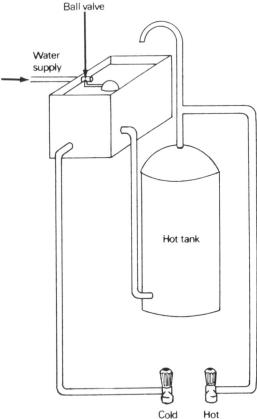

Fig. 4.8   Hot and cold water systems

The shampoo bottles should of course always be clean. They should be kept full, with a clearly labelled tag stating which type of shampoo is contained. There are ranges of shampoo dispensers that do away with shampoo bottles entirely and are practical and economical in use.

Design of containers. The design or shape of the shampoo bottle or container dispenser is important. The graceful line of an elegantly tinted bottle is more pleasing than some of the ugly square bottles that have been, and still are, used. Manufacturers spend a great deal of money on bottle design and its effect on the customer, and they know the difference it has on increasing sales figures. (Fig. 4.10).

Not quite as important perhaps, but still effective, is the colour of the shampoo. The material with which the bottle is made may disguise the shampoo colour, but where it is visible a light subtle colour is more pleasing. A lightly perfumed shampoo is usually appreciated, particularly one that does not clash with the client's own perfume.

Water and art. Water has through the ages aroused interest among artists. The lines of movement, the undulations of waves, the forcefulness or gentleness of water flow, are examples which may stimulate and encourage works of art. The various shades of colour, the eddies and shapes produced by the currents, the sounds of water flowing and the texture and feel of water, are patterns or impressions that may be used in the field of art. Some of these may be seen when using water, and shampooing, coupled with the lines of movements and the circular, rhythmic motions of hair, hands and water, forms a point of contact, though remote, between art and hairdressing. (Fig. 4.11).

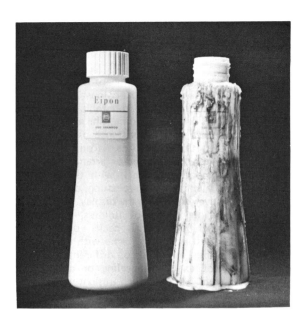

Fig. 4.9   Clean and messy containers

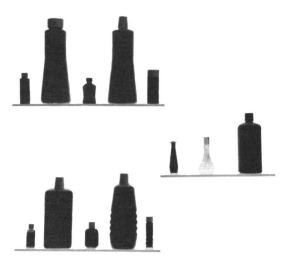

Fig. 4.10   Variety of bottle shapes

Fig. 4.11   Water cascade shape

Revision test 1

Q. 1   Describe the position and action of the hands when shampooing.
Q. 2   Why is a client irritated by the application of a bad shampoo? Give reasons.
Q. 3   Briefly describe a method of shampooing.
Q. 4   Describe the differences between methods of shampooing.
Q. 5   List the precautions to be taken when shampooing.
Q. 6   What is shampooing and what does it do?
Q. 7   How does water arrive at the salon and how is it stored?
Q. 8   What may cause client discomfort when shampooing?
Q. 9   Why is good hygiene in the shampoo area necessary?
Q.10   How is waste water carried away from the salon?

Revision test 2

Complete the following sentences:

1   The word 'shampoo' is derived from the Hindustani word ...., which means to ....
     or ....
2   Three types of shampoo basin used in the salon are called the ...., the .... and the
     ....
3   The hands, when shampooing, should be .... so that the .... may be used.
4   Before applying water to the head it should be ....
5   When shampooing always use clean .... and ....
6   After shampooing, check the ...., ... and .... to make sure it was
     thoroughly done.
7   The shampoo area should always be .... and ....
8   Water which does not form a scum with soap shampoo is called .... water.
9   Shampoo should be placed .... or .... the hand and not directly on to the scalp.
10   The hair should be combed without .... after shampooing.

Revision test 3

Complete the following sentences with the word or words listed below:

Fingertips. Fingernails. Hot water. Warm water. Hard water. Soft water. Hygiene. Infection. Scalp. Waste pipe.

1   After shampooing, rinse the hair with ....
2   When using soap shampoo .... should not be used.
3   Soap or soapless shampoo may be used in ....
4   The hands should be held so that the .... may effectively be used and the .... will not tear the skin.
5   When rinsing the hair very .... should not be used.
6   The application of good .... in the salon will help to prevent the spread of ....
7   An opening in the S-bend or trap enables a blockage to be removed from the ....
8   If the .... is scratched or torn infection could result.

Vocabulary

Aesthetics	The science, study or theory of beauty and the beautiful.
Bacteria	Small disease-causing organisms.
Germs	
Bactericide	A substance that kills bacteria.
Champo	The Hindustani word meaning to press or rub.
Dilute	To weaken or thin with water or other liquids.
Dirt	Particles of dust, grease or oil, anything that will harbour germs.
Disease	An illness, or ill health of mind or body.
Dispenser	A container which distributes its contents or a person who distributes materials.
Germicide	A substance that kills germs.
Hygiene	The science of health and sanitary living.
Hygienic	The application of hygiene.
Sanitary	
Infection	Acquiring disease without actual contact.
Insoluble	A substance that will not dissolve.
Irritating	A substance or chemical that causes skin to itch or become inflamed.
Plumbing	The arrangement of water and waste pipes.
Professional	To act in a manner suitable to the high standards of one learned in a profession.
Psychological	Affecting a person's mind, or attitude.
Reservoir	A place where water is collected and stored.
Scalp	The skin and muscle covering of the head.
Shampoo	Act of shampooing, or material used to cleanse.
Solvent	A chemical that will dissolve another chemical.
Stagnant water	Dirty or impure water.
Sterilized	Free from germs and bacteria.
Texture	The fineness, coarseness or quality of the hair or material.
Undulation	The rise and fall of waves and wave shapes.
Waste trap	Placed in waste pipes. Prevents, by means of a water seal, the backflow of water and
S-bends	gases, and enables pipes to be unblocked.

Shampooing and Shampoos

9. The first type of shampoo was probably water. The water of lakes, rivers and seas is still used in many parts of the world for washing hair, clothes and bodies. Many substances have been used throughout the course of time, e.g. spirit, soap, and now the modern soapless detergent. The chemistry of shampoo is a complex study, and much research has yet to be done on the cleaning of natural and man-made fibres, e.g. human hair and nylon.

Generally, modern shampoos are divided into two categories as regards the needs of hairdressers and hairdressing: the 'wet' and the 'dry' shampoos.

10. The wet shampoo is almost exclusively used in the modern salon. Any shampoo involving the use of water, to rinse or wet the hair, is termed a wet shampoo.

All kinds of soap and soap shampoo have been used over the years. Soft and hard block soaps, green, yellow and white soap have all been used, the commonest probably being the green soft soap made from vegetable oils and potassium hydroxide.

Soft soap shampoo can be made by dissolving the soap in spirit or alcohol, with an alkali, e.g. potassium carbonate, and adding preservative, colour, perfume and water. This type of shampoo should be used in soft or softened water. If used in hard water an insoluble scum is formed between the salts in the water and the chemicals in the soap, which is deposited on the hair. This scum can be easily removed by rinsing with vinegar or acetic acid, or lemon juice or citric acid, diluted with water. Suitable and effective acid hair rinses can be made by adding the juice of one or two lemons, or 20 g of citric acid crystals, to 1 litre of water, or adding 56 ml of vinegar or 6% acetic acid solution to 56–250 ml of water. Owing to the modernizing of water supplies in many parts of the country, water is now too hard for soft soap shampoo to be used generally without acid finishing rinses being applied after shampooing.

11. Chemicals contained in water determine the type of water, e.g. permanently hard, or temporarily hard (see 'Supply of water', page 36). Permanently hard water contains calcium and magnesium sulphates which cannot be removed by boiling. Temporary hard water contains calcium and magnesium bicarbonates, which are easily removed by boiling. If the salts or chemicals in permanent or temporary hard water are not removed, they join with chemicals in soap to form insoluble scum deposits, e.g. if sodium stearate (hard soap) is used with hard water containing a calcium salt, then calcium stearate (an insoluble scum) and a soft water containing a sodium salt is formed. Soft water is water free from calcium and magnesium salts, or water softened by a special process, which readily forms a lather and does not produce a scum deposit when used with soap.

Water softening. Hard water can be softened by several processes. The mineral ion-exchange process, which uses sodium aluminium silicate and exchanges calcium sulphate for sodium sulphate, is one way of removing scum-forming chemicals. The demineralization process, which more thoroughly removes water hardness, is another. Both processes are fitted to the water supply of the salon. (Fig. 4.12). Other means of softening hard water involve the use of sodium carbonate, slaked lime, i.e. calcium hydroxide, and sodium hexametaphosphate. More lather is formed between soap and soft water than between soap and hard water. Mineral salts in hard water reduce the foaming action of soap.

12. Soapless shampoos are effective in hard and soft water without the formation of scum deposits. The first soapless shampoos were very degreasing and caused dryness of the hair and skin. Though now made in gentler form, it is necessary to use a little of them and to rinse from the hair thoroughly. It is possible for a client to react or be allergic to a soapless shampoo.

The bases from which soapless shampoos are made are sulphonated fatty alcohols or oils, e.g. triethanolamine lauryl sulphate, commonly known as T.L.S. The sulphonated oils are the products of sulphonation, i.e. vegetable oils treated with sulphuric acid under the influence of heat and in which some atoms of the sulphur are linked with some atoms of the carbon in the oil. Sodium hydroxide may be used to neutralize and form a neutral sulphonated oil. Sulphonated castor oil or Turkey red oil is used in making oil shampoo.

Synthetic detergents, surface active agents or

Hard water

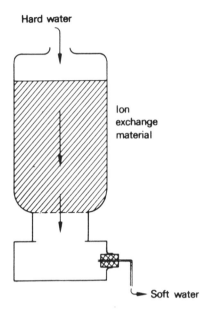

Ion exchange material

Soft water

Fig. 4.12   Water-softening system

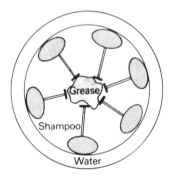

Fig. 4.13   Detergent action

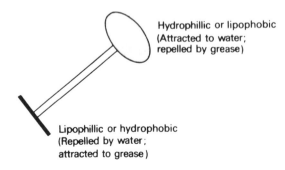

Hydrophillic or lipophobic (Attracted to water; repelled by grease)

Lipophillic or hydrophobic (Repelled by water; attracted to grease)

Fig. 4.14   Detergent molecule

surfactants are terms given to the soapless detergent bases of many shampoos. They are classified according to their chemical properties which include, for example, anionic, cationic, non-ionic and ampholytic, terms used to refer to actions or reactions in solutions, and when in contact with various surfaces, e.g. the scalp. Anionic detergents, which include soap, have negative electro-chemical actions. Cationic detergents, e.g. cetrimide, have electro-chemically positive effects. Non-ionics are considered to be electro-chemically neutral and are used mainly as foam boosters and stabilizers. The ampholytic detergents may be either negative or positive in reaction, depending on the acidity or alkalinity of the surface on which they may be used. The effects of these chemicals, and their reactions with other materials, particularly as more are incorporated in hairdressing products, should prove an interesting development of hairdressing chemistry.

13. The action of the shampoo depends first on its ability as a wetting agent, i.e. substances which lower or break the surface tension of water, in this case used initially to rinse the hair. Surface tension is an elastic force in the surface of a liquid which it causes to contract. Grease and dirt particles are then surrounded by the shampoo water solution, are emulsified or suspended, and finally removed by further rinsings. (Fig. 4.13).

The action involves the different ends of the molecules of the detergent shampoo. One end is called hydrophilic, i.e. water-loving, and the other end is called hydrophobic, i.e. water-hating, or lipophilic, i.e. grease-loving. With one end of the detergent molecule attracted to grease and the other to water, both combine in such a way that the removal of grease and dirt is made easy. (Fig. 4.14).

14. Variations of shampoos are made to suit different types of hair. This applies to both soap- and soapless-based shampoos. The form in which the shampoo is made will vary as often as fashion dictates. At one time a cream shampoo is popular, then a liquid, semi-liquid or powder type becomes more in demand. In whichever form the shampoo is made, the ingredients and purpose of the shampoo to deal with a certain type of hair or condition are of more importance. The shampoo usually derives its name from the active ingredient in the shampoo, e.g. lemon shampoo is so called because lemon essence or citric acid is incorporated. This gives rise to a large number of shampoos with different names and varying effects.

One of the most popular, at the moment, is the *medicated shampoo*. This is intended for use on hair and scalps that need a bactericide to deal with certain conditions, e.g. scaling or dryness of skin and slight irritations. Most medicated shampoos are intended to prevent, rather than cure, conditions of the hair and scalp.

Treatment shampoos are designed to treat certain states or conditions of the hair and scalp. These shampoos may contain various substances, e.g. cetrimide, selenium sulphide or zinc pyrithione. If these types of shampoo are used in the salon, protect the client's eyes, and clean hands and fingernails after use. Many medicated and treatment shampoos are toxic and may irritate the eyes. Some clients may be allergic to some medications used, and blonde or bleached hair may be darkened by them. Infectious scalp conditions or diseases should be treated by a doctor.

Oil shampoos may contain pine, olive, palm, almond, coconut and other vegetable oils, and are usually intended for use on dry hair and scalps. The aim of an oil shampoo is to clean and deposit a small amount of oil on the hair. An application of oil is more effective and often to be preferred to an oil shampoo.

An oil application or treatment consists of warm vegetable oil, e.g. olive, being applied to the dry hair. It is left in contact with the hair for 5–15 minutes. Shampoo is then applied to the oiled hair which is rinsed and washed in the ordinary way. Application of the shampoo direct to the oily hair is important, before rinsing, to enable the shampoo to emulsify the oil. Steam or heat from a steamer or hot towels will aid the process by allowing the hair to swell and the oil to penetrate. Oil shampoos which contain sulphonated castor or olive oil may be used similarly to an oil application. These have the advantage of not requiring another shampoo since they are sufficient cleansers themselves (see Chapter 13, page **184**).

Egg shampoo can be made from real egg or a substance known as lecithin, which is found in egg yolk and the soya bean. The best egg shampoo is made from real egg, which acts as an emulsifier, i.e. it combines with grease and rinses easily. Raw egg is good for both dry and greasy hair. The yolk should be used on dry hair, and the white used on greasy hair. The egg yolk or white may be mixed with a little water, soapless shampoo or used by itself. When using real eggs for shampooing never use too hot water; not only could the client's head be scalded, but hard-boiled egg is difficult to remove from the hair!

Lemon shampoo contains citric acid, found in real lemon, and may be used on greasy or dry hair. This type of shampoo, like acid rinses, is best used on the fine, fluffy, flyaway type of hair which is then left in a shiny, dressable and manageable condition.

Beer and champagne shampoos usually contain acid and other materials which are used for the finish given to the hair. Due to the bottling, these usually look or appear more like the real substances than they really are. These shampoos may be used on dry or greasy hair. Real beer and champagne are best used as a rinse after washing, and act as good setting lotions to give the hair body and lustre.

Types of shampoo which are named after one ingredient contained in them are many, e.g. oil of orange and cactus, attar of roses, egg flip, but the final guide for their use must be the results achieved and the reputation of the maker. If a shampoo does not achieve the results claimed for it, then products known to be reliable and effective should be used. Often too much is expected of a shampoo, and where other than cleansing properties are required, the application of substances made for specific purposes should be made, rather than relying entirely on the shampoo.

Dry shampoos are of two kinds, the liquid spirit type, and the dry shampoo powder. *The liquid spirit* type of dry shampoo was, and still is, used more in men's salons than in ladies'. The liquid spirit is sprinkled on to the hair and then massaged or frictioned with the hands for a few minutes. The spirit dissolves the grease and dirt which is then removed from the hair and scalp by rubbing with a towel. No water is normally used.

The dry shampoo powder is used to clean hair when the application of water is not required. The powder is sprinkled on to the hair, where it mixes with the dirt and grease, which is then removed by firm brushing. A certain amount of grease and dirt is removed this way, but it cannot be favourably compared with a good wash.

These dry shampoos may be made from orris root, the root of a species of iris, starch, mild alkali and absorption detergents or absorbent powders, mainly talc or chalk.

Powdered soap or soapless shampoo in powder form, normally mixed with water to form a wet-type shampoo, should not be confused with dry shampoo powder.

Dry cleaners are made from liquid solvents, e.g. white spirit, petrol and other branded substances. These may be used for cleaning hair, postiche and other fibrous materials. The disadvantages of the use of these dry cleaners must be considered, e.g. the inflammability of petrol and spirit, and the evaporation of harmful fumes. Petrol and spirit are best used in the open air. Carbon tetrachloride should only be used where there is suitable ventilation and care taken to avoid contact with eyes and skin — gloves must be worn. There should be no smoking when using these cleaners. New products are now being introduced which do not have these disadvantages, e.g. trichloroethylene.

15. The choice of a shampoo is determined by (a) the type, texture and condition of the hair; (b) the type of water used in the locality or the salon; (c) what is required of the shampoo; (d) the treatment the hair is to receive after shampooing.

(a) *The texture* of hair is its size and quality. Fine hair usually lacks body and bounce and is soon impaired or damaged. Shampoos which degrease or fluff the hair are best avoided. The best to use with this type of hair are those that add body, e.g. beer and champagne, or leave an acid finish on the hair surface, e.g. lemon. The most difficult of hair, the fine, lank, greasy hair, requires specially made shampoos which contain, e.g., borax, or other alkalis which seem to have a drying effect on the hair. Coarse hair is more often dry than greasy and requires shampoo which contain egg yolk, oil or lanolin. Citric or acetic acid may be used on coarse or fine hair, either in shampoos or rinses. Whatever the hair condition, only shampoos specially made to remedy the condition should be used. Excessive dryness or greasiness may be helped by the use of special shampoos. (Fig. 4.15 a, b & c).

Fig. 4.15(a)   Cross section of hair, fine — coarse

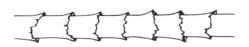

Fig. 4.15(b)   Coarse dry hair — open surface

Fig. 4.15(c)   Fine hair — smooth surface

(b)   The type of water used in the salon or the locality helps, initially, to determine the correct shampoo to use. Soap-based shampoos should not be used with hard water without scum-removing rinses being used afterwards. If the water is soft, or specially softened with water softeners, then most shampoos can be practically and economically used. The type of water used is not considered each time the shampoo choice is made, but when the salon is making its choice of suitable shampoos to stock or order.

(c)   What is required of the shampoo, whether it is to clean or remove excessive grease, lacquer, colour, or to treat a condition, should always be considered before each shampoo. Lacquer-removing shampoos contain lacquer solvents and are usually applied direct to the hair before applying water. For the removal of colour, special colour solvents or strippers are used.

The removal of nits or lice requires special treatment shampoos or applications containing, e.g., lethane, gammexane or derris creams, specially made for the treatment of pediculosis (see Chapter 14, page 191). These special chemicals will kill the lice and the nits will then need to be removed from the hair. Acetic acid or vinegar rinses will help to loosen the eggs or nits on the hair which may be easily removed by a fine toothcomb. Normally the material that exudes from the body of the nit hardens around the hair, and the only way it can be moved is by sliding it along from root to point.

(d)   The treatment that the hair is to receive after shampooing is another consideration in the choice of a suitable shampoo. Hair to be bleached, coloured or permanently waved should not be washed with shampoos that leave chemical deposits, i.e. oil or colour, in the hair which may affect processes to follow. Chemicals, e.g. tar derivatives, found in many medicated shampoos, could affect the resulting colour of a tint. Oil shampoo and conditioners may coat the hair and block the action of permanent waving lotions, preventing the 'perm' from taking. Bleached or blonde hair may become discoloured by several materials. It is wiser to use a bland, gentle shampoo, which will leave no chemical traces to interfere with the hairdressing process the hair is to receive after shampooing.

16. **Before shampooing,** examine the scalp and assess the type and condition of the hair. Consider what is required of the shampoo and the process to follow. Then after taking these points into consideration, choose the shampoo. If there are any spots, areas of inflammation, sores or severe tenderness present, the manager or manageress should be informed and they may advise the client to visit her doctor. No shampoo or treatment should be given if there are any signs of disease, or the condition of the scalp is in any way doubtful.

17. **During the shampoo** (see above, page 34), the blood flow throughout the scalp is affected by the massage movements, the water temperature, and the positions of the client. The blood supplies to the head are transported from the heart by means of the aorta to the common carotid artery in the sides of the neck. This subdivides into the internal carotid arterial branch which passes through the skull and deep into the head for supplies to the brain, and the external carotid arterial branch which subdivides in the neck to form three branches, the facial, temporal and occipital. The hair follicles are supplied by blood from the temporal and occipital branches. (Fig. 4.16a).

Blood is returned to the heart from the head by means of the jugular veins, situated in the sides of the neck. The jugular veins subdivide into the internal and external branches. The internal branch drains off blood from the deeper parts of the head. The external branch removes blood and waste material from the

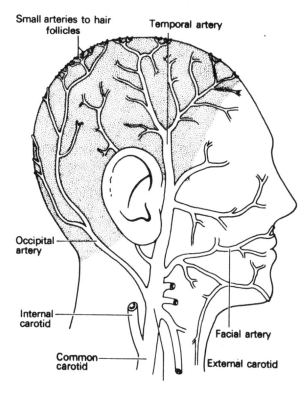

Small arteries to hair follicles

Temporal artery

Occipital artery

Internal carotid

Common carotid

Facial artery

External carotid

Fig. 4.16(a)   Path of arterial blood to head and neck

hair follicles and scalp. The jugular veins carry the blood into the superior vena cava which in turn carries the blood back to the heart and lungs. (Fig. 4.16b).

18. After shampooing, the operator's hands need some consideration. Heads may be washed once or twice a week, but the hands are shampooed several times a day in the salon. This causes the hands to dry, crack and become roughened. To prevent this, rinse the hands thoroughly after shampooing with warm clear water. Pat the hands dry, gently, with a clean towel. A suitable barrier cream may be used for protection at the start of the day, and an oil or skin cream used in the evening. A little care for the hands each day may prevent a lot of worry, discomfort and lost time.

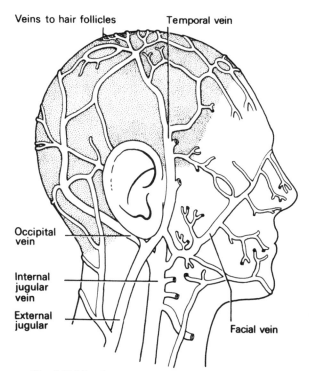

Veins to hair follicles

Temporal vein

Occipital vein

Internal jugular vein

External jugular

Facial vein

Fig. 4.16(b)   Path of venous blood to head and neck

Revision test 1

Q. 1   Describe the effects of soapless and soap shampoos on hair. List the advantages and disadvantages of each.

Q. 2   Name three different types of shampoo, their uses, effects and types of hair they are best used on.

Q. 3   Describe the blood supply to the scalp and how this is affected when shampooing.

Q. 4   What are the considerations for choosing the correct shampoo? List reasons.

Q. 5   What are the differences between dry and wet shampoos and dry cleaners?

Q. 6   What are the differences between medicated and treatment shampoos? Give an example of each.

Q. 7   How should lacquer 'build-up' be removed from hair?

Q. 8   Name five chemicals used in shampoos and on which type of hair these shampoos may be used.

Q. 9   Briefly describe each of the following terms: (a) T.L.S. (b) Medications. (c) Detergency. (d) Acid rinses. (e) Absorption detergents.

Q.10   Briefly describe each of the following terms: (a) Insoluble scum. (b) Water-softening process. (c) Sulphonation. (d) Hydrophobic. (e) Egg shampoos.

Revision test 2

Complete the following sentences:

1   The choice of a suitable shampoo is determined by:
(a)   ....
(b)   ....
(c)   ....
(d)   ....

2   A suitable acid rinse can be made by adding .... of .... to .... of water.

3   Three methods of water softening are:
(a)   ....
(b)   ....
(c)   ....

4   Soapless shampoos may be made from .... which are called .... or ....

5   Three medicaments used in medicated shampoos are:
(a)   ....
(b)   ....
(c)   ....

6   Three medicaments used in treatment shampoos are:
(a)   ....
(b)   ....
(c)   ....

7   Dry cleaners are made from liquid solvents, e.g.
(a) ...., (b) ...., (c) ....

8   A sulphonated oil is produced by the action of .... on a .... An example is ....

Revision test 3

Complete the following sentences with the word or words listed below:

T.L.S. Spirit. Turkey red oil. Lipophilic. Sulphonated oil. Absorption detergents. Insoluble scum. Carbon tetrachloride. Acid rinses. Hydrophobic.

1   The following shampoos contain: dry liquid— ...., soapless— .... and dry powder shampoo— ....

2   A soap shampoo used in hard water may produce an .... which can be removed with ....

3   An oil used in the making of soapless shampoos is a .... and an example is ....

4   The grease-attracted end of the shampoo molecule is called ...., and the opposite end is

called ....
5   An active ingredient of a dry cleaner is ....

Vocabulary

Allergy	Reaction to a chemical or substance.
Bland	Mild, smooth or gentle.
Carbon tetrachloride	A dry cleaning fluid used for postiche.
Carotid arteries	Vessels carrying blood to the head.
Colour stripper	Solvent used for removing synthetic colour.
Condition	The state of the skin or hair.
Demineralizing	A water-softening process.
Detergent	A substance that cleans.
Emulsifier	Combines oil and water in solution.
Evaporates	Passes off in vapour.
Hydrophilic	Water-loving end of shampoo molecule.
Hydrophobic	Water-'hating' or grease-'loving'.
Infectious	Disease that may be caught without contact.
Inflammation	Areas of redness or pinkness of the skin.
Ion exchange	A water-softening process.
Jugular veins	Vessels carrying blood from the head.
Lipophilic	Grease-loving end of detergent molecule.
Lustre	Brightness, sheen or gloss.
Medicament	An active chemical in medicated lotions.
Nit or ova	The egg of the louse.
Pediculosis capitis	Infestation of the head by lice.
Pediculus capitis	The head louse.
Postiche	A hair piece.
Selenium sulphide	A medicament used in treatment shampoos.
Sodium hexa-metaphosphate	A chemical used in water softening.
Sulphonated oil	A vegetable oil after sulphonation.
Sulphonation	Process of subjecting oils to sulphuric acid.
Synthetic	Artificially made.
T.L.S.	Triethanolamine lauryl sulphate.
Tar derivatives	Chemicals and medicaments from tar products.
Vegetable oils	Oils of olive, pine, coconut, almond, etc.
Zinc pyrithione	A medicament used in treatment shampoos.

Perming—Sectioning and Winding

1. Perming is the name given to the physical and chemical process of permanently waving or curling hair. It is a word used commonly in the salon for all kinds of permanent waving processes.

Learning to perm involves an understanding, and practice, of sectioning and winding the hair. After learning techniques, e.g. shampooing and curling, etc., perming preparation naturally follows. This allows further developments of hand, tool and hair control to be achieved and a new skill to be embarked upon.

Artificial curl or wave in the hair remains 'permanently' until it is either cut off or grown out. If the hair or curl is not cut it will gradually grow further away from the scalp until the hair reaches the end of its growing period and falls out.

The physical part of most perming processes involves winding the hair, by one method or another, around a curler. The hair is then softened, by chemicals or heat, and takes the shape of the curler around which it is wound. Since the chemical structure of the hair is being acted upon, it is necessary to understand, and be fully competent in, each of the techniques concerned with perming.

2. Sectioning generally is the dividing of the head of hair into neat, controllable divisions, which enables the work to proceed with the minimum of inconvenience to the client, the process and the operator. Sectioning the hair for combing, cutting, colouring or bleaching should always be carried out in preparation for each particular process, which is described under respective chapter headings.

3. Sectioning for perming enables the hair to be conveniently divided in small sections, for ease of working, with the minimum of wasted time, and without the perm process being affected. If hair needs to be resectioned during the process, the time taken could adversely affect the perm, e.g. render it over-processed or tightly frizzed.

Method of sectioning for cold perming. (a) After the hair has been carefully prepared and shampooed, it should be cleanly combed and free of tangles. (b) It is then centrally divided from the forehead to the nape. (c) The hair is then divided from ear to ear over the top back part of the head. The top and side hair should be prevented from interfering with further

sectioning by securing with clips. (d) The back hair is then divided in three nape sections and three top back sections. (e) The two sides are divided from the top front section, approximately at mid-eyebrow level. Nine sections should be produced and this is referred to as the nine-section method. (Fig. 5.1).

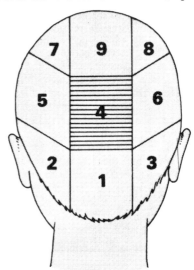

Fig. 5.1   Nine-section method

There are many variations of sectioning methods; some produce eight sections, others more or fewer. For basic work it is convenient to practise with the nine-section method. Once this is achieved, other methods are easily adapted to.

Tools required for sectioning are: a tailcomb which is used for dividing the hair, securing clips to prevent the sectioned hair falling, and at least one of the curlers to be used in the perming process. This may be used to check the length and depth of the section and to ensure the correct size. At a later stage it is necessary for rubber gloves, to protect the hands, to be worn, and it helps considerably to practise wearing them.

Manufacturers recommend a sectioning method to be used with their products, and it is invariably the best fitted. Regardless of sectioning method, provided the end result is suitably achieved then the method is justified, but all methods of working should be efficient and precise.

Many experienced operators will basically divide the hair in four sections. They then take the smaller sections required and wind immediately without any apparent further sectioning. To the untrained it appears that sectioning is not being attempted, but in fact it is. Senior assistants know from practice and experience what size section to take, at which angle and at which part of the head. Taking the time to practise sectioning methods in the early stages will considerably speed up working processes at a later date.

Sectioning for tepid perming is similar to cold perm sectioning, i.e. the nine-section method may be used, but the sub-sections for winding need to be almost twice as large. This is necessary for the heater clamp, i.e. the means of transferring heat to the wound curler, or the heat-producing pad used in tepid systems of waving, to fit over or on to the wound hair. The hair sections required for tepid perming should measure 75 mm by 18 mm approximately. (Fig. 5.2).

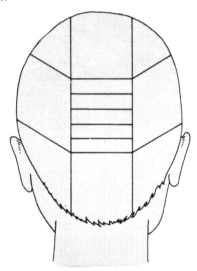

Fig. 5.2   Tepid perm sectioning

Sectioning for hot perming varies considerably and is dependent on the system used. Generally oblong sections, 75 mm by 25 mm, or 25 mm square, are divided all over the head. In the older spiral wind systems, i.e. winding the hair from roots to points, small square sections were used. With the more recent though now infrequently used hot perming systems, larger oblong sections are divided. (Fig. 5.3).

Practice. It is necessary to practise the various ways in which hair can be sectioned. To subdivide the hair into small 'parcels' is, at the beginning, a

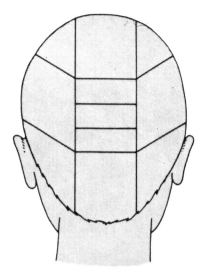

Fig. 5.3   Hot perm sectioning

cumbersome exercise. As the student becomes more proficient in the use of comb and control of hair, so the technique becomes easier and work is quicker and neater. At first confine practice to a practice block until the actions are speeded up. Practise sectioning a dry and a wet head of hair. Do not be disappointed if the first attempts at sectioning a live head do not compare with those achieved on the practice block. Movements of the live model, texture, length and general condition of the hair will take some time to adjust to.

4. Winding is the process of placing the sectioned hair on to suitable shapes and sizes of sticks, bigoudi or curlers so that the perming action may be carried out. The movement is a rolling, turning or curling of the hair on to the curlers.

Method of winding a cold perm curler. (*a*) A section of hair no longer or thicker than the size of curler to be used should be sectioned and cleanly combed directly and firmly, not tightly, out from the head. (*b*) The hair points should be level with the section centre and placed on the middle of the curler. (*c*) The points may be held and controlled by the finger and thumb, thumb uppermost, with one hand. (*d*) With a turning wrist action the hair points are directed round and under. The aim is to lock them against the main body of the hair around the curler. (*e*) After the first turn the curler is transferred to the opposite hand and turned again. The thumb should not be allowed to push the hair away from the curler or the points will loosen. (*f*) After two or three turns are completed the hair points should be firmly secured in position. The curler is then wound down to the scalp.

When one hand is winding and turning, the other hand should be directing any loose hairs on to the

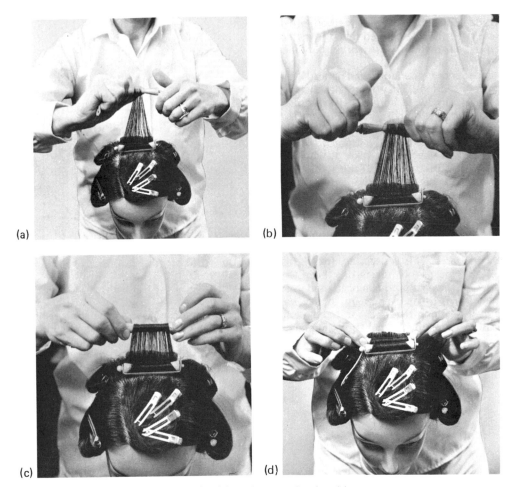

Fig. 5.4(a) – (d)   Winding – hand positions

curler. It is important that, when starting to wind, the thumb is in an uppermost position. If it is held underneath the curler the turning movement is restricted and unable to lock the hair points. (Fig. 5.4 a & b).

The winding of a curler is comparatively simple when all the important points concerned are considered, which is the aim of practice. To ensure correct winding and positioning of curlers, in the minimum of time, the following points should be noted:

(a) Cleanly comb the hair together or pieces will slip and make the winding difficult.

(b) Place the hair points centrally on the curler or the hair will bunch on one side and be loose on the other.

(c) Hold the hair directly out from the head. If it is allowed to slope downwards the curler will not sit centrally on the base section. This will cause the curlers to overlap and rest on the skin.

(d) Angle the curler to correspond with the position of the head on which it is to rest before winding to ensure a neat fit on the head.

(e) Firmly hold the hair, but do not stretch it, to lock the hair point cleanly at the beginning of the wind, or the hair will become bent or buckled or fish-hooked.

(f) Keep the curler level as winding proceeds. If it is allowed to move from side to side, or up and down, the hair will fit the curler unevenly.

(g) Complete the wind and place the curler in the centre of the section. If it does not fit centrally, rewind.

(h) Secure the curler carefully to prevent loosening and without pressing into the hair. The hair is softened during the perming process and bad curler fixing could cause the hair to break.

(i) Each hand should be in complete control,

particularly when transferring the curler from one hand to the other. Undue rocking or movement may cause the ends to slip, the hair to bunch and firmness to slacken.

(j) The hair should feel evenly wound, look neat, without any pieces sticking out and with the points cleanly wound.

(k) Modern cold waving requires the hair to be wound firmly and evenly but never stretched, which could cause hair breakage and over-tight results. (Fig. 5.5).

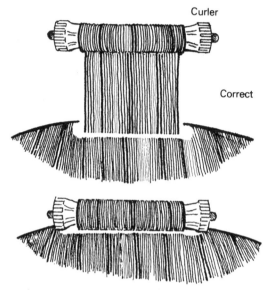

Fig. 5.5   Curler and hair positions

5. Winding aids. The tail of a tailcomb is useful for directing small pieces of hair on to the curler, but it should not be allowed to pass around the curler. This may cause unevenness of winding or small pieces of hair to slip from the curler.

End-papers or wraps are specially made as a perm winding aid. They ensure winding control if neatly folded on the hair, not bundled up, after combing the hair. The paper should overlap the ends of the hair so that the paper is wound first which prevents fish-hooks. If small pieces of hair are to be wound, e.g. short nape hair, half an end-paper should be sufficient; a full piece may cause unevenness of the hair. Specially made end-papers should be used and not other kinds of tissue or paper which may absorb the perm lotion from the hair and cause the points to be straight.

Crêpe hair is an old aid for securing the hair points when winding and is still in use today. Small pieces of crêpe are pulled from a 'rope', i.e. a length of wefted hair on threads or strings, and placed around the hair points slightly overlapping the ends. This allows sufficient grip for winding and prevents the hair points slipping. Like perm end-papers, too much should not be used or the hair will be made to bunch.

Curlers used for cold perm systems are many and varied. Coloured plastic, wood, bone and china are used, the different colours being used to indicate size. The bigger the diameter of curler used, the bigger the wave produced. The reverse applies to the smaller curlers. The smallest curlers are used for winding the short hairs of the nape or for producing tightly curled hair. Most curlers are now made with smaller diameter centres than the ends. This enables the thinner wound hair to fill the concave part neatly and evenly. This applies particularly to tapered hair, i.e. hair sections which taper to a point. Clubbed hair, i.e. hair bluntly cut across and not tapering to a point, should be evenly placed across the curler centre.

6. Winding practice. Practise winding the hair when it is wet; it may be dampened down with water, not lotion. Dry hair is difficult to wind and rarely necessary for most perming systems. In the beginning practise without the use of aids, e.g. end-papers or crêpe hair. When the winding technique is mastered, aids may be used to speed the process. Control is then achieved by practice which will be most welcome in the event of winding aids not being available. Practice should take place on live heads or models as soon as possible to enable the different types of hair and head to become adapted to.

Models used for practice winding will in the early stages present problems. Each model head will be a little different as regards size, hair texture, type and size of curler required, and one may be more sensitive or tender than another. Having arrived at the stage where a 'block head' can be wound in a reasonable amount of time, e.g. 40–60 minutes, new techniques will need to be developed which will, at first, slow down the whole operation and also make the use of a live model necessary.

It is soon learnt that small pieces of hair cannot be wound on the largest curlers, and that talking to the model when trying to wind the shortest hairs in the nape does not help. The model's head should be gently positioned to enable the hair to be wound comfortably. Towels placed incorrectly cause inconvenience, and no doubt many other little points will be met, tackled and overcome with practice.

The time is soon reached when 'live perming', i.e. using perm lotions on real hair, may be considered. The time taken for winding a whole head of hair should then be reduced to approximately 20–30 minutes.

Angles of winding should be correct and maintained throughout the whole process of winding. For even winding the hair should be held out from the head with the points in line with the centre of the section. The curlers should not be 'dropped' or 'dragged', i.e. allowed to drop below the hair section, particularly as winding progresses further up the head. This is a common fault and causes the curler, and the wound hair, to rest on the skin. This may result in sore or broken skin and possibly lead to infection. (Fig. 5.6).

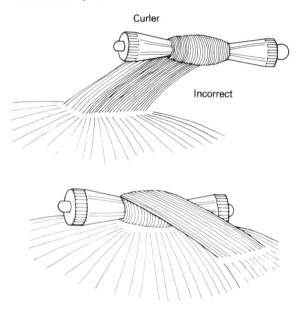

Fig. 5.6   Wrong curler position on scalp

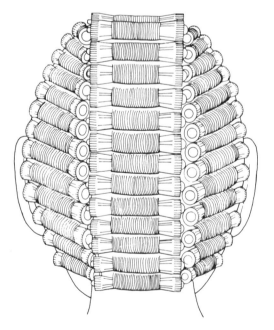

Fig. 5.7   A wound head of hair

After winding is complete, checks should be made for curler positions, firmness of curlers and any unwound pieces of hair. The hair should then be ready for the chemical processing which usually follows. (Fig. 5.7).

7. Preparation for perming, as for other processes, is necessary to save a lot of otherwise wasted time and inconvenience. All curlers should be placed in separate sections in a tray, depending on their size. Tools, winding aids, reagents or lotions and other materials should be close at hand, and collected together beforehand. Good preparation enables the fullest attention to be given to both the client and the techniques concerned.

Hands are affected by cold perming reagents. The skin is softened, similarly to the hair, the natural oils dry out and the skin becomes sore and tender. In this state the hands are liable to become infected. Fine rubber or plastic gloves, or a suitable barrier cream, i.e. a cream which resists or retards chemical reaction with the skin, should be used to protect the hands. If gloves are not worn, at least rinse and dry the hands thoroughly after using the reagent and apply hand creams and oils. If repeated perming is to take place, the only safe measure is the use of a protective covering. Gloves should be kept clean, well washed and powdered, and not worn longer than necessary.

8. Perming. The common factor in all methods or systems of perming the hair is that it is softened by chemicals or heat, applied by one means or another, made to take the shape of whatever it is wound upon, and then allowed to cool, harden or be brought back to its natural 'hair' state.

Application of a cold permanent wave is a process without heat. Prior to the invention of the cold wave system, heat was used in nearly all commercial waving systems. The application of cold waving consists of preparing the hair, i.e. shampooing, sectioning and winding, applying cold waving lotions or reagents to the hair, processing and normalizing.

Shampooing before the perm, the pre-perm shampoo, consists of cleaning lacquer or other material from the hair which could prevent the reagent from penetrating the hair shaft. No deposit or coating should be left on the hair that will in any way interfere with the chemical processing. Combing and brushing should be kept to the minimum to prevent scalp scratches, and the scalp should be free of any abrasions or disease. If perming reagents are used on sore or infected skin, the conditions may be aggravated and made worse.

When working 'live', it is important that all the points made on sectioning and winding (pages 48 and 51) are carefully applied.

Reagents, commonly called lotions in the salon, are made for use on a variety of hair textures and conditions, e.g. bleached, tinted, or porous hair. These may be applied with a sponge, brush, or special applicator, but in such a way that scalp contact is avoided, no closer than 12 mm from the scalp. Always check manufacturer's instructions for their use. Some lotions may be applied before winding commences, i.e. pre-saturation, and others may be applied after winding.

Processing commences after completion of winding and the application of reagents. The timing of processing will vary with the individual heads of hair, system of waving used, the temperature of the salon, method of winding and the texture of the hair. Processing consists of causing the hair to expand, lifting of the cuticle to allow reagent penetration into the cortex, and activation of all the chemicals concerned in the process.

Hair texture, e.g. coarse and dry, will usually absorb reagents, activate and complete processing quickly. Fine, greasy hair can be very resistant and the reagent penetration prevented. A coating of grease will slow or prevent activation of the reagents. Normally, fine hair 'takes', i.e. processes, quicker than coarse hair.

Bleached or tinted hair or hair which has been chemically treated previously will usually absorb the reagent quickly. The state of the cuticle readily allows the reagent to pass through to the cortex. Because of this speed of absorption care must be taken when processing and timing the perming of these hair conditions. The manufacturer's timing guidance for different hair textures, e.g. normal, bleached, tinted, dry, greasy, fine or coarse, should be followed.

Temperature in the salon has a marked effect on processing and timing. If the salon is very cold the process is slowed down. If the salon is very hot the process may be very much speeded up. The heat of a person's head is usually sufficient for most cold perm reagents to start acting. Some perming systems require heat, either from a dryer or an accelerator, to activate the reagents. These are usually accompanied with instructions to cover the wound hair with a paper or plastic cap. If the hair is placed under heat without covering, evaporation of the reagent may take place before the perming process is complete.

Since normal head heat activates, padding between the curlers with cotton wool should be avoided. The cotton wool absorbs the lotion, causing it to make contact with the skin which may become sore or painful and possibly infected. This is what correct sectioning, winding and lotion application is designed to prevent. For similar reasons the wound head of hair should not be wrapped in a towel.

Normalizing, commonly called 'neutralizing' in the salon, is a process which stops the chemical action of cold perming. For this oxygen is used in the form of hydrogen peroxide, mixed with a thickening or foaming agent, e.g. a conditioning or hair aid, and water. Special normalizers may be supplied which oxidize the chemicals in the hair and stop the processing action.

Thorough rinsing of perm reagents from the hair is necessary before applying normalizers. Surplus water is absorbed by carefully dabbing each curler with cotton wool to prevent dilution of the normalizer. The normalizer is applied carefully and thoroughly, without disturbing the hair, to each of the wound curlers. If a foaming normalizer is used it should be made to foam well to allow the maximum of oxygen to be liberated. The normalizer is left in contact with the hair for 5–10 minutes, depending on the type used, and then reapplied and left for a further period.

When normalizing is complete the curlers are unwound and taken from the hair. Care should be taken at this stage, because stretching or undue pulling of the hair may straighten the curl. This applies particularly to inefficiently normalized hair, where the hair may not be completely 'hardened' or returned to its normal state.

After removal, the curlers should be rinsed and dried to prevent the remains of water, reagent or normalizer adversely affecting the next perm. Rubber on the curlers may be powdered to prevent it softening. Much time and trouble is saved if the curler sizes are separated and returned to different sections of the perm tray. Other tools and equipment should be cleaned and made ready for use again.

9. Cold perming faults and corrections:

(*a*) *Perm slow to take.* Winding too loose, too large and too few curlers used, wrong type of lotion used, hair sections too large, cold salon, and lotion absorbed from the hair.

(*b*) *Scalp irritation,* skin breakage, soreness or tenderness. This could be due to securing the curler too tight or resting the wound curler on the scalp, packing cotton wool between the wound curlers, tightly pulling the hair when winding, or using too much lotion or allowing it to run on to the scalp.

(*c*) *Straight ends, pieces or fish-hooks.* Perm curlers or hair sections for winding too large. Not winding the hair points cleanly. Incorrect use of hair aids.

(*d*) *Hair breakage.* Winding too tightly. Tightly securing the curler. Curler band pressing or cutting the hair. Incompatible reaction, i.e. the hair possibly coated with chemicals which react to chemicals in reagents.

(*e*) *Straight perm* or no perm result. Wrong lotion used. Not processing long enough. Too large curlers used or hair sections wound. Insufficient normalizer or normalizing. Hair possibly coated with chemicals or materials which do not allow penetration or absorption. Poor shampooing or the use of conditioners or other materials before perming.

(*f*) *Frizz.* Lotion used too strong. Winding too tightly. Too small curlers used. Over-processed or too much heat used, timing or length of processing too long. Normalizer not applied thoroughly or quickly enough.

(g) Curl weakening, or perm gradually dropping out. Incorrect application or timing of normalizing. Incorrectly made or wrong normalizer used. Before correcting, by re-processing, check for straight frizz, i.e. over-permed.

(h) *Straight pieces* at the sides of the head and neck. Incorrect angling and placing of curlers. Too large curlers used on very short hair. In other parts of the head: too large section of hair wound at the wrong angle; carelessly leaving pieces of hair out of the curler; lack of hair control when winding.

(i) *Discoloration of hair.* The use of metal tools or containers could react with lotions used, and metallic materials coating the hair could cause discoloration.

10. Before the perm examine the hair and scalp for signs of infection, cuts or abrasions, incompatible chemicals or other materials that may be coating the hair. If there is any sign of abnormality, do not perm.

During the perm treat the hair gently, particularly during the softening stage of the process. Do not allow the processing to remain unchecked for more than 5 minutes, unless otherwise directed by the instructions. Do not leave the client unattended, particularly when the hair is being processed.

Tests. If there is any doubt as to what may be coating the hair shaft, test small cuttings of hair by immersing in 20-volume hydrogen peroxide, made alkaline by the addition of a few drops of ammonium hydroxide solution, and a small amount of the perm lotion to be used. This should be carried out before the reagents are applied to the 'live' head of hair. If any discoloration of the hair, or heating of the liquids, occur, do not attempt to proceed with the perm.

The hair should be tested at regular intervals when processing by unwinding curlers in different parts of the head to note the amount of wave or curl developed. When an S-shaped movement has developed, without too much spring or looseness, it should be ready to rinse and normalize. The normalizer should be made immediately before rinsing and applied directly afterwards to prevent the possibility of over-processing, e.g. perming too tight.

After the perm, check the hair for any signs of breakage, for strength of curl and evenness of wave, and for the condition of the hair. If there is any sign of perm failure, do not hurriedly set the hair in the hope that the client will not notice; she may the next day. Try to correct any fault while the client is still in the salon. If the time does not permit this, then arrange a suitable time when it can be done.

Setting the perm. After permanently waving the hair it is usual to place the hair in temporary set for the final required shape or style. This requires special and careful attention, to avoid tightness and kinking. The hair should be dressed so that no perming effects are obvious; the modern trend is for the unpermed look.

Revision test 1

Q. 1   What is meant by 'perming'?
Q. 2   Describe preparation of a head of hair for perming.
Q. 3   Why is a head of hair sectioned for perming?
Q. 4   Describe a method of sectioning.
Q. 5   What aids and tools are used for perming?
Q. 6   List four cold perming faults and corrections.
Q. 7   What precautions should be taken before, during and after a cold perm?
Q. 8   Why are curlers concave in shape?
Q. 9   Apart from preparation, what are the main processes of cold permanent waving?
Q.10   Describe each of the following terms:
         (a) Fish-hook. (b) Tension. (c) Crêpe hair. (d) Frizz. (e) Incompatibility.

Revision test 2

Complete the following sentences:

1   Permanent wave remains in the hair until it is either .... or ....

2   Sectioning for perming reduces inconvenience to the ...., the .... and the ....

3   The aim of good winding is to place the hair on to suitable shapes and sizes of .... or ....

4   The wound hair or curler should not be allowed to rest on the .... or ....

5   Hair points bent back or buckled are called ....

6   Incorrectly secured curlers mark or .... the hair.

7   Winding, for basic perming, requires the hair to be .... from the scalp, ... placed on the curler and .... wound.

8   Perming aids, e.g. .... or ...., should be used to speed winding after hair control is learnt.

9   The hands and skin should be protected by using .... or .... when perming.

10   Another name for a perming lotion is a ....

11   Perm lotion penetrates the cuticle and acts on the keratin in the .... of the hair.

Revision test 3

Complete the following sentences with the word or words listed below:

Bigoudi. Temperature. Heat. Neutralizing. Oxidizer. Taken. Soft. Hard. Angle. Frizz.

1   The processing time of a cold perm may be affected by the .... of the salon.

2   Cold perms are usually carried out without the use of ....

3   Hair wound on too small curlers or over-processed will ....

4   Normalizing is another name for ....

5   A curler or .... is used to wind the hair around.

6   When an S-shaped movement is produced in permed hair it is said to have .... and is ready for normalizing.

7   Hair becomes .... when cold perm lotion has been applied.

8   Hydrogen peroxide is used as an .... when normalizing.

9   After normalizing the hair is made .... again.

10   Curlers should be wound and placed at the correct ....

Vocabulary

Cold perming	Chemical permanent waving process without heat.
Crêpe rope	A length of coiled crêpe hair, used as an aid when winding.
'Dropped' curler	Not centrally placed, allowed to rest on the skin.
End-papers	Winding aids which help prevent fish-hooks.
Fish-hooks	Bent or buckled points due to bad winding.
Hot perming	Heat and alkaline lotions for permanent curl.
Incompatibility test	A test to detect incompatibles; a small cutting of hair is placed in 'peroxide' or perm lotion.
Incompatible	A chemical or substance that will not mix, or reacts, with another chemical or substance.
Normalizing	Commonly called 'neutralizing', re-hardens the hair by oxidation after chemical softening.
Oxidizer	A substance that liberates oxygen.
Perm 'burn'	Stretched skin exposed to excessive reagent or heat. *Pull burn* is the common term in hot perming.
Permanent set	Another name for permanent wave or curl.
Perming	Common name given to methods of permanent waving.
Practice block	An implanted model head of hair used for practice.
Pre-saturation	Wetting the hair with reagent before winding.
Processing	The chemical action of reagents on hair.
Reagent	Solution which reacts with chemicals in hair.
Sectioning	The division of the hair in suitable-sized sections for perm processing.
'Taking' *'Taken'*	Names used for processing and processed.
Tension	The stretch or stress placed on hair.
Tepid perm	A permanent wave system which uses low alkaline strength reagents and temperatures.
Test curlers	Used in cold perming to check curl strength, by unwinding a curler, and in hot perming to assess heat required for the process.
Winding	The physical wrapping of hair round a curler.

Perming

11. History of perming. Permanently curling hair goes back to the beginning of civilization. The early Egyptians wound hair round sticks, coated it with clay and baked it in the sun. The old wigmakers or perruquiers found that permanent curl could be produced by wrapping the hair round sticks and boiling in water.

At the beginning of this century a system of perming was introduced which consisted of winding the hair, spirally, from roots to points, around sticks or curlers, securing the points by tying with string. A borax paste was coated on to the wound hair. Muslin, paper and flannel were used to cover and protect the hair. Heat was applied to each of the wound curlers and allowed to cool. Specially designed irons, similar to the older crimping irons used to form lines and crimps in hair before S-shapes were the fashion, were used to apply heat. Later electric heaters took the place of the heating irons and the first electric hot perming system was produced.

Hot perming systems were used, in many forms, up to the end of the Second World War. The first systems had the disadvantage of excessive heat being used over prolonged periods. This resulted in dry hair and scalp burns. The early electric machines produced shocks and discomfort to the client. Later systems were introduced which consisted of lower alkaline reagents, lower temperatures, better curlers, protective water jackets and safer electrical machines. (Fig. 5.8a).

Wireless and machineless systems then followed which did not require clients to be directly attached to an electric machine. This was another disadvantage of earlier systems, the attachment of the client to a machine by wires. These newer systems consisted of winding the hair from points to roots, i.e. croquignole method, the application of kinder reagents to the hair, and applying heat from heaters detached from a machine. An electric machine heated specially designed heater clamps which fitted over the wound curler. In some systems a rubber jacket was used to protect the hair.

Tepid perming was introduced about the same time as the first wireless and machineless systems, but was a method of perming which did not require the

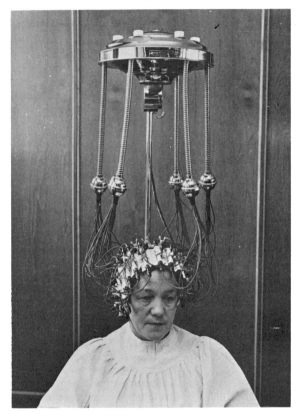

Fig. 5.8(a)   Hot perm machines

use of a machine. Tepid perming consisted of croquignole winding, the application of a reagent, not unlike a weak cold perm lotion, and covering the wound curlers with sachets after being dipped into water. The sachets contained calcium oxide and the action of water produced sufficient heat in the sachet to activate the reagents used on the hair. This system did not become popular until recent times, and became known as the 'exothermic' perm. The advantages of this, and the newer tepid systems, some of which include the use of a machine, are the low alkaline reagents used, less heat, hair left in better condition and improved client comfort and safety. (Fig. 5.8b).

When the *cold perming system* was introduced in this country on a large scale, in 1946, its action on hair was harsh and rough, but it soon became the most popular system in use. It is now vastly superior to the earlier methods and the hair is left in a far better state.

Despite the many improvements of hot, tepid and cold perming systems, hair is still wound on to sticks or curlers and processed in a similar way to that used by the early Egyptians. Today, however, the hair is more naturally processed with a softness and safety other systems were unable to produce.

hair. In the cold wave system hair is physically wound round a curler. Reagent is applied which penetrates the cuticle and the cortex. The keratin structure in the cortex is acted upon. The chemical structure of keratin is compared to a number of long chains, each link cross-linked to other chains. These long chains are known as polypeptide chains, chemically composed of amino acids. The connecting links are composed of disulphide, basic, acid and salt bonds or linkages. The chemicals of the reagent react with those contained in the hair. The normal straight alpha keratin state of hair is stretched into the beta keratin position by the physical process of winding. The links or bonds are broken and moved into new positions when the hair is soft. The disulphide linkage, usually the most resistant, is finally broken after processing with substances like thioglycollic acid and ammonium hydroxide. (Fig. 5.9).

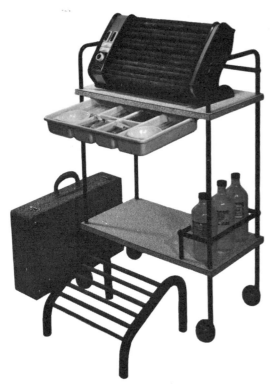

Fig. 5.8(*b*)   Tepid perm machine

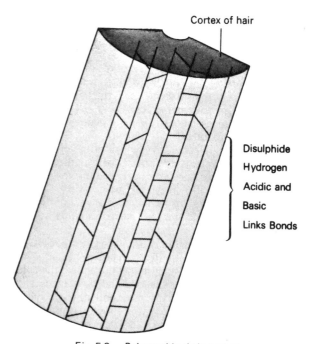

Cortex of hair

Disulphide
Hydrogen
Acidic and
Basic
Links Bonds

Fig. 5.9   Polypeptide chain system

Recently *semi-permanent waving* systems have been introduced which produce a curl in hair which gradually relaxes over a period of six to eight weeks. These are popular since gentle effects and enough body to hold modern styles are produced. This system involves the use of large curlers with a cold waving-type reagent which is activated by the heat of a dryer.

The search for newer and better methods of perming continues, and the system which does not rely on winding, reagents and heat is yet to be found.

12. Science reference: the action of perming on

When enough bonds are broken or chemically undone they are made to reform, but in their new form or beta keratin position. This is achieved by normalizing the hair. An oxidizing agent is applied to the softened hair and the liberated oxygen rejoins the bonds and balances the hair structure. The hair is hardened and the new chemical links retained, and this produces the permanent curl or wave shape required.

The effect of heat on the hair is to soften the keratin content so that the chain cross-links are able to be broken. The new positions forced by the very tight winding are held by the curlers until the hair re-hardens, the cross-links are reconnected and new curl positions are attained. These are features of the hot perming systems.

Tepid systems rely on a chemical breakdown of the chain-link systems, activated by a certain amount of heat, and normalized by oxidation and cooling. With the newer types of tepid waving an oxidizing normalizer stops the chemical activation.

13. The chemistry of perming. All methods of permanent waving consist of processing keratin or the chemical structure of the hair. This occurs whether weak or strong reagents, low or high temperatures, or no heat, are used. During chemical processing the hydrogen bonds, salt links and disulphide bonds are acted on. This action is one of reduction, i.e. the removal of oxygen or the addition of hydrogen. When this occurs the bond is broken which is later reconnected by the addition of oxygen. (Fig. 5.10).

Cold wave reagents commonly contain ammonium thioglycollate, i.e. the salt of ammonium hydroxide and thioglycollic acid, chemicals which contain hydrogen sulphur bonds in their formula, known as mercaptans. During processing an exchange of oxygen between cystine, i.e. an amino acid in hair, and the mercaptan of the reagent, converts cystine into cysteine, i.e. another amino acid. (Fig. 5.11).

The perming action is stopped when the normalizing oxidizer is applied, e.g. hydrogen peroxide. The released oxygen reforms disulphide bonds in their new positions. Other oxidizers, e.g. sodium perborate, percarbonate and bromate, and potassium bromate, may be used. Very strong oxidizers form acid links which do not retain the curl or wave effect as do the reformed disulphide bonds. (Fig. 5.12).

Hot perming reduction takes place when a solution of sodium sulphite is applied to hair and heated. This action reduces cystine to cysteine, but unlike the cold perming action the curl is retained as it cools and hardens. Oxygen is not directly applied, but oxygen in the atmosphere has its effect. Ammonium hydroxide and borax are old hot perm reagents. Steaming and boiling of hair, i.e. the old board-workers' method, produces curl or wave permanence.

Tepid perming utilizes weaker types of cold perm reagents and lower temperatures. The action is similar to the cold wave process except that heat is used to activate. Heat is applied by lime, i.e. calcium oxide, or potassium permanganate-filled sachets first dipped in water and placed over the wound hair. Exothermic, i.e. chemical action evolving heat, methods of perming rely on dryly stored sachets; damp activates them and renders them ineffective for perming.

14. Permanent curling in boardwork. Hair to be made into postiche is often required to be permanently curled. Three main methods are used, each involving the principle of boiling.

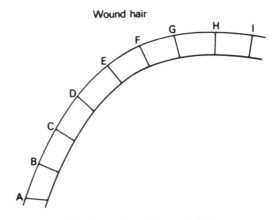

Fig. 5.10   Magnified chain links

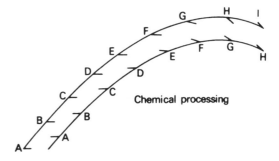

Fig. 5.11   Keratin structure — broken bonds

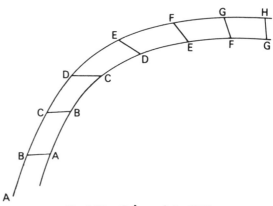

Fig. 5.12   Reformed structure

(a) *Frissure forcée* is used on hair 150 mm or more in length. Small bundles of hair are secured at the root end in a jigger, i.e. a boardwork tool which consists of a looped string-type clamp. The hair is wound from points to roots and the points are secured by wrapping and tying with string. The hair required is wound on a number of curlers, usually made from bone, wood, china or glass, so that they

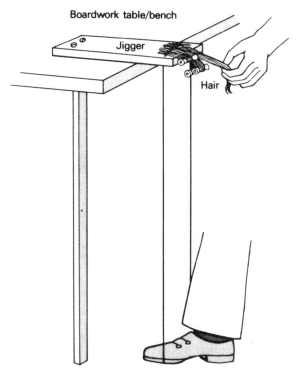

Fig. 5.13 Jigger hair winding

do not melt, and immersed in boiling water for a minimum of 30 minutes. The spiral method of winding may be used if a soft wave shape is required at the hair points and a firm movement required at the roots. (Fig. 5.13).

(b) *Crop curling* is used on hair 75–100 mm long. Curls may be formed on curlers or similarly to the en papillote method, and placed in boiling water for 30 minutes. The curls are then dried and stored until required for use. This method produces the soft curl or wave shapes required for some modern pieces of postiche.

(c) *Creoling* is a method of producing soft permanent waves in hair longer than 300 mm. It consists of plaiting lengths of hair and boiling in water for at least 30 minutes. The softness of wave produced is useful where added bulk is required by the type of postiche, e.g. two- or three-stem switches.

Permanently curling postiche. The hair of postiche may be permanently curled, after it has been made up, by the use of any of the hairdressing perming systems, e.g. cold, tepid and hot perms. When using these systems care must be taken to prevent the reagents, or the high temperatures, from damaging the postiche base. There is the possibility of reaction between reagents used and some postiche colourings. It is best to test for incompatible chemicals before using these processes. Where possible, permanently curl hair before making into a hair piece, and always use particular care when dealing with a ready-made piece.

15. Aesthetics of perming. The internal structure of hair offers an infinite variety of shapes and patterns. These are continually being brought out by microscopic and electromicroscopic investigations into the effects of perming on hair. The long chain-type molecules of keratin, with its numerous interconnections of cross-links, form spiralling interlinking shapes which are aesthetically stimulating. These, and the basic shape with which perming is concerned, the repeating S-shaped pattern of curl and wave, form the basis of many arrangements of beauty and shape.

In permanent waving chemistry a variety of science and art can be found closely integrated. The end product of perming is an aid to beauty, but the intermediate products, e.g. reagents, machines, curlers and other equipment, are those of science, which all require aesthetic design.

Design has a large part to play in the presentation, as well as the application, of the perming process. The simple design of a curler, its shape, colour and method of securing, has proved to be very useful. The concave curler shape enables the wound hair to fit evenly, its colour ensures quickness of selection, and its material resists the effects of handling and chemicals, and allows hair to be safely curled against it.

From the simplicity of curler design to the more complicated shape of waving machines indicates the range of art involved. A modern waving machine needs to be attractive; many look frightening, but compared to earlier machines they are tame and gentle in appearance and action. The old machines were functional and produced only the heat required. Today the professionalism displayed by the appearance and effects of modern waving machines owes much to art as well as to science.

Angles. An important part of the perming process is the variety of angles used, e.g. the angling of sections, winding and curler placing. Unless the curlers are correctly angled, outlining the head and the desired perm result will not be achieved.

Illustrations, e.g. sketches and diagrams, used in answering questions in written examinations, can save a lot of time and writing. This applies to many aspects of hairdressing, but in particular the theory of perming. A simple sketch may be the means of fully expressing a point rather than a lot of time-consuming words.

The shape of the hair produced by perming should be natural and look 'unpermed'. This basic shape is used to create further shapes and styles. The lines, movements, impressions or feelings created by well-permed hair are essentially based on aesthetic appreciation, and as scientific as perming undoubtably is, art forms an integral part of it.

Revision test 1

Q. 1   Outline the physical and chemical processes of perming.
Q. 2   Name some of the disadvantages of a hot perm system.
Q. 3   Describe the chain-link system in hair and how it is acted on in the cold perm process.
Q. 4   Describe the tests used in permanent waving.
Q. 5   What are the differences between hot, tepid and cold perming?
Q. 6   Describe two perming faults and how they may be corrected.
Q. 7   Name and describe three chemicals used in perming.
Q. 8   Describe a wireless or machineless perming system.
Q. 9   Describe methods of producing permanent curl in boardwork.
Q.10   Briefly describe each of the following terms:
        (a) Croquignole. (b) Spiral winding. (c) Mercaptan. (d) Frissure forcée. (e) Disulphide links.

Revision test 2

Complete the following sentences:

1   Name four methods of producing permanent wave, and the active chemical, agent or action:
     (a)..
     (b) ....
     (c)..
     (d) ....
2   The names given to keratin links or bonds are ...., ... and ....
3   The amino acid .... is converted into .... in the cold perming process.
4   Winding too tightly, over-processing, and using too small curlers could result in .... and ....
5   Before perming the scalp should be thoroughly .... Perming should not be carried out if there are any .... or ....
6   Perm systems which use heat-producing chemicals, e.g. .... and ...., are called .... perming systems.
7   Hair aids, e.g. .... and ...., may be used to speed winding and prevent ....
8   Winding too loosely, using large curlers, and under-processing could cause the perm to be ....

Revision test 3

Complete the following sentences with the word or words listed below:

Frissure forcée. Calcium oxide. Spiral. Ammonium thioglycollate. Croquignole. Hydrogen peroxide. Ammonium hydroxide. Thioglycollic acid. Frissure forcée. Calcium oxide. Potassium permanganate. Creoling.

1   The main chemical in a cold wave reagent is ...., made from .... and ....
2   The names given to two methods of winding are .... and ....
3   Two chemicals used in tepid perm systems are .... and ....
4   Two methods of producing permanent curl in boardwork are .... and ....
5   An ingredient in a cold wave normalizer is ....

Vocabulary

Alpha keratin	Keratin in an unstretched state.
Beta keratin	Name given to keratin in a stretched state.
Chain links or bonds	Chain-forming chemicals in hair, e.g. salt, acid and basic links, hydrogen and disulphide bonds.
Crop curling Creoling	Boardwork methods of permanent curling.
Croquignole	Winding from points to roots.
Cysteine	An amino acid converted from cystine.
Cystine	An amino acid in hair.
Exothermic	Heat-producing chemicals used in tepid perms.
Frissure forcée	Boardwork method of permanent curling.
Hot perm reagents Sodium sulphite Ammonium hydroxide Borax	Used in hot perming systems.
Jigger	Clamp-like boardwork tool used for holding hair to be curled.
Machineless Wireless	Names of perm systems where clients were not attached to machines by wires.
Mercaptans	Thio-alcohols which have hydrogen sulphur links in their formulae.
Normalizing	Correct term for the common 'neutralizing'.
Oxidizers	Substances which add oxygen to others.
Perruquier	The French name for a wigmaker.
Reduction	Removal of oxygen or addition of hydrogen.
Sachet	Container of heat-producing chemicals.
Sodium perborate Sodium percarbonate Sodium bromate Potassium bromate Hydrogen peroxide	Used to oxidize or normalize the chemical action of cold wave reagents.
Spiral winding	Winding from roots to points.
Tepid perm Exothermic perm	A system using cold wave-like reagents and low temperatures of heat.
Tepid perm reagents Calcium oxide Potassium permanganate	Exothermic heat-producing chemicals.

Perming

16. Hair straightening is a process of reducing or relaxing naturally curly or wavy hair to straighter hair. Permanent waving systems may be used to achieve these effects. Although the main aim of good perming is to reproduce natural soft, curl and wave in straight hair, this too is equally desired by those with very tight curly or frizzy hair. Others with slight wave movements may require their hair to be completely straightened.

The demands for a 'straight look', i.e. hair with no wave or curl, and very curly effects, vary periodically. The demand remains constant from those with very tight, kinky or negroid hair for soft wave and curl, which requires some method of straightening.

17. Temporary straightness may be achieved by most methods used to curl or wave hair. Kinky frizzy hair may be set on large rollers to produce a straightened effect. Tension or stretch will need to be applied to wet hair and dried in position. The use of heated rollers or irons (see Chapter 7) achieves temporary straightness by setting dry hair on large rollers, or stroking hair straight with the hot irons. These methods are not entirely satisfactory since moisture in the air is soon absorbed which causes the hair to revert back to its naturally curly state.

Hot combs are commonly used for hair straightening. A metal or alloy comb is heated and repeatedly combed through tight curls. This achieves a temporary straight effect similar to that produced by heated rollers and irons. An added disadvantage with the hot comb method is hair breakage, particularly at the front hairline. A common condition of the hair after repeated hot comb straightening treatments is traction alopecia, i.e. balding areas due to the hair being cut, dragged and broken by excessive heat and physical combing.

18. Permanent chemical straightening may be achieved by the application of permanent waving reagents, commonly cold wave lotions, or the specially made straightening creams or lotions, which are to be preferred for their special and safe effects. The use of too strong a cold wave reagent could have a depilatory effect, i.e. remove or destroy hair. (Fig. 5.14).

The principle of permanent hair straightening is

Before lotion application

After application and processing

Fig. 5.14   Chemical hair straightening

identical with permanent waving methods. Instead of the hair being made to form small curl or wave shapes as when permed, the straightening process forms the hair in large, loose or soft wave shapes. The effects on the keratin content of the hair are similar when chemical methods are used. The hair is first softened, the chain-link system in the hair is acted on, links or bonds are broken, moved into a new position and finally hardened by normalizing and the new shape retained.

Excessive use and amounts of straightening reagents must be avoided or the skin and scalp will become softened, sore, and open to infection. Do not use metal tools or equipment; hair discoloration and breakage could occur with straightening reagents. Dealing with negroid hair requires particular care. Although the hair appears short, it may be 225 mm or more in length, and the tight coiling will make combing difficult. Always use correct combing techniques and work on a small section at a time. Protective gloves or barrier creams should be used and vaseline may be applied to protect the scalp and hairline.

A method of hair straightening. Divide the hair in four sections, centrally from forehead to nape and from ear to ear. Subdivide the nape sections in small sections and apply the straightening reagent. Avoid contacting the skin with the reagent. As the hair begins to soften, gentle combing movements with a wide-toothed comb may be used to relax the hair gradually. The hair may be left in a combed straight position. Do not continually comb the hair when it is in a soft state, or harshly apply the comb, or the hair will soon break.

The length of processing will depend on the type of hair and reagent used. Soft curly or wavy hair will soon relax, but tight kinky hair will take considerably longer. When processing is complete (5—10 minutes is usually sufficient), a normalizer may be applied, after which the hair is set in the shape required. The hair will remain in its straightened state until it is either cut off or falls out.

Another hair-straightening method, commonly used, may be applied as follows: Wind the hair, as for cold perming, on large perm curlers or non-metallic setting rollers. The reagents may be applied before or after winding. Processing and normalizing take place as for normal cold waving. The result achieved is a softer, larger wave shape, ideal for tight curly hair. This is generally considered to be a safer method since repeated combing is not necessary.

The two methods outlined above are particularly effective when using cold waving reagents. Make sure when using special straightening creams or lotions that manufacturers' instructions are carefully followed and applied.

Restraightening or retouching will be required as the new hair grows from the scalp. These hairs will appear tightly waved in comparison with the straightened lengths, and noticeably in need of restraightening. When the regrowth is approximately 12 mm, straightening reagents may be applied but to the regrowth only. If the lengths are repeatedly processed, hair breakage and poor condition will result.

Revision test 1

Q. 1   What is hair straightening and what are its uses?
Q. 2   Describe two temporary hair-straightening methods.
Q. 3   What is traction alopecia and how may it be caused?
Q. 4   Describe a method of permanent hair straightening.
Q. 5   Describe the chemical action of straightening.
Q. 6   List the dangers and precautions of hair straightening.
Q. 7   How should regrowth be dealt with after straightening?
Q. 8   Why should softened hair not be repeatedly combed?
Q. 9   Describe the correct combing required for curly hair.
Q.10   Briefly describe each of the following terms:
      (a) Depilatory. (b) Negroid hair. (c) Hot combs. (d) Chemical hair relaxing. (e) Restraightening.

Revision test 2

Complete the following sentences:

1   Name three methods of temporary hair straightening:
    (a) ...., (b) ...., (c) ....
2   Excessive heat and repeated combing may cause ...., and a condition called ....
3   Hair straightened temporarily reverts back when it becomes ....
4   To protect the hands or skin, ... or .... may be used.
5   Hair-straightening processing time is determined by ...., ... and ....
6   A depilatory action is one that .... or .... hair.
7   List three hair-straightening precautions:
    (a)..
    (b)..
    (c)..
8   Metallic tools or equipment may cause .... or ....
9   When restraightening, reagents should be applied to the .... only or .... will result.

Revision test 3

Complete the following sentences with the word or words listed below:

Hot combs. Heated rollers. Cold wave reagents. Straightening creams. Frizzy. Kinky. Temporary. Permanently. Regrowth. Hair lengths.

1   Permanent straightness may be produced by .... and ....
2   Temporary straightness may be produced by .... and ....
3   Negroid hair may be .... and ....
4   Stroking the hair with heated irons is a .... method of straightening hair.
5   The application of perming systems may be used to .... straighten hair.
6   When applying reagents for restraightening they should be confined to the .... only and not allowed to contact the ....

Vocabulary

Chemical straightening	Terms given to the process of straightening hair.
Hair straightening	
Permanent straightening	
Temporary straightening	
Hair relaxing	
Unkinking	
Depilatory	Substance used for hair removal.
Hot combs	Usually alloy combs, heated and used for temporary straightening.
Kinked Hair	Terms given to very tight curly or wavy hair.
Kinky hair	
Frizzy hair	
Negroid hair	
Regrowth	New hair regrown after straightening.
Restraightening	Straightening application to hair regrown since the last process.
Retouching	
Straightening reagents:	Chemicals or lotions used for hair straightening.
Ammonium thioglycollate	
Barium hydroxide	
Sodium hydroxide	
Traction alopecia	Baldness due to pulling or dragging hair.

Finger Waving and Blow Waving

1. Finger waving is a method of moulding the hair into S-shaped movements with the hands, fingers and comb. It is also called water waving or setting. A finger-waved head of hair was an accepted style or fashion, but now the technique is used as part of a hair style, in the training of hairdressers, and in some competitions and displays.

Apart from the style effect of finger waves, mastery of the technique achieves four aims: (*a*) appreciation of wave shape, the basis of styling; (*b*) control of hands, comb and hair; (*c*) exercise of the muscles of the hands, arms, back and body; (*d*) self-discipline is learnt, which is so essential for the successful professional hairdresser.

Practice for finger waving should begin on a practice block. As with other techniques, the sooner work on live heads can take place the sooner the problems and difficulties of working 'live' are overcome.

The hair should be washed, well combed and free of tangles. Rough hair condition should be treated with suitable conditioners, to ease combing and enable free flow for waving.

Practise the wave formation at the back of the head, below the crown and parting, before attempting to wave the whole head of hair. Medium-fine texture hair approximately 100 mm long is usually the best for practice. Slightly wavy hair is easiest, and coarse, lank or tightly permed hair the most difficult. Waves should be uniform and shapely and an acceptable wave size for practice is 30 mm between crests.

Setting lotion helps to bind the hair so that a firm shape can be made. Setting gels, emulsions or viscous-type mucilages are suitable, preferrably those which do not flake. These are now used to assist waving rather than the retention of waves for two to four weeks as was the practice when finger waving was a style requirement. A setting lotion is particularly useful when waving short hair.

Positioning the hair for finger waving is important. It should be cleanly combed back and, if a parting is used, made to lie evenly and at equal angles from the parting. The hair should be returned to this line after each wave movement is complete. This ensures the direction and position intended for the waves. Parting

Fig. 6.1   Position of hair and parting

the hair in line with the middle of the eyebrow distributes the hair evenly. (Fig. 6.1).

The position of the body, hands, arms, fingers and comb are all equally important. Standing correctly, i.e. upright with legs slightly apart, and the body square with the part of the head to be worked upon, will help. The elbow and arm should be held above the hand when placed on the head. Only one finger, the index finger, should be allowed to contact the head. This position will at first feel awkward and uncomfortable but achieves the required control and pressure to be placed on the hair. Correctly hold the comb in the opposite hand and apply the combing action. When waving, do not allow the arm to drop or pressure is removed from the finger and control lost. In the beginning this is not easily seen, but it is a vital part of the waving process. A comb with close and widely spaced teeth is suitable for waving. (Figs. 6.2 & 6.3).

2. A method of finger waving. The following points should serve as a guide to finger-waving practice:

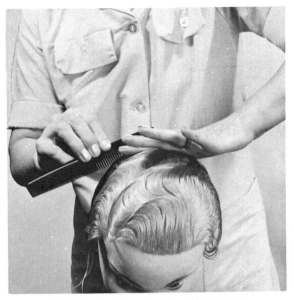

Fig. 6.2   Position of hand and finger wave

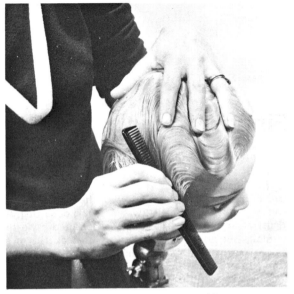

Fig. 6.3   Incorrect waving position

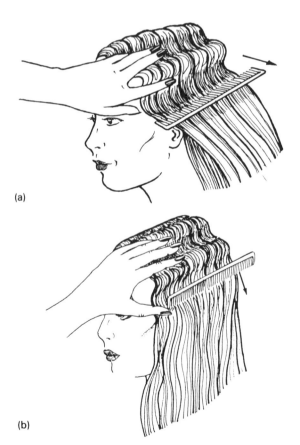

(a)

(b)

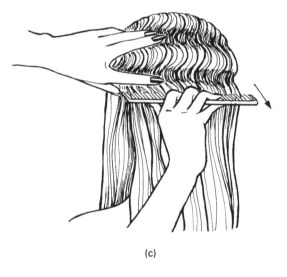

(c)

Fig. 6.4(a) — (c)   Finger-waving method

(*a*) Place the index finger on the head, with arm and hand above the finger. Do not allow the hand to rest on the head. The index finger determines the position and direction of the wave crest, the size of the wave or the distance between two wave crests, and control of the hair.

(*b*) Hold the comb in the opposite hand and, using the coarse end, place in the hair close to and level with the finger. Comb only when the hair is firmly held.

(*c*) With a movement directly to the left or right, without turning or twisting, comb and form the first crest. The angle of combing determines the height of the crest.

(*d*) When the first part of the crest is formed, replace the index finger with the second finger, and place the index finger directly under the crest.

(*e*) Comb the hair cleanly, with the crest firmly controlled, first with the coarse and then with the fine end. At the same time position the hair for the next part of crest formation, without twisting or turning the comb.

(*f*) The crest is continued by placing the index finger above the line of the crest already formed. The hair is then combed at the same angle as when forming the first part of the crest. This angle should be clearly visible if the finger is placed above, and not in line with, the formed crest.

(*g*) These movements are repeated and the crest continued across the head until one long crest is in position.

(*h*) The second crest is commenced, to complete one full wave, by placing the index finger below the first and repeating the combing action but in the opposite direction. If the first was formed by combing to the right, the second is formed by combing to the left.

(*i*) This is continued across the head where the third crest may be commenced, followed by more crests, until the lower part of the head is reached. The waving proceeds from side to side, gradually progressing lower.

(*j*) When smooth, even and well-shaped waves can be formed, without breaks between crests, attempts should be made to wave completely a full head of hair. (Figs. 6.4 a b c & 6.5).

3. Waving the complete head should commence approximately 75 mm from the front hairline, at the parting. The finger should be placed at right angles to the parting and the crest curved round to the front. If no parting is used, commence at the hairline on one side.

To encircle the head with waves, a crest, usually on the small side of the parting, is 'lost', i.e. the depth of the crest is gradually diminished by careful positioning. Do not wave too deeply at the crown or near the parting; maximum depth should be at the front and back. Shallow waving at the crown enables

the hair to be positioned so that waves on one side fit neatly with those on the other side. (Fig. 6.6).

The waves formed should be slightly smaller than finally required to allow the hair some spreading when dry. Do not use clips, grips or wave claws which usually distort and encourage slack waving. Sufficient control should be exercised to place the hair without the need for hair-holding aids. One or two rows of curls may be placed beneath the lowermost crest of the completed waves. These should be made to fit the waves and form a V-shape.

Dressing. If the waved head of hair is to be dressed it is not usually brushed. The dressing should disturb the positions of the waves as little as possible. Loosen the curls and place the coarse end of the comb

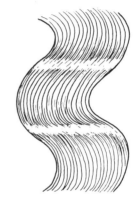

Fig. 6.5   Crest formed — section

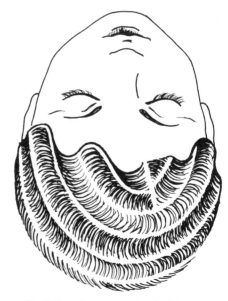

Fig. 6.6   Finger-waved head with parting

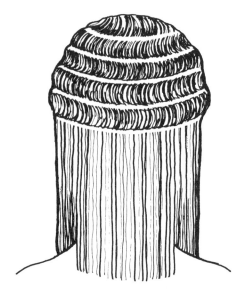

Fig. 6.7   Horizontal waving

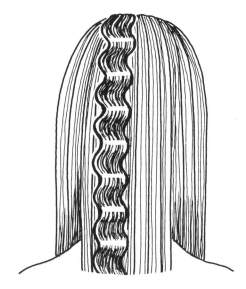

Fig. 6.8   Vertical waving

between the two lowest crests and comb through to the ends. Repeat this between the next higher crests. Support and hold the crests and hair above the combing to prevent dragging. A slight pushing and moulding action with the hand produces full, soft wave shapes. Complete dressing with the fine end of the comb. Curls may be reformed over the finger and tailcomb. Correctly formed waves should retain shape.

Horizontal waving is the name given to the method described above, working from one side of the head to the other. (Fig. 6.7).

Vertical or 'strip' waving is another method of finger waving, forming waves, from top to bottom of the head, in strips approximately 50 mm wide. The technique is similar to horizontal waving except that the joining up of the strips requires the comb to be angled to prevent disturbing the waves formed. Better control and hair positioning may be more easily attained with the horizontal method, particularly at the crown and parting areas. As with most method variations, those that individually suit and achieve the best results are most acceptable. (Fig. 6.8).

Two- and three-wave sets are terms applied to finger-waved heads of hair. A two-wave set refers to a head of hair with two full waves moving forward, on the large side of a side-parted head, and with one full wave on the small side. A three-wave set refers to a set with three full waves moving forward over the front hairline on the large side and two full waves on the small side.

Pompadour is the term given to a completely waved head of hair without a parting. The hair may be lifted at the front to give the full Pompadour

effect or it may be left flat. (Fig. 6.9).

4. Waving faults. One of the most common faults in finger waving is pinching or forcing the crest. If the hair is controlled and the correct combing angle used, forcing is not necessary. This only distorts the wave, and if dried in a forced position it soon drops to present an uneven and untidy appearance.

Allowing the arm to drop and wrapping the hand around the head is another common fault. This restricts hair control and disturbs waves formed, causing repeated and needless waving movements.

Repositioning of the hair after each combing movement is often neglected, causing uneven, ill-shaped waves. If the comb is used to force more hair into the crest to form a deep-looking wave when wet, the hair will soon fall and look uneven when dry.

Precautions. The comb should be used in an upright position without a great deal of pressure being exerted on it. This could tear or scratch the scalp and is easily done in the early stages of learning to wave. Carefully place a net over the waved hair so that it is not disturbed when drying, which could make dressing difficult. Waves are more easily formed if the hair is kept moistened with water or setting lotion. Do not attempt deep waves on short hair; a wave shape which will be retained is sufficient.

5. Modern finger-waving fashions require fullness rather than flatness of style. Completely waved heads of hair are now rarely required, except for practice. Finger waves may, however, be incorporated in modern styles with good effect.

The lower part of the back of the head is a common and suitable area for finger waves. They appear to look and fit better when positioned at a

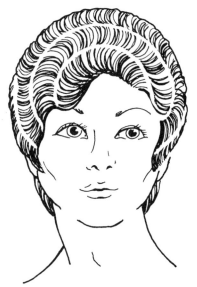

Fig. 6.9   Complete finger-waved head — Pompadour

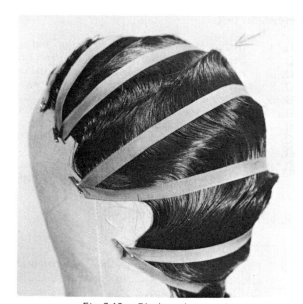

Fig. 6.10   Block waving, taped

slanting angle. A wave or two at each side, with the hair swept behind the ears, may be suitable on some heads. A flat, short finger wave, one side of the front hairline, can be an attractive position. There can be no hard-and-fast rules since the features of each client need careful consideration.

6. **The effect of finger waving** on hair is similar to other methods of temporary curling or waving. The waves diminish or 'drop' as moisture is absorbed by the hair. Modern lacquers and setting agents help to resist the effects of moisture. The hair reverts back to its original straight, waved or curly state as soon as it is washed again.

7. **Finger waving in boardwork** is applied similarly to the waving on a live head. The waves need to be a little smaller to allow for more movement and relaxing when fixing. The postiche is secured to a malleable block, i.e. a soft 'block' head, by postiche pins. If these are angled, rather than pushed straight in, they will hold the piece firmly.

When combing postiche the comb needs to be angled so that the teeth do not catch, tear or break the foundation. It is customary, but not necessary, to tape the waves in position. This is done by placing 18—25 mm wide tape along the trough or between the wave crests. One end is secured by a postiche pin, the tape laid along the wave, pinned and turned at each end, so that it continuously passes backwards and forwards along the waves. Setting lotions which do not affect postiche foundations should be used. The hair piece should be thoroughly dried in a postiche oven, or placed under a dryer, before dressing. (Fig. 6.10).

Revision test 1

Q. 1   What determines the depth, direction and position of a finger wave?
Q. 2   Describe the position of hands, arms and fingers when finger waving.
Q. 3   What is the difference between horizontal and vertical methods of finger waving?
Q. 4   Describe the uses and purpose of finger waving now that it is no longer a fashion style requirement.
Q. 5   Describe a method of finger waving.
Q. 6   Describe the method of finger waving a complete head.
Q. 7   Describe two common finger-waving faults.
Q. 8   How does finger waving affect the internal hair structure?
Q. 9   How is postiche finger waved?
Q.10   Briefly describe each of the following terms:
        (a) 'Joining up'. (b) Pompadour. (c) Water wave. (d) Three-wave set. (e) Vertical waving.

Revision test 2

Complete the following sentences:

1   Finger waving achieves the following when practised:
     (a)...
     (b) ....
     (c)..
     (d) ....
2   The best length and texture of hair to practise finger waving on are .... and ....
3   The terms given to two methods of finger waving are (a) .... and (b) ....
4   When finger waving the .... finger is used for control and direction of the .... or hair.
5   These two points ensure even, smooth waves:
     (a)...
     (b) ....
6   When about to wave a complete head of hair the finger is placed at .... to the parting, approximately .... back from the front hairline.
7   The index finger determines:
     (a)...
     (b) ....
     (c)..
8   Names given to finger-waved sets or styles are (a) ...., (b) ...., (c) ....

Revision test 3

Complete the following sentences with the word or words listed below:

Angle. Line. Crests. Trough. Size. Depth. Height. Horizontal. Vertical. Direction.

1   The .... of the crest is determined by the amount of hair combed into it.
2   The size of a wave is the distance between two ....
3   Waving backwards and forwards across the head is called .... waving.
4   Waving the hair in strips is called .... waving.
5   Two crests and one .... make one full wave.
6   The .... of the crest is determined by the placing of the index finger above the crest formed.
7   The .... of the wave is determined by the .... of combing.
8   The .... and position of the wave is determined by the placing of the index finger.
9   Approximately 30 mm is the generally accepted wave ....

Vocabulary

Crest height	The amount of hair combed into the crest determined by the angle of combing.
Wave depth	
Emulsions	Terms given to mixtures used for waving.
Setting gel	
Mucilage	
Finger wave	Wave shape formed with finger, comb and hair.
Full wave	Two crests and one trough.
Horizontal waving	Waving the head from side to side across.
Index finger	The first finger next to the thumb.
Joining up	The blending of one wave crest with another or continuing a crest.
'Lost' wave	Diminished crest enabling wave to fit at the crown.
Malleable block	A soft, sawdust-filled canvas block used for setting and dressing postiche.
Parting	Division of hair, placed for finger waving at mid-eyebrow for equal hair distribution.
Pompadour	A famous dressing named after the Marquise de Pompadour. Hair dressed high and back in front, without parting, waves encircling.
Postiche foundation	The net, silk or base on which hair is knotted or sewn to form hair piece.
Postiche oven	Heating oven for drying hair pieces.
Second finger	The finger next to the index finger.
Strip waving	Vertical waving of 50-mm strips of hair.
Taping waves	Fixing finger waves in postiche.
Two- and three- wave sets	Names given to finger-waved styles.
Vertical waving	Waving down in strips.
Viscous	A thick liquid.
Wave direction	The angle, position and placing of the wave determined by placing of index finger.
Wave size	The distance between two crests.
Wave trough	The dip or hollow between two crests.

Finger Waving and Blow Waving

8. Blow waving is a method of temporary waving produced by a comb or brush and heated air from a hand hair dryer. The hair is held in a wave position and a flattened nozzle dryer attachment directs and concentrates the flow of heated air. This is a waving method commonly used for men's styles and now becoming popular for women's hair fashions.

The control required to form wave shapes is determined by movements of the comb or brush and dryer, in relation to the hair position. Repeated combing and dryer movements are necessary to shape the hair.

9. Tools required are a fine cutting or dressing comb, and a hand hair dryer. The dryer should preferably be switched for half and full air flow and heat, and have a nozzle to direct the air flow. Metal combs and high temperatures must be avoided; metal conducts heat and may burn the fingers or the client's scalp.

Preparation of the hair follows the same procedure as for other forms of temporary waving, but for blow waving the surplus water left after washing is removed by towel drying or roughly drying with the hand dryer. A hood dryer may be used at this stage. The hair is then combed in the position in which it is to be finally shaped and dressed.

10. A method of blow waving. Commence at the front hairline and follow any natural wave movement. The comb is inserted in the hair, using the coarse end, and with a backward combing movement made to grip and hold the hair in a wave crest shape. Hot air is then directed on the wave trough below the wave crest. The angle of the air jet should be directed opposite to the direction in which the comb is holding the hair. The movements of both hands should be co-ordinated and repeated. Half, not full strength of air flow, should be used or the force will blow the hair out of the comb. Continually move the dryer along the hair. This serves two purposes: the heat is evenly directed and the head is not burnt. (Fig. 6.11).

The second crest is formed similarly to the first. Always direct the air flow along the line in which the hair was originally positioned. This retains the required line and shape without ruffling.

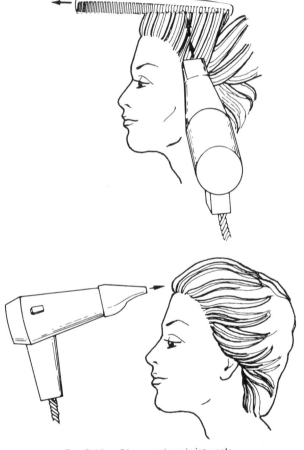

Fig. 6.11   Blow-waving air jet angle

When parts of the hair are too short to wave, angle, position and dry the hair in line with the waves formed. Use of the coarse end of the comb enables the air flow to penetrate and speed the process; the fine end may be used for finishing.

Setting lotions may be used after towel drying. Depending on the type, texture and condition of the hair, the quicker-drying, spirit-based setting agents are usually suitable. Do not attempt to blow wave the

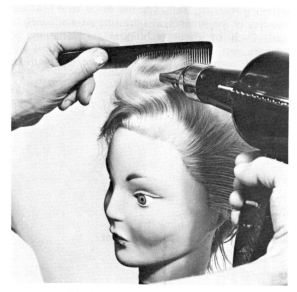

Fig. 6.12   Completed blow wave

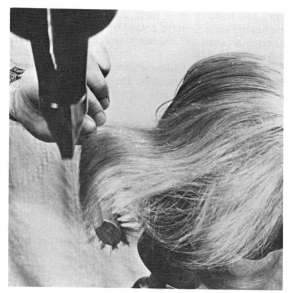

Fig. 6.13   Blow drying

hair when it is too dry; too much time and heat will be required to mould it.

When the hair is waved, dressing cream, oil or lacquer may be applied to complete the dressing. Small amounts should be used or the hair will become flat and lank. A net stretched over a wire frame is sometimes used for dressing. This prevents the hair fluffing when the air jet is directed on to it. (Fig. 6.12).

11. Blow drying is, at its simplest, drying the hair with the hand hair dryer. It is particularly useful for producing a straight effect on long hair if a controlled blow-drying technique is used. This requires the hair to be divided in 25-mm sections, commencing in the nape, and placed on a rounded firm bristle brush. The brush, held in one hand, should continually turn and lift the hair at the root ends. The other hand holding the dryer directs warm air on to the hair, particularly the roots, firmly held by the brush. Sections above are treated similarly and each dried section allowed to fall on to the previously dried ones. Do not allow wet hair to fall on to the dried hair, or repeated drying and loss of shape result. The brush should be gently eased through the hair without pulling. Practice ensures a continually moving brush with the lift and control required, Blow drying is best used on coarse types of hair; very fine hair does not respond favourably to this method. Simple lifted, full shapes may be achieved. (Fig. 6.13).

12. Blow combing is a method of drying hair with a blow comb, i.e. an electric comb with heated jets of air flowing over or between large spaced teeth. It is used to dry hair loosely or to produce wave shapes in long hair. It may be used by repeatedly

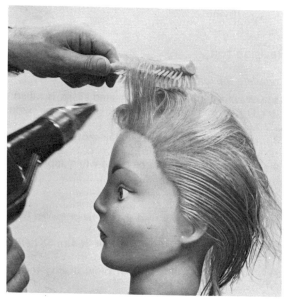

Fig. 6.14   Hair stretching

passing through the hair, or made to hold the hair, in a similar way to blow waving, to form wave shapes. Blow combs are designed for home use but there are restricted uses for them in the salon.

13. Hair stretching is the name given to the technique of stretching hair, rather than waving. A brush is placed in, under or on sections of hair and turned to grip and slightly stretch the hair. It produces soft, slightly lifted shapes on very short hair. The hand dryer is used, as in blow waving, and the heated air is directed on to the stretched hair. It is commonly used on women's and men's short hair styles. (Fig. 6.14).

The principles of blow waving, blow drying, blow combing and hair stretching are essentially the same as other setting methods with the use of heat, i.e. softening the hair, moulding the shape with heat and a variety of movements, and dressing after allowing to cool. Each of these techniques are variations of ordinary setting methods. The science of curls and curling (Chapter 3) applies equally to the methods described in this chapter.

Revision test 1

Q. 1 What is blow waving?
Q. 2 Describe a method of blow waving and list tools required.
Q. 3 Describe the scientific aspects of hair moulding with heat techniques.
Q. 4 What are the effects of and uses of blow waving, hair stretching and blow drying?
Q. 5 What precautions should be taken when using hair-moulding methods involving heat?
Q. 6 What is the difference between blow waving and waving with irons?
Q. 7 How does blow waving differ from finger waving?
Q. 8 What is blow combing?
Q. 9 Describe a method of hair stretching.
Q.10 Briefly describe the meaning of the following terms:
       (a) Hair moulding. (b) Blow or electric comb. (c) Temporary waving. (d) Hair stretching. (e) Blow drying.

Revision test 2

Complete the following sentences:

1 Waving with a comb and heated air jet is called ....
2 Other methods of moulding the hair with heat are called ...., ... and ....
3 Four tools or aids used in hair-moulding techniques are:
   (a) ...., (b) ...., (c) ...., (d) ....
4 Three precautions to be taken when applying hair-moulding techniques are:
   (a)...
   (b)...
   (c)...
5 Hair to be blow waved should be prepared by .... and .... to remove tangles and loosen dirt.
6 When hair stretching, the hair is firmly held by the .... and the .... from the dryer softens or .... it.
7 To produce fullness when blow drying the hair should be held out from the scalp and dried at the .... ends.
8 Setting lotions may be applied .... the hair is dried.
9 The hand dryer .... or concentrates the .... or air flow which softens and moulds the hair.

Revision test 3

Complete the following sentences with the word or words listed below.

Heated rollers. Waving with irons. Hair stretching. Blow waving. Brush. Comb. Setting net. Setting lotions. Soften. Cooling.

1 Moulding the hair into wave shapes with a hand dryer is called ....
2 Producing full straight effects in hair is a technique called ....

3   Two other methods of moulding hair shapes with heat, without a hand dryer, are called ....
    and ....

4   Usually stretched over a wire frame, a .... may be used to finish a blow-waved head of hair.

5   The heat of a hand dryer will .... hair which may be dressed after ....

6   Each of the following may be used in methods of heat moulding of hair: ....,
    .... and ....

Vocabulary

Air jet	The stream of air from hand hair dryer.
Blow combing	Drying or waving with electric or blow comb.
Blow drying	A technique using brush and dryer where hair is lifted and dried in position.
Blow waving	Waving hair with comb, brush and heated air.
Dryer attachment	The nozzle which fits on a hand dryer and directs heat and air flow.
Electric or blow comb	Wide-spaced toothed comb with heated air flowing through, used for blow combing.
Hair moulding	A term given to softening and shaping hair.
Hair stretching	A technique using a brush and dryer where the hair is stretched and laid in position.
Hand dryer	A small dryer held in the hand which directs a stream of heated air on to the hair.
Heat hair-moulding techniques	Methods of hair shaping with heat, e.g. blow waving, drying and combing, hair stretching, setting heated rollers and irons, heated comb straightening.
Hood dryer	A dryer used for wet setting which covers the head and hair.
Part drying or towel drying	Removal of surplus water after washing.
Setting net for blow work	A net stretched over a frame used with 'blowing' techniques to hold hair in place.

Chapter Seven

Waving with Irons

1. Waving with irons is a method of producing temporary wave shape in hair. Heated irons are used to soften and shape the hair. The effects obtained may be compared with other hair-softening and moulding techniques, e.g. heated rollers and blow waving.

Marcel waving. Before 1872, when Marcel Grateau revolutionized the methods of wave formation, waving was a series of straight-line crimps. By reversing the age-old process of hair crimping, Grateau was able to form S-shaped undulations with a simple sequence of movements. This became known as Marcel waving and was founded on three basic rules: (*a*) Part of the waved hair should be used as a guide to shaping the unwaved hair. (*b*) The waves should encircle the ears. (*c*) The grooved iron should be below the rod when waving

Varieties of waving developed from Marcel waving, which like most original methods soon became adapted and changed. Though basically all similar, the term 'waving with irons' is used to describe a variety of iron waving.

Uses of iron-waving methods are applicable to everyday style and fashion. Although the 'iron wave' is no longer fashionable it remains an excellent exercise of hand, tool and hair control. The appreciation of wave shape and self-discipline derived from the practice of this technique is invaluable. Modern aspects and applications of waving with irons are: formation of pli with curls using heated irons, either the Marcel or electric large-barrelled type, and heated rollers, to produce fashionable shapes and styles.

2. The tools and equipment required for waving with irons are: two pairs of waving irons, Marcel or modern, a dressing or waving comb, a suitable iron heater or stove, a practice weft or switch of hair and a malleable block and stand on which to work.

Marcel-type waving irons are made in several sizes, each marked with the letter A, B, C or D. A is the smallest, and is used for curling and tight work. B and C are larger and more commonly used for waving. D is the largest and is used for producing larger, softer wave shapes. The modern types of irons are not marked in this way. Two pairs of the Marcel type are

used and while one is being applied, the other is heated and made ready for use.

A professional waving or dressing comb should be used, and practice wefts, purchased or made, 150–250 mm wide with hair 250 mm long, or longer, are suitable.

Waving irons consist of two lengths of shaped metal. One is hollowed into a groove or trough, the other is a solid rod, which when closed fits into the groove. These are pivoted at the centre and terminate in two handles. The irons should be freely movable, balanced and suitable for waving. Well-made irons are necessary to produce good-quality work. The electric waving irons based on the Marcel type, not the large-barrelled ones, are popular for traditional work. These have heating elements in the rod or barrel and do not require to be heated in stoves.

Heaters or stoves are used to heat the irons to the required temperature, determined by the texture and quality of the hair. The electric, thermostatically controlled stove is now commonly used. Older methods of heating irons include gas flames from specially designed gas wall brackets, spirit stoves, or the flames from heating blocks, similar to modern firelighters. The modern stove is far safer and more efficient in comparison. Care must be taken when using naked flames for iron heating. There should be nothing over or near the flame, e.g. towels drying or inflammable materials stored or placed nearby.

3. Use of irons. It is essential that the movements required of the irons, when in use, are well practised before attempting to wave hair. Ungainly, jerky movements will not allow even, round wave shapes to be formed. At first the comb may be discarded for waving until shape and control is attained, and brought into use at a later stage.

Exercises with irons ensure the flexibility and control required for successful waving. The following are designed to help the beginner:

(*a*) *Holding the irons.* The handles of the irons should lie across the palm of the hand, diagonally, from the base of the index finger. They may be supported by the thumb resting across the handles. First practise holding in this way, palm uppermost, and then with the hand turned, palm facing downwards. The irons in use should be held in a horizontal position, with the elbow held away from the body and level with the irons. (Fig. 7.1).

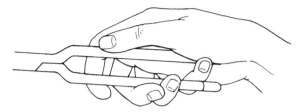

Fig. 7.1   Holding the irons when closed

(b) *Opening the irons.* By slipping the little finger behind one of the handles and allowing the thumb to grip the other, the irons may be opened and closed, after a while, comfortably and easily. If the little finger is too short the next finger may be used. (Fig. 7.2).

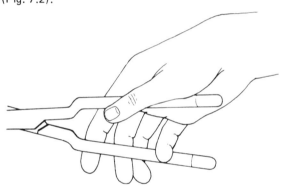

Fig. 7.2   Opening the irons

(c) *Turning the irons.* Allow the irons to return to the 'hold' position and practise turning the irons, over and over, first one way then the other. When this is comfortably achieved, practise pointing the irons in all directions whilst still turning them. Do not allow the hand to slip up towards the crutch or pivot; it should remain on the handles.

(d) *Cooling the irons.* Hold one handle and allow the irons to open. Direct the points downwards and let them swing in the palm of the hand and then allow them to spin round in the hand, first one way then the other. This helps to gain control and is used to cool very hot irons. (Fig. 7.3).

4. Preparation for waving requires the hair to be clean and dry; greasy hair resists heat and causes uneven waves. Dirty hair should be shampooed and dried before waving is commenced. Heaters should be prepared and irons heated and tested for the correct waving temperature, which varies according to type of hair.

Testing waving heat. A piece of tissue paper is

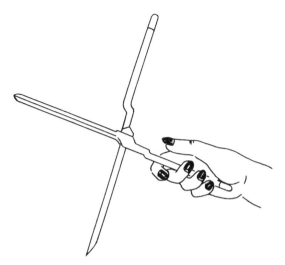

Fig. 7.3   Turning the irons

pinched between the irons and if no charring or marking occurs the irons may be used on the hair. If there is any smoke or marking they should not be used on the hair until cooled. Other methods of testing, e.g. placing the irons near the nose or cheek and assessing the amount of heat by experience, is for use by the professional only. This method is considered dangerous and unsuitable for use by the inexperienced junior.

5. A method of waving. The following points should serve as a guide to waving the hair with heated irons:

(a) Comb the hair thoroughly, and determine the natural hair fall and direction of any wave shape.

(b) Lift a section of hair, approximately 50 mm wide and 12 mm deep. The trough or grooved iron should be placed below the hair section, and the edge nearest the operator should contact the hair first. If both edges of the trough are closed on the hair, two ridged marks will result.

(c) The irons are gently closed, and at the same time rolled up towards the head, without contacting the scalp. A tight grip or pressure is not necessary. (Fig. 7.4).

(d) As the irons, and the hair, are rolled up, the hair is carefully directed to one side. This must be done gradually as the irons move up, or ridges may be produced.

(e) Allow the heat from the irons to penetrate the hair, then unroll the irons. Open them and place the grooved edge, that furthest from the operator, in contact with the underside of the crest formed. Gently close the irons and turn a half turn under. (Fig. 7.5).

(f) When the irons are in this position, the hair and hand are positioned for the next crest. Unroll the irons and slide them down to where the second crest is to be formed. The distance the irons slide determines the size of the wave. The generally accepted wave size is approximately 31 mm between crests. (Fig. 7.6).

(*g*) When the irons are in place for the second crest to be formed, roll the irons and the hair up to the previously formed crest. (Fig. 7.7).

(*h*) It is important to direct the hair to the left or right when rolling up the irons. If the hair is directed right on the first crest it should be directed left on the second crest, and right on the third, etc.

(*i*) For even wave shapes to be produced it is essential that the hair, hands or comb, heat and irons are controlled.

(*j*) Repositioning of hair, hand or comb may be done when the irons are in the under-crest position. (Figs. 7.8 & 7.9).

Joining up the waves requires part of the waved hair to be used as a guide to the shaping of the next, unwaved, portion of hair. This allows the waves to run evenly, across and down, as they do in a natural state. When joining up, warm, not hot, irons must be used or the previously waved hair will become distorted. (Fig. 7.10).

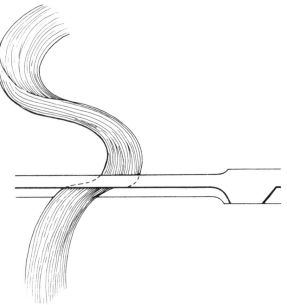

Fig. 7.6   Repositioning hair and irons

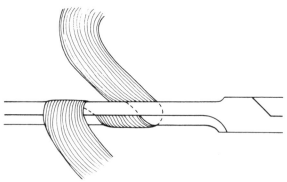

Fig. 7.7   Rolling up, second crest

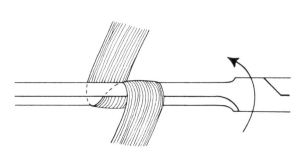

Fig. 7.4   Commencing waving — rolling up

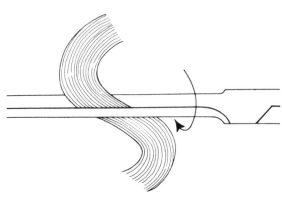

Fig. 7.5   Waving — the turn under

Fig. 7.8   Finished wave shape

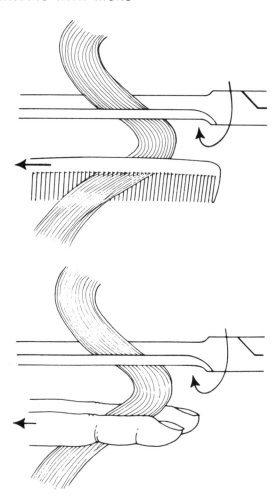

Fig. 7.9   Waving with and without comb

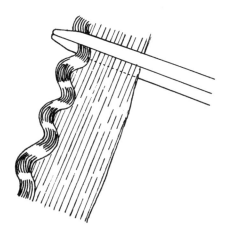

Fig. 7.10   Joining up

Underwaving, or waving the underneath sections of hair, is achieved similarly to the joining-up process, except that part of the top, waved section is used as a guide to shaping the underneath, unwaved hair.

The practice weft is best waved in strips, along its length, joining one strip to the other as waving progresses. When the top section is waved and joined, underwaving may be carried out. Commence by using a warm iron to form the first shapes and deepen them by waving with a hotter iron afterwards.

The hair must be reasonably straight to start with; do not attempt to wave a crimped piece of hair, i.e. ridged or lined, or unsatisfactory shapes will be produced. If square waves are formed, lack of iron control, incorrect positioning of hair, or tightly pulling the hair may be the cause.

Do not attempt to straighten out marked or crimped hair, or ill-formed waves, by overwaving, i.e. waving over shapes already formed, with hotter irons. The hair may be straightened by damping, combing and gently stretching and dried by stroking with warm irons.

6. Curling with irons is a technique of rolling, turning and positioning hair to form various curl shapes and effects. Traditionally hair was curled up to the lowest crest in the nape. Modern styling requires hair to be curled in a variety of shapes which are slipped from the irons, clipped in different positions and dressed when cool. Different effects are produced by varying heat, tension and shape.

Types of curl produced with irons are as varied as those used for wet setting. Three traditional curls are the Digite, or ringlet curl, formed spirally from roots to points; the Bombage, formed croquignole fashion; and the Francois curl, formed similarly to the Digite, but with extra root tension.

Methods of forming a curl. The warmest part of the irons is usually the point ends; the coolest part is near the crutch or pivot. A curl formed at the iron points will be tighter than that formed at the pivot end. Tighter or looser effects may be produced by varying the time the curl is held by the irons, e.g. a curl held till the irons cool will be tighter than a curl held for a short while only.

Forming a ringlet curl requires a small hair section to be placed near the root end, between the irons. These are rolled under, and up towards the head, gradually feeding the lengths of hair into the irons. By slightly opening the irons on each turn the hair may be slipped from the point end until all the hair is curled. As the irons are turned, slightly opened, and the hair slipped into the irons, the point ends of the hair should be untwisted and allowed to spiral round the irons as rolled. The ringlet formed will be close to the head with a looser hanging point. (Fig. 7.11).

If a looser root-end ringlet is required, the hair may be formed croquignole fashion; this will also form firm points.

The barrelspring curl may be formed by gripping the hair points, at the pivot end of the irons, and rolling up to the head. The root stem, which determines the curl direction, is positioned accordingly, by turning the irons. As the handles of the irons are moved, so the directed points position the curl base or curl stem. (Figs. 7.12, 7.13 & 7.14).

Short hair may need to be curled by the points of the irons and slightly opened after one or two turns to form an open centre. As soon as the curl is formed it should be positioned and clipped on the head. (Fig. 7.15).

Softening and curling the hair is a method achieved by stroking the hair lengths with hot irons and shaping and placing, as for wet setting. The heat softens the hair and the shape is retained by the curl when cool.

Full waves may be achieved by the application of reverse curling with hot irons. When cool the hair may be lightly combed and the resulting wave shapes 'ironed' over by using the iron-waving technique. A full waved head of hair may be quickly achieved by this method.

Waving and curling on live heads presents difficulties not encountered on the practice weft. Apart from wave and curl formations, style directions and suitability must be considered. When an all-waved head can be successfully completed it becomes easier to adapt and produce variations.

Waving the head of hair in the traditional manner, without a parting, requires determining natural hair fall, particularly at the front hairline. The points of the irons should be used to form the first crest, and without great depth or height in this position. Small sections of waved hair should curve on to the forehead. Following waves may be deeper and continued across and round the head. Sides may vary but should generally encircle the ears. When the top sections are waved and joined, underwaving may be started. Complete by curling up to the lowest crest in the nape.

Dressing the waved hair may be commenced when it has been allowed to cool. The hair in a warm state is soft and if dressed before cooling will lose its curl or wave shape. Dressing or control creams may be applied and dressing out completed as for a dried wet set.

7. Modern styling or pli with irons requires a variety of curl shapes and positions depending on the line of the style. The pli is built or designed similarly to that required for wet setting. The difficulty of styling short hair may be overcome by taking small sections of hair which will enable them to be gripped by the irons. (Fig. 7.16).

The electric waving irons are similar to the Marcel type except that an electric element is situated in the rod, which enables them to be heated. Other electric styling irons consist of larger barrels and troughs and

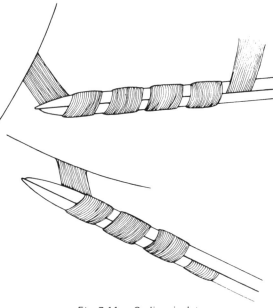

Fig. 7.11   Curling ringlets

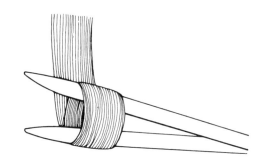

Fig. 7.12   Barrelspring curl with irons

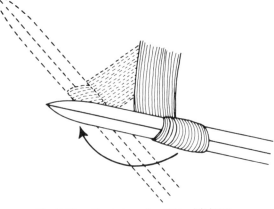

Fig. 7.13   Root stem direction with irons

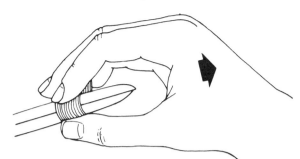

Fig. 7.14   Barrelspring curl — slipping the hair

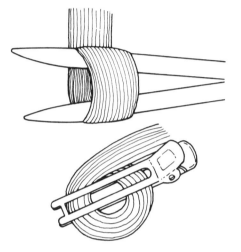

Fig. 7.15   Barrelspring curl — clipped to head

Fig. 7.16   Modern pli with irons

are designed for curling and shaping rather than waving. The barrel of this type of iron may be filled with an oil which is spread on to the hair during waving. The waving temperature may be pre-set by a control on the electric irons. The modern, larger curl, e.g. barrelspring or roller type, is best formed with the large-barrelled styling irons. The traditional waving and curling methods are best produced by the Marcel-type irons or the electric waving irons.

The practical, scientific, aesthetic and boardwork aspects of other hair-moulding, heat-softening techniques, e.g. heated rollers, blow waving, combing and drying, have been dealt with previously (see Chapters 3 and 6, which should be read and compared with the work of this chapter).

8. Dangers and precautions:

(*a*) Heated irons should never be used on hair without testing for temperature, or burns and ruined hair result.

(*b*) When working close to the scalp, place the comb between the irons and head to prevent discomfort and burning.

(*c*) When finished with heating stoves, disconnect and place, with the irons, in a suitable position for cooling. Do not place hot heaters or irons in cupboards until they are cool.

(*d*) Do not use very hot irons on white or blonde hair; high temperatures will discolour the hair.

(*e*) Do not allow the irons to overheat in stoves; red-hot irons are dangerous, become brittle and may break if dropped on the floor.

(*f*) Hold irons by the handles; remember the irons are hotter near the pivot.

(*g*) Never play around or fool about with hot irons; accidents happen all too easily.

(*h*) Make sure that all equipment, particularly electrical, is in good order. Unclean or poor-conditioned equipment is dangerous and may hamper the ease of movement required to produce good results.

Cleaning the irons, particularly those heated in stoves, is necessary to remove surface residue produced by heating and materials used, e.g. setting agents and oils. A light rubbing with emery cloth removes this, and remaining grease may be removed with spirit. The irons should be lubricated with sterilizing oil and stored in a dry place to prevent rusting.

Treatment of burns. Minor burns, without blistering, may be treated by running under cold water, application of a suitable burn cream and covering with a clean dry dressing. Severe burns, with blistering, should be covered with a clean dry dressing, the person treated for shock, i.e. kept warm and comfortable and quiet, until a doctor or medical aid arrives. The employer, manager or senior assistant should always be notified of any accident to client or staff.

Fire. If a heating appliance causes a fire, disconnect any electrical supply, and apply water, fire blanket, sand or carbon dioxide from a fire extinguisher. Do not use water on electrical appliances connected to the mains supply because of the danger of shock. Uncontrollable fires should be dealt with by the fire brigade who should be informed as soon as possible. In this event escort all clients from the area and sound the alarm or warn others in the salon or area.

Revision test 1

Q. 1   What is 'waving with irons'? Describe its uses.
Q. 2   List the dangers of iron waving and the precautions to be taken.
Q. 3   Are waves produced with irons temporary or permanent?
Q. 4   Explain and list the tools used in iron-waving methods.
Q. 5   Describe the hottest and coolest parts of irons and how this may affect curling.
Q. 6   List the modern equipment and applications of waving with irons.
Q. 7   Describe a method of waving with irons.
Q. 8   Describe a method of curling with irons.
Q. 9   How and why is the hair prepared for iron waving?
Q.10   Briefly describe each of the following terms:
        (*a*) Wave size. (*b*) Size of irons. (*c*) Joining up. (*d*) Testing the irons. (*e*) Underwaving.

Revision test 2

Complete the following sentences:

1   The name of the man who revolutionized waving with irons was ....
2   Three basic rules of this type of waving are:
     (*a*)..
     (*b*) ....
     (*c*)..
3   The term given to all forms of 'iron' waving is ....
4   Straight lines or marks made in the hair with irons are called ....
5   Three tools required for waving with irons are:
     (*a*)........................, (*b*)........................, (*c*)........................
6   Name three different types of waving irons:
     (*a*)........................, (*b*)........................, (*c*)........................
7   Describe three points of iron-waving hair preparation:
     (*a*)..
     (*b*) ....
     (*c*)..
8   Hot irons should always be .... before use.
9   A wave consists of .... and one ....
10   The size of a wave is the distance between ....
11   Waving underneath sections of hair is called ....
12   Three traditional curls formed with irons are called (*a*) ...., (*b*)........................,
     (*c*)........................
13   Hot irons and stoves should not be placed in .... until they are ....

Revision test 3

Complete the following sentences with the word or words listed below:

Tight. Pressure. Ringlet. Styling irons. Sizes A, B, C, D. Hottest. Coolest. Croquignole.

1   The irons should not be gripped with too much ...., or held too ....

2   The points of the irons are ...., and the crutch or pivot end the ....
3   The hanging spiral curl is called a ....
4   Curling hair from points to roots is called ....
5   Size .... irons are used for tight work, sizes .... and .... for general work, and size .... for large loose work.
6   The large-barrelled, electric, oil-filled irons are generally called ....

Vocabulary

Crest	The ridge of the wave.
Crimp	A straight line or mark in the hair.
Croquignole	Term given to winding from points to roots.
Crutch of iron	The centre pivot part of the irons.
Digite, Bombage, François curls	Names of traditional-type curls formed with heated irons.
Gas brackets	An old design for heating irons.
Groove	The concave or hollow prong of the irons.
Hair weft *Practice weft*	Wefted hair used for iron-waving practice.
Heat moulding	Softening process of heated irons in use.
Heater, stove	Means of heating waving irons.
Iron exercises	Enable hand and tool movements to be practised.
Iron work or waving	Waving and curling with irons.
Joining up	Joining one strip of waves to another.
Marcel Grateau	Revolutionized iron waving by producing S-shaped waves, in 1872.
Marcel waving	S-shaped undulations of Marcel Grateau.
Pli with irons	Modern curl styling with irons.
Ringlet	A hanging spiral curl.
Rod	The solid, rounded prong of the irons.
Sizes	Marcel-type iron sizes: A for tight work, B and C for general work, D for loose work.
Spirit stove	Used for heating irons.
Styling irons	Large rod and groove, sometimes oil-filled, electric irons used for modern iron work.
Testing irons	Heat test: tissue paper is placed between irons. If charring and marking occurs they are too hot for use.
Thermostat	Bimetal strip which expands and contracts and controls iron temperature.
Underwaving	Joining up the underneath hair sections.
Undulation	The wave shape or form.
Wave	Two crests and a trough, an undulation.
Waving with irons	Name given to all forms of iron waving.

Haircutting—Introduction and Tools Used

1. Cutting the hair to the shape of the head is essential for good hairdressing, and forms the basis of all hair shapes and styles. It affects the way in which hair hangs or falls from the head and, in the final result, all other processes. A well-cut or shaped head of hair should be pleasing to look at and easy to manage.

2. Tools used for cutting should be clean, sharp and balanced, they should fit the hand and feel comfortable in use. Tools commonly used are: scissors, thinning scissors, razors or hair shapers, combs, and hand or electric clippers.

Scissors. A wide variety of scissors, with straight or curved, short or long blades, are used. A good pair of scissors should be made of well-tempered steel with freely moving, sharp-edged blades. They should not be too heavy or too long to control; a common length for the small hand is 150 mm, and for the larger hand 175—187 mm. Scissors need to be reground and set occasionally, i.e. resharpened, so a spare pair, preferably of the same type, is required.

Parts of the scissors commonly referred to are: the blades, points and heel, shanks, rivet or pivot, and handles. Haircutting scissors should not be used to cut other materials or the edges will be made blunt and will drag or pull and be difficult to use until resharpened. There are reputable firms who specialize in servicing scissors and fine-edged tools. (Fig. 8.1a).

Holding scissors correctly, with the thumb through one handle and the third finger through the other, ensures ease of use and control, and allows the movements required. (Fig. 8.1b).

Practice with scissors when purchased, particularly for the first time, is necessary so that the weight and feel may become accustomed to. Straight, long, curved or short-bladed scissors are equally popular and good results may be achieved with each type if carefully and correctly used.

Simple *exercises* help the hand to move the scissor blades into the many angles and directions in which they will be used, and practice of the following will help:

(a) Hold the scissors correctly and, if held in the right hand, point them to the left. Place one blade on to the back of the left hand and open and close the

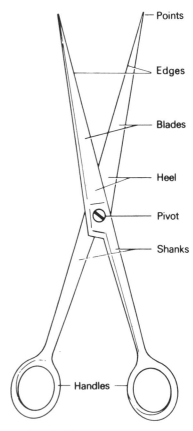

Fig. 8.1(a)   Scissor — parts

blades by allowing only the top blade to move. After a while practise this movement without resting them on the hand. (Fig. 8.2a).

(b) Practise moving the points of the scissors into different positions by slowly turning the wrist, first in one direction and then in another. Then practise opening and closing the blades as they are being turned. (Fig. 8.2b).

(c) Place the scissors handles in the palm of the hand, and with the thumb and index finger grasp them at the pivot and simply turn them, in a closed

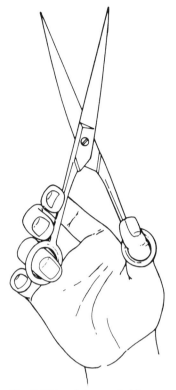

Fig. 8.1(*b*)   Scissor – hold

position, first one way and then another. Occasionally place the finger and thumb into the handles, without the use of the other hand, and hold the scissors correctly. (Fig. 8.2c).

Razors. Open razors, e.g. the smaller, solid-bladed French razor, or the larger hollow-ground blade German type, and the modern safety, guarded-blade razor or hair shaper, are all commonly used in methods of cutting. These tools have very sharp edges, or should have, and care must be taken when using them. (Fig. 8.3).

The parts of a razor are the blade, edge, point, heel, back, tang and handle. The handle is used as a cover for the blade edge, but take care that the edge does not protrude from the handle. (Fig. 8.4.). *The modern hair shaper,* designed similarly to the open razor, has a removable blade with a metal guard attachment. Some have handles like open razors, others have a straight fixed one.

The edges of open razors must be kept sharp and keen by setting, honing or stropping (terms used for sharpening techniques), or sent to specialists for servicing.

Razor setting was more often learnt by men's, rather than ladies' hairdressers, as part of their work. There are few craftsmen who work with sharp-edged tools who are unable to set or maintain them. A razor is set to sharpen its edge, and various types of stone, e.g. slate, water or Belgian oilstone, are used. The

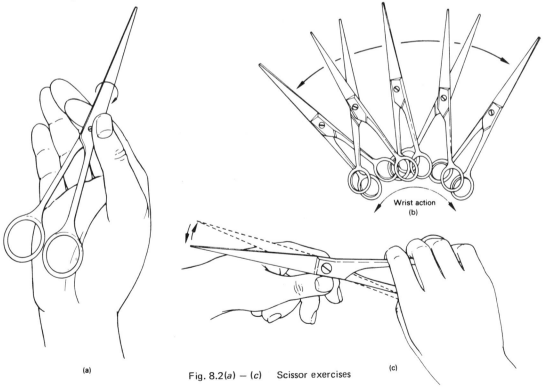

(a)

Wrist action
(b)

(c)

Fig. 8.2(*a*) – (*c*)   Scissor exercises

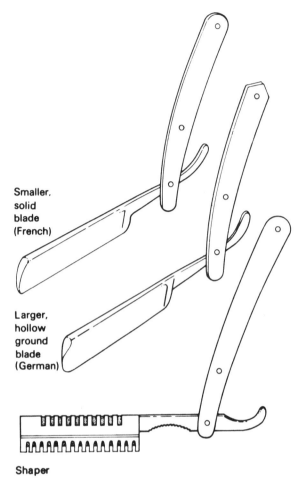

Smaller,
solid
blade
(French)

Larger,
hollow
ground
blade
(German)

Shaper

Fig. 8.3   Razor types, and hair shaper

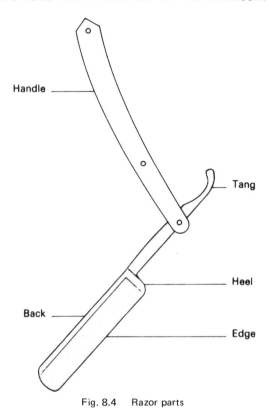

Handle

Tang

Heel

Back

Edge

Fig. 8.4   Razor parts

stone is lubricated, depending on its type, with water, spirit or oil. The blade of the razor is placed flat, with its edge towards the centre, on one end of the stone. It is then slid, across and along the stone, from heel to point. The blade is turned, on its back, held flat on the opposite end and then slid back along the stone. These movements are repeated, using little pressure, and the blade is moved backwards and forwards over the stone. The cutting edge may be tested by gently placing on the fingernail, and if it grips or tugs the nail the edge will be keen. (Fig. 8.5 a & b).

The edge is then stropped or smoothed by gently stroking up and down a clean leather strop, taking care not to knock the edge. *The stropping action* is reverse to the setting action. The blade is placed flat on the leather, with the edge away from the centre, and drawn down the leather. It is then turned, on its back, and gently pushed up the leather. Several strokes will be required and the edge will, if set correctly, easily cut a single strand of hair. (Fig. 8.5c).

Holding a razor. The handle is opened and the thumb and index finger hold the back of the blade between the heel and the handle. The two middle fingers rest on the back and the little finger rests on the tang, on the other side of the handle. This hold enables the razor to be moved in different directions without restriction. The razor may be held in a straight position, like the hair shaper, for some movements. (Fig. 8.6a).

The modern razor or hair shaper has a guarded replaceable blade, with a fixed or movable handle. They have the advantage of not needing sharpening and are safe to use. The guard restricts some razoring movements, but this may be overcome. It is held similarly to the open razor but used with shorter stroking movements. (Fig. 8.6b).

Thinning or tapering scissors are designed with one or both blades with serrated edges. They are used to remove part of a section of hair with opening and closing movements. They cannot be used in a slithering action as with ordinary scissors. Carefully handled they are a valuable tool, but with restricted uses. They should be held similarly to scissors. (Fig. 8.7).

Clippers, both hand and electric, have restricted use in the salon. They consist of two blades with sharp-edged teeth; one blade remains fixed while the

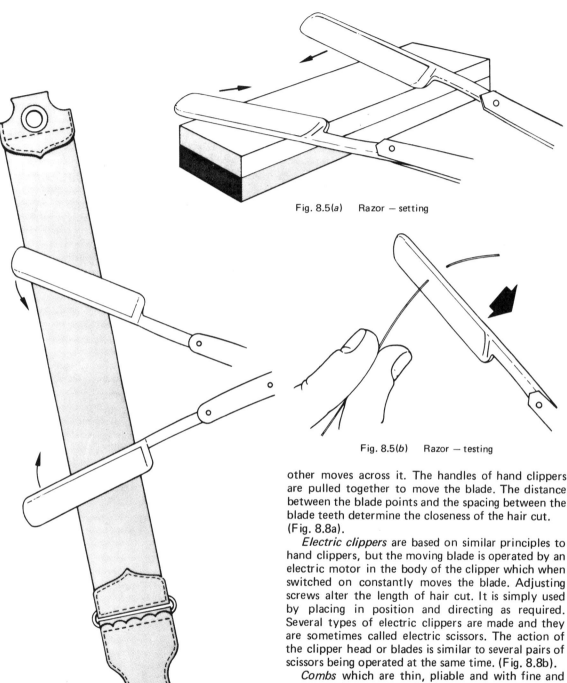

Fig. 8.5(a)   Razor — setting

Fig. 8.5(b)   Razor — testing

Fig. 8.5(c)   Razor — stropping

other moves across it. The handles of hand clippers are pulled together to move the blade. The distance between the blade points and the spacing between the blade teeth determine the closeness of the hair cut. (Fig. 8.8a).

Electric clippers are based on similar principles to hand clippers, but the moving blade is operated by an electric motor in the body of the clipper which when switched on constantly moves the blade. Adjusting screws alter the length of hair cut. It is simply used by placing in position and directing as required. Several types of electric clippers are made and they are sometimes called electric scissors. The action of the clipper head or blades is similar to several pairs of scissors being operated at the same time. (Fig. 8.8b).

Combs which are thin, pliable and with fine and coarse teeth are most suitable to use for cutting. The fine teeth enable the hair to be controlled and closely cut, e.g. when cutting neck hairs over a comb; the coarse teeth are for repeated combing and positioning of the hair. A variety of suitable comb shapes are available; choice is an individual one, but they should feel comfortable and be easily positioned in the various parts of the head.

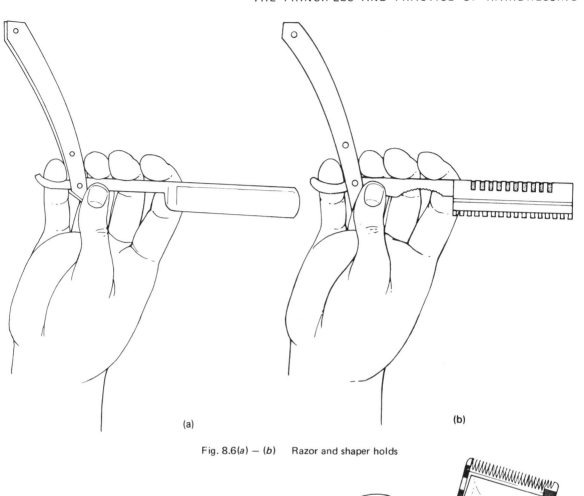

(a)

(b)

Fig. 8.6(a) — (b)   Razor and shaper holds

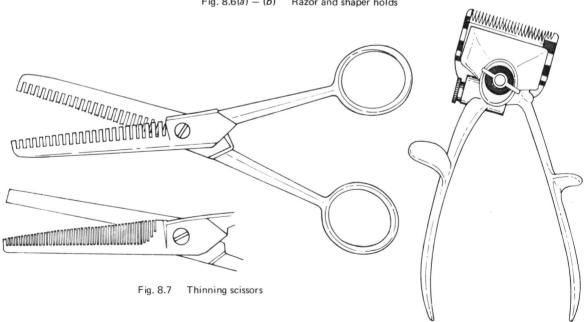

Fig. 8.7   Thinning scissors

Fig. 8.8(a)   Hand clippers

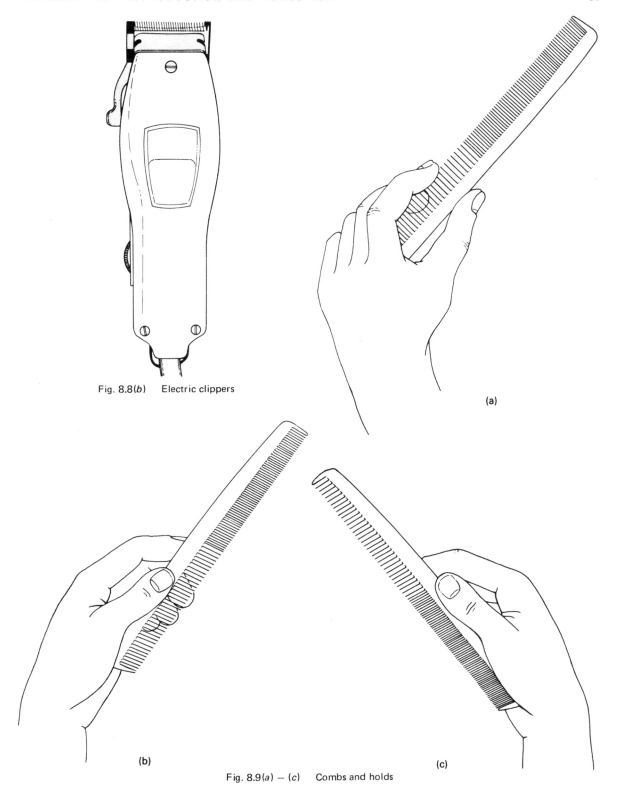

Fig. 8.8(b)   Electric clippers

(a)

(b)   (c)

Fig. 8.9(a) – (c)   Combs and holds

Holding combs depends on the cutting techniques used. For cutting over the comb, one end is held between the index finger and thumb, the finger on the teeth edge and the thumb on the back of the comb. As the comb is turned the finger and thumb grasp the back of the comb. Simply holding and turning the comb backwards and forwards serves as a good exercise. (Fig. 8.9 a & b).

Used for sectioning, the comb is held centrally with the thumb on one side and the fingers around the other. For normal combing and disentangling, use as described earlier (see Chapter 2). (Fig. 8.9c).

Cutting aids, e.g. gowns, hygienic paper strips and towels, are used to prevent short cut hairs falling down the neck. A long, soft-bristle brush should be repeatedly used to clear hairs from the face and skin. Powder from a spray is useful, particularly if the skin is hot and sticky, to loosen and free hairs on the skin. (Fig. 8.10).

3. Cleaning tools. Metal cutting tools may be cleaned by removing all loose hairs with clean tissue, grease may be removed with spirit, and lubricating oil used to lubricate and disinfect. They should then be placed in dry sterilizing cabinets, e.g. an ultra-violet-ray cabinet, until required for use. Some liquid disinfectants and vaporizing sterilizing cabinets blunt and corrode metal tools left in them too long. The manufacturer's advice for the use of these cabinets should be checked first. Do not allow the tools to become rusted or corroded by chemicals or liquids; place them on dry working surfaces away from all solutions. Some rusting and corrosion may be removed by lightly rubbing with emery cloth, but badly marked tools will need to be cleaned when sent for servicing.

Do not use dirty tools; germs breed in the many corners and are easily spread. Scissors and razors are easiest to clean, but clippers are more difficult. Hand clippers may be dismantled for cleaning, but it is not advisable to take electric clippers apart, although the clipper head may be removable for easy cleaning. Servicing and repairs should be carried out by the manufacturers or an electrician. With the combination of suitable disinfectants, sterilizing oils and cabinets, cleaning metal tools is now no longer a problem.

4. Dangers and precautions. Do not place scissors or sharp tools in overall pockets; this is unhygienic and dangerous, as they may fall on to the feet, stab into the body, or become damaged. (Fig. 8.11a).

It is easy to slip on loose, cut hair if it is not cleared from the floor, and accidents can result. Sweep cut hair as soon as possible and place in covered bins. Allowing it to accumulate looks most unsightly and breeds germs. (Fig. 8.11b).

Take care when replacing hair-shaper blades and when using open razors.

If clippers pull the hair, clean and adjust them

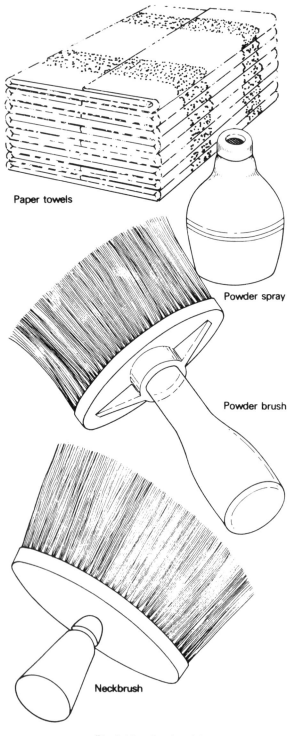

Paper towels

Powder spray

Powder brush

Neckbrush

Fig. 8.10   Cutting aids

with the tension or adjusting screw. Do not use clippers with broken teeth; the wider spacing will drag hair and tear skin.

Use only sharp tools or the hair will be dragged, split or broken. Clean tools after use and store them in a safe, dry place away from hairdressing chemicals.

First aid. If the skin is cut, bathe immediately with clean water, apply an antiseptic cream, and cover. If the cut is severe, try to stop the bleeding by pinching together, keep clean to prevent infection, treat for shock, and call the doctor or seek medical help as soon as possible.

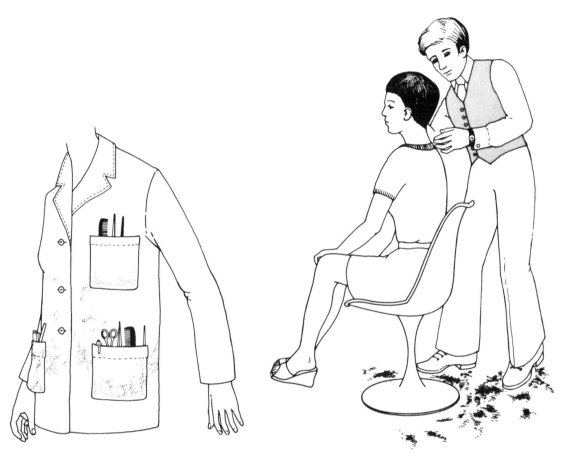

Fig. 8.11(*a*)   Tools in pockets

Fig. 8.11(*b*)   Loose hair on floor

Revision test 1

Q. 1   Describe the correct holding techniques for scissors and razors, and a practice exercise for each.
Q. 2   How are cutting tools kept clean?
Q. 3   What is meant by 'setting and stropping'?
Q. 4   List the precautions to be taken when using cutting tools.
Q. 5   How do thinning scissors differ from ordinary scissors?
Q. 6   What are the differences between hand and electric clippers?
Q. 7   Describe two cutting aids, not tools, and state how and why they are used.
Q. 8   Describe what should be done if a client had a minor or severe cut on the ear.
Q. 9   What is haircutting and what does it do?
Q.10   Describe the different parts of an open razor.

Revision test 2

Complete the following sentences:

1 Good shape and style is based on good ....
2 Two commonly used cutting tools are .... and ....
3 There are two particular types of open razor, the .... type and the .... type.
4 The open razor has been largely replaced by the modern ....
5 Scissors are held by placing the .... finger and the .... through the handles.
6 To sharpen an open razor it is .... and ....
7 The distance between the clipper blade points and the space between the teeth determines the ....
8 Another name for an electric clipper is ....
9 A good cutting comb should be .... with .... and coarse teeth.
10 Metal cutting tools may be lubricated with a suitable .... and stored in a .... cabinet.
11 Placing scissors or sharp tools in overall pockets is both .... and ....
12 If a client's skin is cut or broken, always try to prevent .... by using suitable antiseptic creams.

Revision test 3

Complete the following sentences with the word or words listed below:

Spirit. Dirty. Clean. Hair shaper. Razor. Scissors. Sterilizing oil. Hand clippers. Electric clippers. Thinning scissors.

1 .... tools breed germs and spread infection; always .... them after use.
2 The solid, French, open .... is commonly used for cutting.
3 Grease may be removed from cutting blades with ...., and lubricated with ....
4 .... and .... may be used to cut and thin out the hair.
5 When cleaning .... they may be dismantled, but .... should be sent to the specialist if they need repairing.
6 The modern .... is largely replacing open razors.

Vocabulary

Clippers, coarse and fine	The larger the space between clipper blades and teeth the coarser the cut, i.e. leaves hair longer. A close or fine cut is hair cut short.
Corrosion	Surface chemical action on metal by moisture, air or chemicals, e.g. rust.
Curved scissors	Scissors with curved blades.
Electric scissors	Another name for electric clippers.
Haircutting	The process of cutting hair, commonly abbreviated to cutting.
Hollow-ground	Blades of razors may be ground so that their shape is concave or hollow, common with German razors.
Honing	Another name for edge setting, with the use of a hone or stone.
Modern hair shaper	Name given to modern-type razor with replaceable blades and safety guard.
Open razor	A sharp blade covered with a handle which pivots open. May be solid, semi-solid or a hollow-ground blade.
Scissors	A pair of edged, handled blades, with a central rivet on which blades pivot.
Setting hones or stones	Different types of stone used for setting, e.g. slate, water or oilstone.
Solid or semi-solid razors	The solid or semi-solid blade, common with French razors. Quieter in use than hollow-ground blades.
Sterilizing cabinet	An ultra-violet-ray sterilizing cabinet suitable for storing sterile metal tools.

Sterilizing oil	Used for lubricating and disinfecting metal cutting tools.
Strop	A piece of leather, either long with a handle or fixed to wood, used for stropping.
Stropping	The smoothing of a razor's edge on a leather strap.
Thinning, tapering scissors or shears	Used for thinning hair, may have one or both blades with serrated edges.
Tool care	Cleaning, sterilizing, sharpening, safely storing and maintaining sharp edges.
Tool exercises	The practice movements which enable the tools to be freely used correctly.
Tool holds	The correct manner in which to hold tools.
Tool setting	Sharpening of edged cutting tools, e.g. scissors and razors.

Haircutting—Terms, Techniques and Basic Method

5. There are a number of **names or terms of techniques** used with slight differences of meaning. For accurate understanding, communication and application, a short definition of the most common should serve as a guide.

Tapering is cutting hair to a taper, a technique of reducing the length of some hair in a section of hair, enabling it to form easily into a point. It may be used to shorten the length of the whole section at the same time.

Tapering with scissors on dry hair is a slithering, sliding, backwards and forwards movement along a hair section. The blades are allowed to open and close slightly and the hair cut in the crutch of the scissors from the point third of the section, i.e. a third of the length from the points. (Fig. 8.12).

Tapering with a razor, on wet hair, achieves a similar effect. The razor should be placed on or under the section, at a slight angle to prevent dragging, and in a series of slicing actions backwards and forwards allowed to cut the hair. A razor may be used to shorten at the same time as tapering, which should be restricted to a third of the length from the point ends of the hair section.

Point tapering achieves similar tapering effects by the removal or shortening of some hairs from the point end of a section, with the points of the scissors. The hair is held at the required angle, and with a loose wrist action the scissor points are moved backwards and forwards along the section to remove or cut the hair. (Fig. 8.13).

Feathering is another name given to tapering. It also describes the effects produced by dressed, tapered hair, particularly when dressed in a splayed-out effect on the forehead and at the sides. Point tapering may be used to produce feathered effects.

Backcombing taper is another tapering method. A section of hair is backcombed, or pushed back from the points, and the point end remaining in the hand is slither tapered. The amount of hair backcombed will determine the degree or length of taper. If a long taper is required then less hair is backcombed. If a little taper is required a lot of hair is backcombed. (Fig. 8.14).

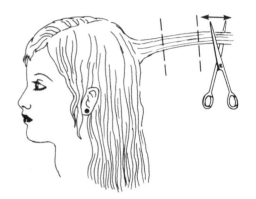

Fig. 8.12   Tapering

6. Club cutting is a method of cutting sections of hair across bluntly. It is used to reduce the hair and section to one length. The angle at which the scissors cut will affect the position of the hair points. Club cutting may be carried out with scissors on dry or wet hair, and with a razor or hair shaper on wet hair. (Fig. 8.15).

If a large section of hair is sharply clubbed the resulting line, described by the hair ends, will be irregular. It is necessary to club cut small sections of hair at a time. A hair section correctly clubbed will form a straight line, as opposed to taper, i.e. ends falling to a point.

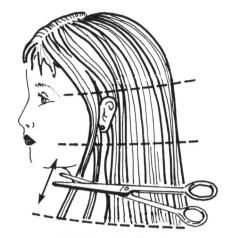

Fig. 8.13   Point tapering

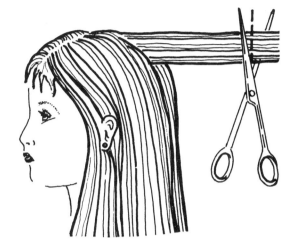

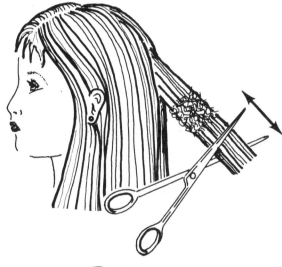

Fig. 8.15   Club cutting

Fig. 8.14   Backcomb taper

Club cutting is commonly used to produce a graduated cut or shape, i.e. hair without steps or divisions with the hair ends forming a slope.

Club cutting over a comb may be used for fine graduations, particularly in the nape; it is commonly used in men's styles and some women's shapes. The hair is lifted with the comb and the protruding hair clubbed or blunt cut. The comb should be correctly held with the points of the teeth directed away from the scalp, or a deep step, i.e. line or division, will result. The degree of the slope or graduation is described by the line in which the comb is moved. (Fig. 8.16).

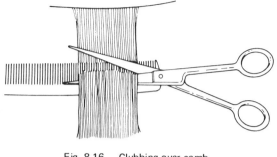

Fig. 8.16   Clubbing over comb

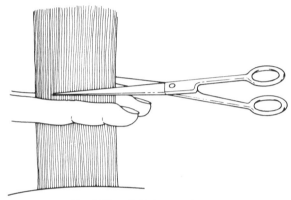

Fig. 8.17   Clubbing over fingers

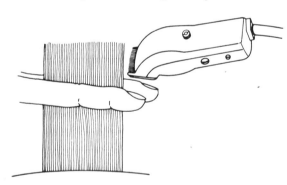

Fig. 8.18   Clipper clubbing

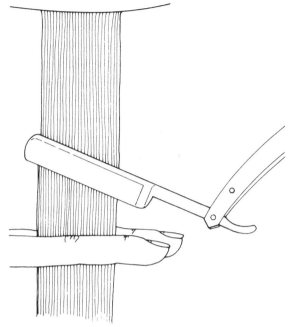

Fig. 8.19   Razor clubbing

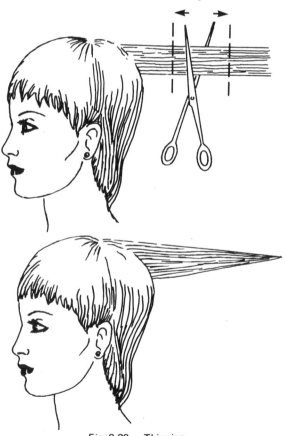

Fig. 8.20   Thinning

Clubbing with clippers is the normal cutting action of hand and electric clippers. These may be used to produce a clubbed graduation in the neck or used similarly to clubbing with scissors over the fingers. All clipper cuts, i.e. cutting a complete shape with clippers only, involve the use of clipper clubbing techniques. (Figs. 8.17 & 8.18).

Razor clubbing may be achieved, though not commonly seen, by holding sections of hair in suitable positions so that the blade edge slices through to produce the blunt clubbed effect. The hair must be held taut, or the blade will not be able to pass through, and cut between the fingers and the head, not over the fingers. The same positioning and angling of the hair as for scissor clubbing may be used. (Fig. 8.19).

7. **Thinning** is a technique of reducing the length of some of the hairs in a section which as a whole is not shortened. The effect produced is a reduction of bulk and a thinner section which forms a long thin taper. The hair is cut or removed at the middle third of the section. If the hair is cut closer than 50 mm from the scalp, short, spiky hairs will stick out through the top layers when combed flat, producing an unsightly effect. (Fig. 8.20).

Thinning may be achieved with scissors used in a tapering action, i.e. the slithering movement, backcombing, taper or point cutting, at the middle third of the section. Thinning or tapering scissors with serrated edges may be used, but few cuts should be made or too much hair will be removed. The first cut should be made nearest the head and following cuts made progressively closer to the points. If the blades are not moved along the hair, too much will be removed from one place.

The razor or hair shaper may be used to thin hair by using long sliding movements from mid-lengths to points. Little pressure should be used or the blade will cut through and shorten the hair more than may be required.

Root thinning may be carried out, with scissors or razor, by cutting small sections of hair level with the scalp. This is a drastic method of thinning and is only used exceptionally. Some competition shapes may require root thinning, but this technique is rarely used, or necessary, in the salon or on the average head of hair. The term *point thinning* is used to describe the removal of hair bulk in a similar way to point tapering, but from the middle third of the hair section.

8. **Wet and dry cutting** are terms used to describe methods of scissor or razor cutting. Scissors may be used on wet or dry hair, but rarely with a taper action on wet hair because the blades are soon blunted and the hair control restricted. Scissor clubbing may be used on wet and dry hair.

The razor is commonly used to produce taper, club and thinned effects in wet cutting, but dry cutting should not be attempted with the razor. The hair is dragged and broken, the process painful, and the cutting edges blunted. Scissors, clippers and thinning scissors are best used for dry cutting.

9. **Graduation** is the difference in the apparent length between the upper and lower parts of a section of hair, or the slope produced by the ends of the hair when cut at a certain angle. If a section of hair is held at right angles to the head, i.e. straight out from the scalp, and club cut at right angles to the hair section, i.e. all the hair cut to the same length, the hair will lie evenly on the head when combed flat. Owing to the angle of the cut and the contour of the head, the ends

of the hair will lie neatly on to each other to produce a graduated curve. Graduation is used to refer to the slope of short to long hair produced in some styles by clubbing. (Fig. 8.21).

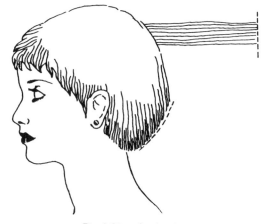

Fig. 8.21   Graduation

A graduated cut is usually produced by clubbing the hair from short in the neck to long at the crown, or by cutting one length all over the head. The neck and back are most commonly graduated in the shortest fashion. (Fig. 8.22).

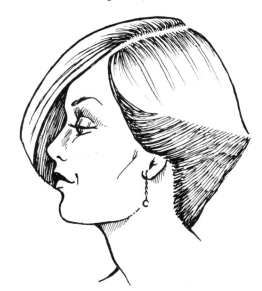

Fig. 8.22   A graduated cut

Reverse graduation refers to the graduated line produced by cutting angles opposite to the contour angles of the head. This is used to produce a longer top layer effect where the ends turn under, e.g. short or long pageboy styles. (Fig. 8.23).

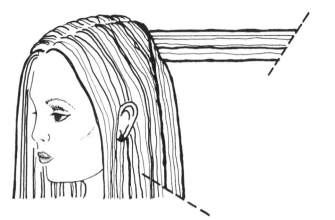

Fig. 8.23   Reverse graduation

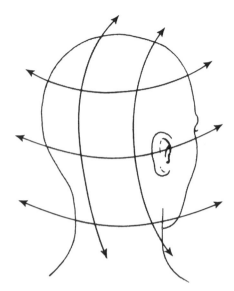

Fig. 8.25   Cutting lines

Angles. There are two important angles to consider when carrying out any method of cutting: (*a*) the angle at which the hair is held out from the head; (*b*) the angle at which the cut is made across the hair or section. Variations of these two angles will produce a variety of results and effects. (Fig. 8.24).

Guides refer to specially prepared sections of hair, cut so that the length and cutting line is determined, and used and followed throughout the cutting process to produce even and precise results. Cutting haphazardly, without guides, produces peculiar and unwanted effects. (Fig. 8.26).

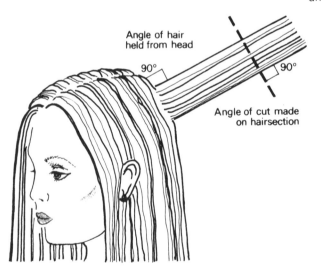

Fig. 8.24   Angles

Fig. 8.26   Cutting guide

Cutting lines are the lines described by the hair ends after cutting, and there are two main ones to consider: (*a*) the head contour from top to bottom; (*b*) the head contour from side to side. Both of these contour lines must be followed throughout any cutting procedure. (Fig. 8.25).

To prepare guide sections the features of the head, e.g. position of eyes, ears, nose, hairline points, etc., should be followed. Further guides may then be prepared in the neck, sides and front, to be followed throughout the cut. When cutting, always use part of the previously cut hair as a guide to the cutting of the next.

Parts of the head which may be conveniently sectioned are determined by the contours of the head, e.g. if a comb is placed flat on the head the point where the head curves away from it usually marks a dividing line.

The back of the head may be subdivided into the top back and the nape; this division is determined by a line passing behind one ear, over the bottom of the crown, and down behind the other ear. The two sides are divided by a line, about mid-eyebrow, intersecting the back line. The top front is divided, approximately 50 mm in from the front, joining the two side lines. The crown or top is that area between the top front, sides, and back dividing line. It is convenient, both for cutting and discussing, to divide the head into separate parts, e.g. the back, two sides, top front and crown. (Fig. 8.27).

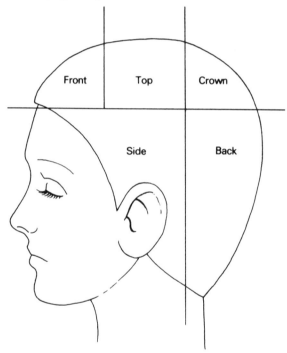

Fig. 8.27   Parts of head sectioned for cutting

Cutting practice cannot of course be carried out on practice blocks — the expense would be prohibitive. The practice of tool movements and positions, combing hair at various angles and the control of hands can be accomplished, to a certain extent, before any cutting is commenced. Live heads are the best for practice, but care, thought and concentration are essential.

Cutting for the first time can be successful if a simple pattern or method is used. Timing at this stage is unimportant; speed of cutting can only be achieved after a great deal of practice, and should never be at the expense of the finally cut shape.

Factors such as the shape and features of the face and head, abnormalities that may be present, or the fashionable and styling effects of cutting, are important and should be considered but concentrated on only when the cutting of basic shapes becomes proficient. Restricting the number of cutting techniques, e.g. using club cutting only to achieve the shape, will be less confusing in the beginning. Later it becomes necessary to use several techniques, e.g. clubbing, tapering, thinning, wet and dry cutting, for each cut.

Satisfactory achievement in cutting basic shapes is necessary for confidence with cutting procedures and style and fashion cutting at a later stage. The basic cut shapes, with variations, become a means of satisfying a number of clients.

10. A basic cut is a head of hair shaped into an unbroken line, or lines, which fit the contours of the head. The hair should be able to be combed, with or without a parting, in any position and allow a variety of suitable and practical styles to be dressed and easily managed by the client. To this end a basic cut will consist of the removal of excess or unwanted hair with the variety of techniques and tools available.

Although methods of basic cutting vary, the end results should not, and whether the cutting method is horizontal, vertical, diagonal, or any combination, the hair should fit the head without steps, broken curves or lines to be seen. The finished cut should not rely on setting and dressing for its shape; these techniques should be used to enhance the cut.

A good method of cutting should provide a suitable starting point, a clear visible guide for a continuous cutting line, and enable excess hair to be easily removed.

Method of cutting a basic shape. The hair and the model should be suitably prepared, e.g. the hair clean and the model comfortable, particularly if cutting for the first time. The application of this method consists of club cutting the hair dry, with scissors. All guide sections should be first cut horizontally and then vertically, and all other sections cut vertically only.

The first cut may be made after determining the cutting lines and final length of hair required.

The first cutting line is determined by combing and holding the centre nape hair down, and by using the two ears as a guide an imaginary unbroken line can be discerned passing 12 mm below one ear down through the centre nape to 12 mm below the other ear. The centre of this line is a convenient place to start to cut, but before this is done the length of the hair which is to remain must be considered.

Basically the hair should not be cut above the nape hairline, and the shortest length may be achieved by the first cutting line passing just below. If a cutting line is 50—100 mm below the nape line, a medium length may be produced, and hair left below this line may be considered to be long. These are general guides only, but basically a short to medium length is required, with allowance made for short or long crown and, later, other style factors.

Once the overall length of the nape hair, the curve and direction of the cutting line, and the point at which the first cut can be made, have been decided, cutting may then commence.

Cutting the nape. A section of hair, 12–18 mm across, should be taken and held horizontally between the first two fingers, resting on the neck. The scissors should be made to club this section with a slicing, rather than chopping, movement, consisting of a number of small cuts. With this done, the first part of the cutting line and the hair length are determined.

Working either side of this central cut, a series of further cuts should be made. The cutting should be directed in an unbroken curve from one ear to the other.

Having reduced the hair length and completed the first cutting line, horizontally, the nape section is then subdivided and cut vertically. This is done to achieve a degree of graduation and determine the second cutting line.

Small vertical sections should be combed and held out from the head at a 45° angle, and the scissor cuts made at a 90° angle to the section. Each section should be firmly held, and overlap, so that the previously cut hair is clearly seen to which it may be made level. When all the nape hair has been carefully cut in this way it may be used as a guide to the cutting of other layers and sections of the back.

The next higher section, approximately 25 mm deep, can then be combed down, subdivided, angled, and cut similarly to the nape hair. Each of these sections is cut vertically only. Cutting progresses further up the head until the top is reached. The completed back hair should fit the head neatly.

If one length of hair is required throughout, the hair sections should be held at right angles from the scalp and cut at right angles to the sections. For longer lengths in any other part of the head the cutting angles should be adjusted accordingly and the line of the scissor cuts should describe the shape outline.

Cutting the sides. The first section or subdivision, at the bottom of the side, is combed and held down between the fingers in a horizontal position. This is lined up with the cut hair of the nape and then cut to continue the curve round to the side. This first section is then combed, angled and cut vertically, but not held too far from the head, or too much graduation may be produced. The higher part of the side may then be subdivided and cut vertically only, but not without using part of the previously cut hair as a guide.

Cutting the top crown and front. When each of the

sides has been cut, the top front and crown hair may be combed down, from a central parting, and cut on to the sides and back. This is done similarly to the previous cutting, i.e. small overlapping section, firmly held, angled and cut in continuous lines, working from top side to the centre parting, first on one side then the other.

Checking the cut. Having cut the hair vertically, comb and check the hair length and blend of sections horizontally. Always check the sections by combing opposite to the way taken when cut. By checking in this way, unevenness is clearly seen and easily corrected.

In the beginning it is difficult to control dry hair, particularly if it is very curly or with the remains of a perm. With more experience it will be found that checking the hair after it has been washed is easier.

During cutting a neckbrush should be continually used to clear cut hairs from the skin. The protective coverings should remain in place throughout the cut. Each section of hair should be cleanly combed and only cut when held at the correct angle. When the cut is completed and checked, the resultant shape may be further improved by setting and dressing.

Adapting the basic shape or cut to simple style shapes is comparatively easy once the beginner is accustomed to a basic cutting method, e.g. the cutting line at the sides may be varied to line up with the chin, mouth, nose, eye or eyebrow. The front hair may be cut in line with various points on the face, the crown hair may be left long or cut short, and the neckline may be cut round, square or pointed. Each of these points may be considered to achieve a varied basic cut, which enables the first style cutting effects to be produced. (Fig. 8.28).

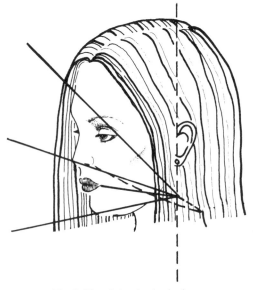

Fig. 8.28   Adapting basic shape

11. Science and cutting. Although perhaps not at first obvious, science plays its part in cutting as in other hairdressing processes. The cutting techniques, how tools are made and used, and the effects and results produced, are better understood when the scientific aspect is considered.

Tools used for cutting are made from steel or a mixture of metals and need cleaning, sharpening and maintaining. Chemicals affect their appearance and efficiency and a tool in good condition helps to produce good results. Tool application is important; most are designed to be used in a certain way, and varied use affects the results produced.

With most tools the principles of leverage or levers are used, i.e. a lever operates around a fixed point, the fulcrum, and lifts weight or controls motion by power or pressure being exerted on either side, e.g. if too little pressure is placed on the handles of clippers, the force applied is not sufficient to cut the hair moving through the blades. (Fig. 8.29).

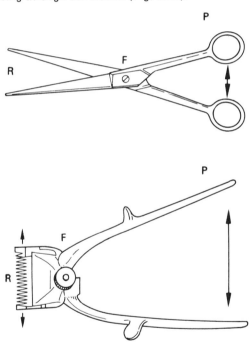

R = Resistance

F = Fulcrum

P = Pressure

Fig. 8.29   Lever action of tools

Using tools, and holding them correctly, enables them to be easily and comfortably applied. If they are not balanced in use, more effort is continually required to counteract the unbalancing. This puts pressure and strain on the hands and muscles; actions are slowed and results affected. Muscles ache when using scissors for the first time until they become used to the movements, but if held and used incorrectly a continual strain may be placed on them.

Cutting and hair growth. Hair grows approximately 12 mm each month and the rate of growth varies throughout the head. This causes the hair to become uneven and untidy a few weeks after cutting, and to maintain a good shape the hair needs to be trimmed or recut. Hair grows vigorously in the early stages of its development, but more slowly towards the end of its life. Fortunately, the hairs on the head are at different stages of development; if they were all at the same stage and grew at the same rate there would probably come a time when all the hair would fall out at the same time, which does not happen.

Distribution of hair on the head allows it to lie naturally forward from the crown. Repeated combing and training, away from the face and eyes, allows the hair to sit back on the head. Most heads of hair may be trained or re-trained to lie in different positions.

Hair streams and *hair whorls* are names given to the natural hair direction due to the arrangement of the hair follicles. In a hair stream the follicles are evenly distributed so that the hair parts. In a hair whorl the follicles are arranged in a circular manner. It is difficult to train these hair patterns, and this must be considered when cutting the hair. To neglect the natural fall, stream or whorl results in difficult-to-manage and unattractive hair shapes. The crown, front hairline and nape are common positions for these patterns of hair growth. (Fig. 8.30).

Angles used in cutting are examples of the use of measurement and calculation in hairdressing processes. An angle is the difference in direction of two intersecting lines on one plane, which is measured in degrees, i.e. 1/360th part of a circle is a degree. Measurement and angles are essential for the complete discussion or description of cutting methods.

The effects of cutting on the hair with blunt-edged tools results in hair being torn, frayed or split, which causes it to become rough and dull. If the hair cuticle is damaged (e.g. razoring dry hair will drag or tear it), uneven absorption of colouring or waving reagents occurs which will adversely affect the results required. (Fig. 8.31).

Hair growth is neither stimulated nor made to grow faster by cutting. All hair growth is determined in the body and skin, and when it grows above the surface where it is considered to be dead tissue, little, if anything, can alter its growth rate.

A single uncut hair naturally tapers to a point which is removed by any form of cutting. The ends of cut hair, particularly if just above the skin level, may feel blunt, bristly and hard, until it grows longer again. It was thought, and occasionally still is, that clipper cutting and shaving made the hair grow

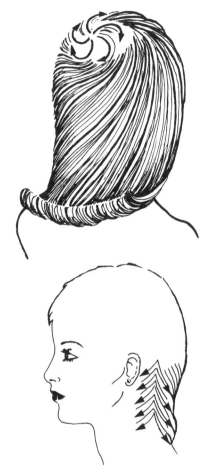

Fig. 8.30   Hair whorls and stream

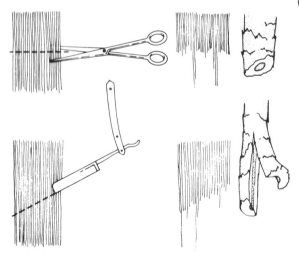

Fig. 8.31   Cutting effects

quicker and thicker than hair cut by scissors. Since the cutting actions are similar the effects produced are similar too. Apart from a certain amount of stimulation applied to the skin with each method of cutting there is insufficient to speed the rate of hair growth. Increasing the thickness of hair means increasing the number of hair follicles, which cannot be done by cutting.

12. Aesthetics and cutting. The shape of the cut hair in relation to the shape of the head and face is an important consideration. The cutting lines should follow the contours of the head and the finished shape depends on the amount or bulk, position and 'fit' of the hair. When dressed the cut shape may be altered, but either shape should be suitable and pleasing. What looks 'nice' is difficult to define, depending as it does on aesthetic appreciation. Generally a round, full, fat face is not improved by hard straight lines cut into the hairlines. Long, heavy hair on a short, full neck does not always enhance face and head shape, but a well-balanced medium length could be ideal.

The length and quantity of hair left after cutting are important aesthetic aspects. This is where haircutting and hairstyling become dependent on one another. When both the practical techniques and aesthetic principles can be applied, high standards of cutting and shaping may be achieved. The successful hairdresser applies both to his work. (Fig. 8.32).

Short hair – round face   Longer hair – round face
Fig. 8.32   Round face shape — hair length and hairline

13. Cutting and boardwork. Cutting postiche is similar to cutting hair on a live head. The techniques are the same but postiche hair does not grow and must be cut exactly and carefully. The cuts should not expose the edges of foundations, particularly of wigs, and should help to correct unnatural hair distribution.

Cuttings is a boardwork term used to describe the hair cut from a head and is one of the main sources of hair used for postiche. (Fig. 8.33a).

The hair, 75 mm or longer, cut from a head, should be placed on to a work surface with the cut or root ends together, overlapping the edge. Placed in this way the cut hair may be suitably prepared for boardwork without being 'turned', i.e. the process of placing all the root ends together. Cuttings differ from combings; the former should not need to be turned, the later will always need turning.

Boardwork clubbing is a term used to describe the clubbing process of levelling the ends of the hair. When hair is being sorted it is placed into hackles or drawing mats, i.e. tools used to hold loose hair, and drawn out with the fingers or the back of a knife and placed level at the root ends. When this is expertly done the ends of the hair look as if clubbed cut, which makes for ease of handling. (Fig. 8.33b).

Boardwork taper. When making some types of hair piece, different hair lengths are used so that a natural taper is produced, e.g. switches which have a full roundness at one end and taper to a point. The degree of taper is determined by the amounts and lengths of hair used. (Fig. 8.33c).

Cutting eyelashes. Eyelashes are made by weaving hair on to fine silks, threads or hairs, and finally trimmed to fit and appear natural. This is done by holding the weft flat and club cutting the length and shape required. If the hair is woven point first, for added lift, the root ends may need to be trimmed.

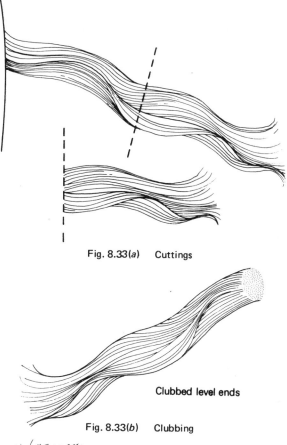

Fig. 8.33(*a*)   Cuttings

Clubbed level ends

Fig. 8.33(*b*)   Clubbing

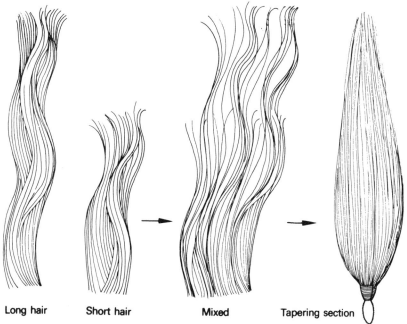

Long hair   Short hair   Mixed   Tapering section

Revision test 1

Q. 1   What is tapering? How and when should it be used?
Q. 2   What is the difference between tapering and thinning?
Q. 3   What are cutting lines? Describe these fully and state how they are determined or decided.
Q. 4   Describe three boardwork terms which may be confused with cutting terms.
Q. 5   Describe methods of clubbing over the fingers, clubbing over a comb and clubbing for graduation.
Q. 6   Describe which tools may be used for clubbing and how they may be used.
Q. 7   What is meant by basic cutting and shaping? Describe a method of cutting a basic shape.
Q. 8   What is graduation? Describe how and when it may be used.
Q. 9   How are angles used in cutting? Describe how the hair should be sectioned and angled for cutting.
Q.10   Briefly describe each of the following terms:
        (a) Feathering. (b) Guide sections. (c) Taper. (d) Clubbing. (e) Hair growth.

Revision test 2

Complete the following sentences:

1   Cutting at the point third of a section of hair and reducing it to a point is called ...., which may be achieved by a .... action with scissors.
2   Reducing the hair length only may be achieved by .... with .... or ....
3   Reducing the hair bulk from the middle third of a hair section is called ...., which may be achieved with ...., ... or ....
4   When cutting a piece of hair it should be lined up with a previously cut piece of hair which acts as a ....
5   Two terms given to certain types of hair growth distribution are .... and ....
6   If a razor is used to cut dry hair it will .... and ....
7   Hair used for boardwork is usually called .... and/or ....
8   In a basic cutting method the nape section is cut both .... and ...., but the following sections are cut .... only.
9   The first cut of a basic shape is determined by the .... required, and the direction of the .... is usually determined by the two ears.
10   The parts of the head which may be conveniently sectioned are the ...., ..., ... and ....

Revision test 3

Complete the following sentences with the word or words listed below:

Clubbing. Vertically. Thinning. Horizontally. Tapering. Wet hair. Feathering. Hair section. Dry hair. Actual cut.

1   Sections of hair may be cut .... and ....
2   Two important angles to consider when cutting are the angle of holding the .... and the angle of the .... across the section.
3   Four names of cutting techniques are ...., ..., ... and ....
4   .... may be cut with scissors or razor, but .... should be cut with scissors only.

Vocabulary

All-clipper cut	A complete cut shape with clippers only.
Boardwork clubbing	Levelling the ends of the hair.
Clubbing	Cutting method which produces level ends; *club cutting* and *blunt cutting* are alternative terms.
Combings	Hair collected from repeated combing and used, after preparation, in boardwork.
Cutting angles	Angle at which the hair is held, and angle of cut across the hair.
Cutting lines	The direction in which cutting is made to follow the contours of the head.
Cuttings	Hair cut from the head, used in boardwork.
Feathering	Tapering action with scissor points.
Graduated cut	A cut producing short neck hair to a longer crown length, e.g. men's.
Graduation	The slope produced by the ends of the hair after any method of cutting.
Guides	Any feature or point on the head, or part of a previously cut piece of hair. The prepared nape section may be used as a guide to cutting the rest of the hair.
Hair shaping	A term alternatively used for cutting.
Hair stream	The distribution of hair due to the positions of the hair follicles.
Hair whorl	
Point tapering	Tapering with the scissor points.
Razor clubbing	Club cutting with a razor.
Razoring	Any method of cutting hair with a razor.
Reverse graduation	Hair cut with the longer lengths on top, e.g. long hair, turning under, may be reverse graduated.
Root thinning	Removal of hair at the root ends.
Slithering	Descriptive term for tapering action.
Tapering	Term used for cutting a taper in hair.
Thinning	Reducing hair bulk without reducing length.
Wet and dry cutting	Cutting the hair when wet or dry.

Haircutting—Fashion and Style Cutting

14. Fashion and style cutting are methods of cutting hair to a particular shape or style which may follow a line of fashion past or present. To achieve the effects required, a variety of cutting techniques and methods may be used. To create any effect 'anything goes', but to create pleasing and unique effects a carefully prepared plan or pattern of cutting should be followed, based on an understanding of hairstyling.

The features of the face and head should be evaluated before starting to cut. The general shape of the head, nose, ears, eyes and mouth should be closely looked at, and note made of the facial profile, e.g. whether it is concave or convex. The lowest point of the chin, in relation to the top, back and nape, should be examined, and positions of facial features in relation to the front hairline should be noted.

The length, quality, quantity, texture and general state of the hair, particularly the effects of previous cutting, must be considered. Abnormal or unusual aspects should be discussed and dealt with accordingly, e.g. a large bump or cyst requires a longer length of hair to be left so that it is not made obvious. Each of these points are important and may be used as guides to cutting lines and angles for the creation of individual shapes.

Techniques and methods to use are decided by initially examining the hair. Some heads of hair may need tapering and lightly clubbing, or first clubbing and then tapering, and thinning may be required if the hair is extremely thick and bulky. The choice of wet or dry cutting is an individual one determined by experience and the hair to be cut.

15. Cutting lines and angles require the hair to be held away from the head. The position in which it is held and cut determines its position when on the head.

A section of hair held at a right or 90° angle from the back of the head, and cut at right angles to the hair section, will produce a 45° angle of graduation, i.e. the gradient between the top and bottom of the vertical section. (Fig. 8.34a).

A section of hair held vertically at a right or 90° angle, and cut at a 45° angle, will produce a steeper

graduation, of use in short nape styles. (Fig. 8.34b).

A section of hair held vertically at right angles and cut at a 145° angle will produce a 'level length', i.e. the ends of the hair will be level without graduation. (Fig. 8.34 c & d).

For all style and fashion shapes the line of cutting, i.e. the silhouette shape produced by combing the hair out from the head, must be adjusted. The angle of cutting will vary with the different lengths required by the shape. As with basic shaping, the first cutting line and length are decided in the neck, i.e. from ear to ear. The second cutting line varies with the different lengths throughout the shape. (Figs. 8.35 a & b — 8.36 a & b).

When cutting side hair, vertical sections may be combed forward towards the face, to vary length or graduation, e.g. the hair nearer the face will be cut shorter than hair nearer the back, when combed in a natural position. This is required for flicking, wispy side effects in short styles.

Variation in angling the hair sections and cutting angles produces a variety of effects. If each of the angle directions are followed, from one section to the next, good shapes may be achieved. If the angles continually vary, section after section, uneven, unwanted effects are produced. It is important to follow the contours of the head, and for the cutting lines to describe the outline of the shape and lengths required. (Fig. 8.37 a & b).

16. Cutting long hair so that it falls evenly at the ends is simply achieved by following the basic pattern. Cutting angles are varied by choosing different guide points, and if the hair is fine then clubbing is best used. The length and first cutting line are determined by cutting, to below each ear, from cheekbone to cheekbone, to the corners of the mouth, or the point of the chin.

Since graduation is not required, and the hair is to fall level, following sections at the back are combed down and cut horizontally, to a point just below the first cut section. This allows for natural hair lift and will not show graduation. If the hair is to turn under, reverse graduation is achieved by cutting a fraction lower than the first cut section. This produces full

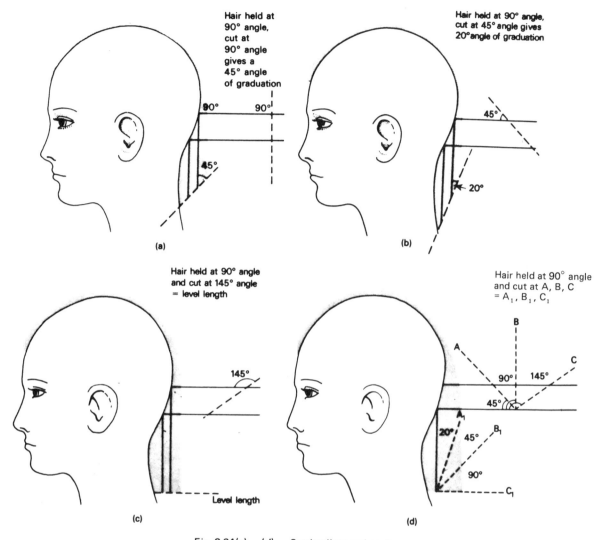

Fig. 8.34(a) — (d)   Cutting lines and angles

swinging hair, i.e. hair level at ends which swings back into position.

If a degree of graduation is required, after preparing the length and cutting line in the nape the following sections are cut on to it by holding them out and cutting at right angles. The determined length must be followed and the angle of cut carefully executed. (Fig. 8.38 a b c & d).

17. Cutting short curly shapes is best done with the tapering technique, as tapered hair holds a curl longer. Prepare the nape hair, cut the length and first cutting line horizontally, then cut the second line and graduation required by taking vertical sections. If the hair is held at a 90° angle and cut at a 90° angle throughout, a short style is produced with a suitable degree of graduation. (Fig. 8.39).

The sides, depending on whether they are to be dressed forward or back, must be angled and cut accordingly. A fringe, commonly worn with short styles, may be cut by combing the hair forward, the length and shape being determined by tapering, using parts of the nose, eyes or brows as a guide. Fringes may be cut similarly to nape hair but directional growth must be considered and allowed for when determining length. If a hard fringe line is not required, do not club cut unless angled correctly.

18. Geometric cutting is used to produce soft or hard effects by varying the cutting lines to different angles. The shape and line of the head, face, hairlines and other features are used to determine angles of cutting, on which geometric effects are dependent. The shorter shapes are more exacting since they cannot be altered or corrected by setting or dressing, and are not usually exaggerated by dressing. Precise

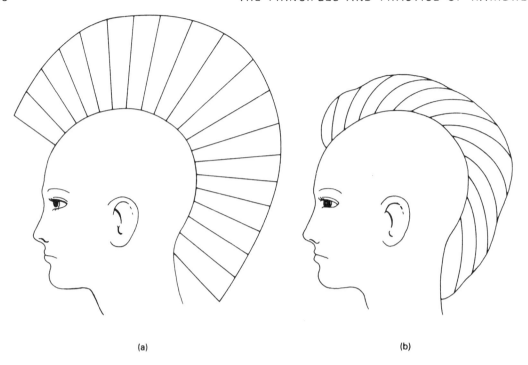

(a)   (b)

Fig. 8.35(a) — (b)   Varied second cutting line — side view

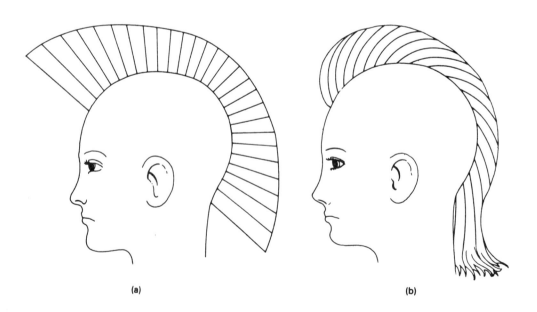

(a)   (b)

Fig. 8.36(a) — (b)   Varied second cutting lines — hair in position

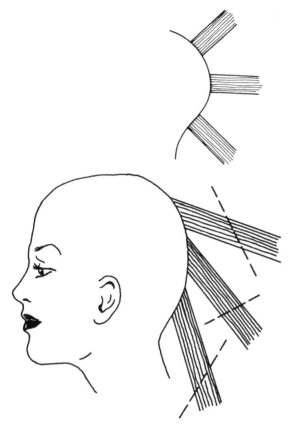

Fig. 8.37(a)   Hair position — cutting

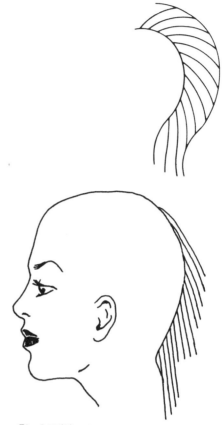

Fig. 8.37(b)   Hair position — placing

and correct cutting is essential and should not be attempted unless techniques and principles are understood. (Fig. 8.40 a b & c).

19. Cutting for long and short effects, in the same style, is a popular and effective means of shaping. The hair is usually cut shortest at the top and back of the head, with the longest lengths at the nape and sides.

The bottom cutting line is determined by choosing a low point, cut straight or curved, and the angle of graduation sharply inclined towards the neck. The following sections are cut with the same degree of graduation but in the opposite direction. Alternatively, the nape section may be cut with little or no graduation and the following section sharply graduated.

The cutting line should be sharply angled to the top of the ears and the reverse angle used to shape the sides, which has the effect of separating the sides from the back. The sides and front may be heavily tapered to produce long wispy effects, and both tapering and clubbing techniques may be used with scissors or razors for these styles. (Fig. 8.41).

Shingles, semi-shingle and Eton crop are some of the names given to short nape styles, common between the wars. The technique of cutting is similar to that required by men's short styles. The technique of clubbing over a comb is used to produce sharp graduated neck sections. The shingle and Eton crop were graduated high in the neck, but the semi-shingle produced a softer effect by the little amount of graduation in the lower part of the neck only. (Fig. 8.42).

20. Cutting men's hair. The main differences between ladies' and men's cutting are the style worn and the shape of faces on which the shapes are cut. Similar techniques are used, but methods of application vary. Cutting short styles requires precision since there can be little or no disguising of mistakes. Clipper cutting was commonly used to produce the 'short back and sides' style, i.e. very closely cropped hair, military fashion, designed more for cleanliness than fashion. Variations of close-cut styles have been worn for a number of years, but recent styles show a return to good shape and fashion.

The styles produced should suit and fit the heads on which they are to be worn, which applies equally

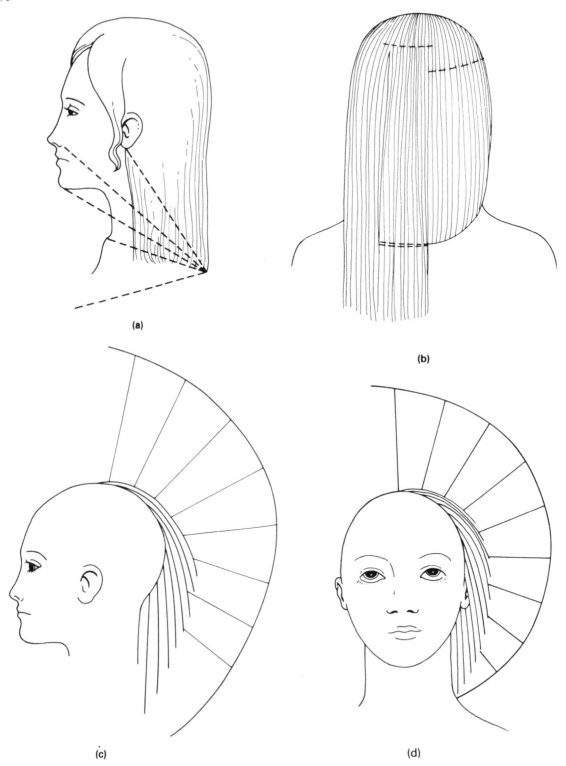

Fig. 8.38(a) — (d)　　Cutting long hair

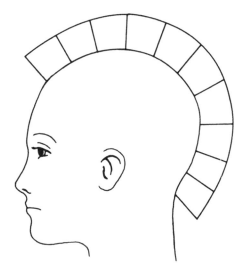

Fig. 8.39   Cutting short curly shapes

to ladies' shapes. Short or skinned heads are rarely suitable, but when short shapes are cut and balanced to allow for fullness they become more suitable.

Longer men's styles may be cut in the same way as ladies' styles, but if too feminine effects are produced the suitability of the style may be as wrong as too masculine effects are on females. Although there are many similarities, each type of cutting requires skill and experience, and no doubt specialization in one or the other will continue, despite the fact that cutting a head of hair, to fit the male or female head, remains basically the same. (Fig. 8.43).

21. Variation of cuts. Cuts are varied to individuals and their requirements. Apart from the similarities of cutting methods, different names may be given to each, e.g. bobbing, layer cutting or layering, bevel cutting, which are the effects of tapering or clubbing. The Eton crop, Egyptian bob and cap cut are some of the names given to different styles or cuts. When a client asks for a named cut, make sure the request is correctly interpreted, e.g.

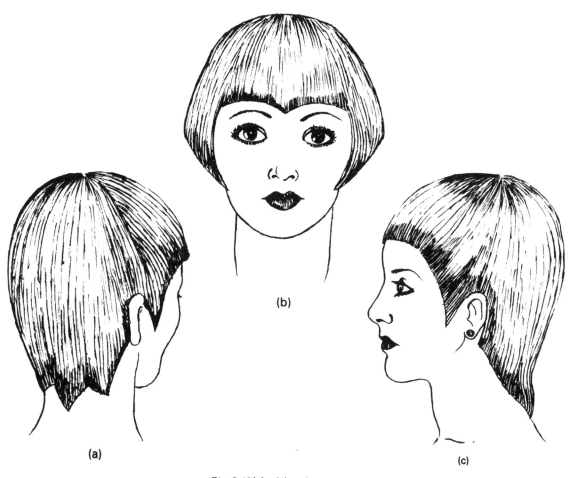

(a)

(b)

(c)

Fig. 8.40(a) —(c)   Geometric lines

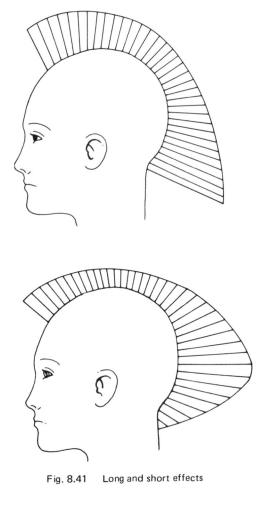

Fig. 8.41   Long and short effects

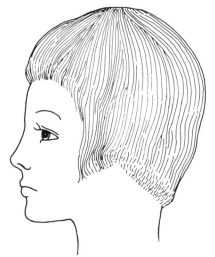

Fig. 8.42   Semi-shingle

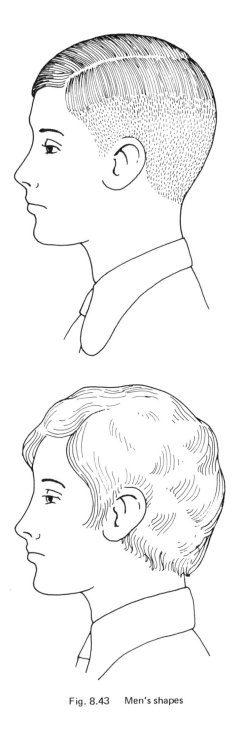

Fig. 8.43   Men's shapes

long, medium and short varies according to each client, and beware the confusion of names.

Necklines may be curved, straight, pointed, or graduated high or low. The lower the graduation the softer the style will appear. Cutting above the natural hairline should be avoided, or·harsh, hard effects are produced. Hair remaining below the neckline may be removed with clippers or points of the scissors. Steps or lines left in a graduated neck will spoil the effect, and it is preferable that all lines be softened unless stark effects are required. (Fig. 8.44 a b & c).

Trimming or recutting is the removal of small amounts of regrown hair, usually to retain the original cut shape. The same techniques, cutting lines and angles should be used if the shape is to be reproduced. If the hair is to be restyled or reshaped, the hair must not be shorter than the length required by the new style; note any abnormalities, and discuss with the client the time that may be required to achieve the desired shape. It is not always appreciated by the client that certain shapes require certain hair lengths and time for it to grow.

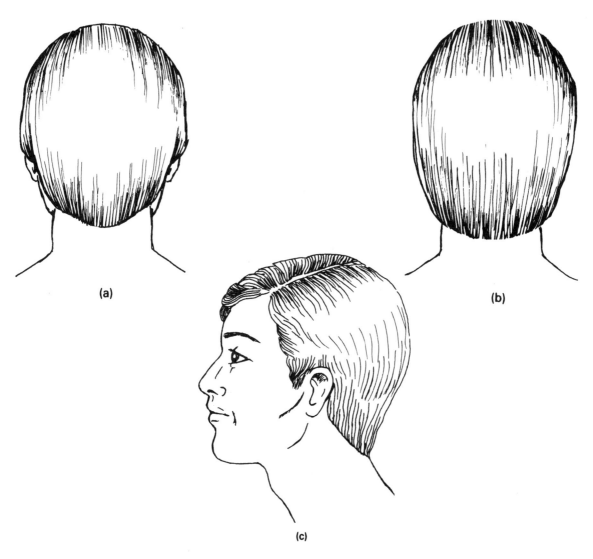

(a)

(b)

(c)

Fig. 8.44(*a*) — (*c*)   Necklines

Revision test 1

Q. 1   What is fashion or style cutting, and how does it differ from basic cutting?
Q. 2   How are cutting lines and angles used for fashion or style cutting?
Q. 3   Describe a method of cutting long hair.
Q. 4   What is geometric cutting and how does it vary from other methods of cutting?
Q. 5   Name and briefly describe three types of hair cut.
Q. 6   What are the differences between women's and men's cutting?
Q. 7   What is meant by reshaping or restyling?
Q. 8   Describe the cutting techniques used in fashion or style cutting.
Q. 9   What is 'trimming' and why is it necessary?
Q.10   Describe each of the following terms:
        (a) Neckline shapes. (b) Short back and sides. (c) Directional growth. (d) Guides to cutting.
        (e) Swinging hair.

Revision test 2

Complete the following sentences:

1   The names given to two tapered effects are .... and ....; they may be produced with .... or ....
2   The technique of .... is used to produce curly effects; to produce hair of one length .... should be used.
3   Cutting other than basic shapes is referred to as .... or .... cutting.
4   Cutting a head of hair after a period of growth is called .... or .... Shaping a full head of hair is referred to as ....
5   A section of hair held out at a $90°$ angle and cut at right angles will produce a ....$°$ angle graduation.
6   List six features or points of the head which may be used as a cutting guide: ...., ..., ..., ..., ..., ...
7   Determining which cutting techniques to use is dependent on .... required and on .... of the hair.
8   The distance between clipper .... and .... determines the closeness or coarseness of clipper cutting.
9   List three precautions to be taken when using cutting or sharp tools:
     (a) ....
     (b) ....
     (c) ....

Revision test 3

Complete the following sentences with the word or words listed below:

Thinning. Clubbed. Tapered. Suitable. Level. Curved. Hair whorls. Square. Hair streams. Guides.

1   Fine hair does not usually require .... and it is better for it to be .... Hair is best .... for curly effects.
2   Directional hair growth, e.g. .... and ...., must be considered when cutting.
3   Necklines may be cut straight, ... or ...., with or without graduation.
4   Swinging hair requires the ends to be ....
5   Shapes cut for women or men should always be ....
6   The features of the face may be used as .... to cutting lines.

Chapter Nine

Dressing

1. Dressing the hair is a process of blending a shape, or shapes, from the directions in which the hair was set. The completed shape is referred to as a dressing, coiffure or hair-do. Several techniques may be used to blend or bind the hair together, e.g. backcombing.

Dressing with a brush is the placing of hair in a finished shape with the use of the brush only. After the hair is set, dried and allowed to cool it is then ready for dressing. The brush is applied to the hair ends and gradually moved up the head and through the set curls and waves. The brushing action should be gentle but firm so that the hair is moulded into shape. Basically the dressing is finished when the hair is moulded into the required position.

Backbrushing is a method of pushing some hair back with a brush so that the main body of the hair stands away from the head. This is done to produce height and to bind the hair together to prevent it from parting or spoiling effects. The amount of hair backbrushed determines the amount of lift or binding. (Fig. 9.1).

A *method of backbrushing* is carried out by holding hair sections from the head, directly or at the angle of final positioning. The brush edge is placed on top of the section, and with a slight turning action made to slide some hairs back towards the head. Too heavy a movement will cause too much hair to be pushed back and the section to flop down.

It is sometimes necessary to lower the hair section gradually in place by slightly lowering after each brushing movement. If maximum lift or height is required the hair is pushed closer to the head with the section held at right angles. If, as is required by many dressings, small amounts of hair are slid back, only the surface is bound together.

The backbrushed hair supports the section and allows a smoothing action with the brush or comb to produce full, light hair shapes. The tangled, pushed-back hair should not be visible on completion of the dressing. (Fig. 9.2).

Backcombing is a dressing technique similar to backbrushing. The comb is used to push back the shorter hairs in a section so that the rest may be dressed high and full from the head. Backcombing

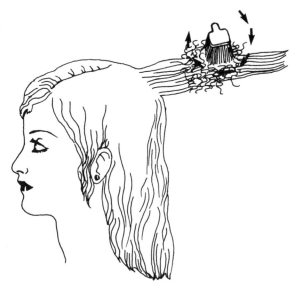

Fig. 9.1   Backbrushing

Fig. 9.2   Backbrushing — stages

may be used where a greater degree of backdressing is required but more hair is pushed back to the head. (Fig. 9.3).

A method of backcombing. Sections of hair are held, directly or at varying angles, from the head, depending on the position required. The fine, closely spaced teeth of the dressing comb are placed on the underside of the section near the root end. The comb is gently turned and pushed back towards the head. The shorter hairs are doubled back and bind or tangle with the rest of the hairs. This action is repeated further along the section until the hair ends are reached. The backcombed section is pushed away so that the following section may be treated similarly. This is continued throughout the head, or parts of the head, that require binding or are to be high and full.

When backcombing is complete the hair may be carefully positioned with the fingers, and finally the wider-toothed end of the comb is used to smooth and line the hair surface. If backcombing is placed under each hair section, surface smoothing is easier, but if placed above, much of the backcombing will be dragged out in the endeavour to smooth the hair. The comb should not be allowed to penetrate too far into the hair or the backcombed hair is loosened and the effects lost. *Backdressing,* i.e. backcombing or backbrushing, may be applied to any part of the hair and commenced at the top, front or nape. (Fig. 9.4 a b & c).

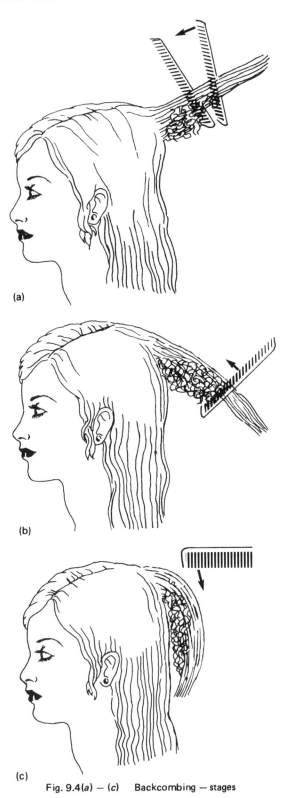

(a)

(b)

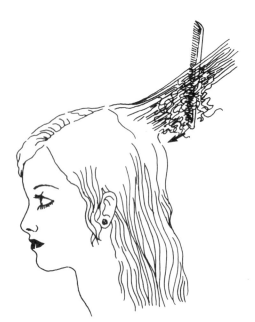

Fig. 9.3   Backcombing

(c)

Fig. 9.4(a) — (c)   Backcombing — stages

Teasing the hair with a pin or the tail end of a tailcomb may be used to complete a dressing. By carefully inserting the pin or the tail into a part or parts of the hair and lightly lifting, balance may be achieved or an exposed area of backcombing may be covered. It is important when dealing with small pieces of hair to work with the fingertips, the point of the comb, the brush edge or the pin tip so that the hair is not generally disturbed when finishing the dressing.

The use of hands is a valuable aid but should be lightly used throughout most dressing procedures. Often the hands are used to pat down the hair continually until all full dressing effects are flattened down. This produces a flatter effect than if no backdressing was used in the first place. The fingertips should be used without the hands resting on or touching the head. (Fig. 9.5).

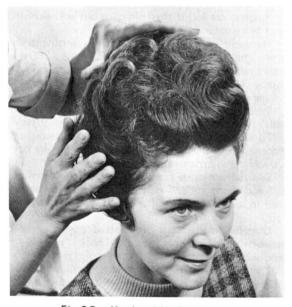

Fig. 9.5   Hand position for dressing

The use of mirrors by the operator to view the progress of the dressing should not be neglected. Used correctly, i.e. carefully looking and watching movements and lines produced, alterations to shape may be minimized, and other suitable shapes, for use on future occasions, may be seen. Looking at one place on the head too long or too closely restricts the overall view. Occasionally step back from the client so that the whole outline or silhouette may be clearly seen. The use of a hand mirror for the client to view finished effects should be used by the operator to check that final adjustments are not required.

2. A simple dressing may be carried out in the following manner:

Brush the hair firmly, from nape to front,

gradually working up the head. When the brush moves freely through the hair, brush against the set and then in the direction intended. With the pli blended the comb or brush may be used to distribute the hair into the desired shape. It is necessary at this stage to follow the movements set. As the comb or brush positions the hair, the hand lightly strokes it, and if height is required pushes it gently from the head. A well-set head of hair may be quickly dressed in this way, without backdressing. This is all that is required by many clients, and for simple styles. The pli should determine the variation of movement in the dressing.

Style dressing requires more height and volume in parts of the head and backdressing is required to exaggerate more fullness than rollers or stand-up curls can produce. The sections of hair requiring fullness are taken, piece by piece, and the amount of backdressing placed where necessary. There usually needs to be a gradual blending from the fuller to the flatter areas of the dressing. Backdressing is reduced and the angling of the sections lowered for the right balance to be achieved. If the pli is followed a dressing is soon realized, but if the pli is to be corrected by dressing, then more drastic backdressing or force dressing is necessary.

Overdressing is one of the commonest faults of dressing. To overdress the hair is to reduce the shape, balance and movement, by continually picking or fiddling with the hair. If the dressing is closely watched the desired shape is soon seen, and for salon work a shape is achieved long before most dressings are completed. Finishing touches should be made but never at the expense of the general shape. The dressing should be planned by deciding what is to be done, where to start and finish, and how it is to be achieved. This will depend on the shape required and the hair texture to be dressed.

Backdressing and the client. Often the client complains that her backcombed hair is difficult to manage. This is usually due to the fact that she has not been told how to deal with it. A few words on correct combing and brushing techniques will help considerably, and should enable her to remove backdressing without tearing or breaking her hair.

3. Dressing long hair in natural, downward positions is not difficult if it has been cut to a good shape. These long flowing shapes may be finished with a hand dryer. Good hair condition will help it to hang well and shine.

When dressing long hair into upswept positions it is important to centralize the weight, i.e. place in a position from which it will not readily fall. Once placed it should be secured with grips, pins, rubber bands, combs, ribbons or plaited hair, but take care not to tangle or damage the hair. If the hair to be dressed is to be plaited, small sections should be taken from positions which will be covered in the final dressing. When the weight and bulk of the hair is positioned and secured, the hair lengths may be dressed into curls, swirls or shapes, and care taken not to loosen the firmness of the base.

Dressing a pleat or hair fold. After thoroughly brushing the hair the top crown hair is secured out of the way. The side hair may be dressed separately or dressed in with the back hair and placed accordingly. Depending on the position of the pleat or fold, the hair is brushed, smoothed and placed, e.g. centrally or diagonally on either side of the back of the head. The hair may be backdressed near the roots to add extra fullness.

If the pleat is to be placed at one side of the back the hair should be brushed smoothly in that direction. The hand is then placed on the head, at the angle the pleat is to lie, the hair firmly gripped in position, and the hair brushed back and placed on the palm of the hand which is able to grasp and hold the bulk of the hair. The other hand, after releasing the brush, takes the hair ends and directs them towards the head, at the same time moving up to the crown. The hand on the head is then released which assists in positioning the hair and holding the pleat until it is firmly secured, through the edges of the pleat, with long hair pins.

When placing the pleat the head should be in an upright position so that any forward movement tightens, rather than loosens, the pleat. If the pleat is placed with the head forward it will loosen or bulge out when the head is held erect.

With the pleat neatly secured, pins should not be seen, and the top and sides may be dressed. This may be done in a variety of ways, e.g. the front or crown may be dressed to cover the top of the pleat or placed under the pleat top, the sides may be waved back, curled, draped or placed in ringlets. The pleat is a common long hair dressing and is often called a French roll. (Fig. 9.6 a b c & d).

Plaiting the hair is a useful means of dealing with long hair, and a variety of shapes and sizes may be used and attractively positioned on the head. The addition of plaited postiche may give further variety. Plaiting postiche, or the hair on the head to be dressed, is achieved by intertwining a variety of hair sections together, one over the other. The three-stem plait, or plait of three, is a common one. Small or large plaits, with three or more stems, may be placed, coiled or draped effectively and are useful for covering separations in the hair dressing.

Dressing and ornamentation. The use of ornaments to complete dressings has been popular throughout the ages. Ornaments of combs, ribbons, jewels, grips, slides, and various other shapes of materials are used to enhance the dressed head of hair. Added hair pieces or postiche are an attractive means of ornamentation, and flowers, glitterdust, colour sprays, beads and sequins are all popularly used.

4. Dressing and postiche. A wide range of shape,

type and size of postiche may be used in a hair dressing. Apart from its use for covering an injury, scar, bald patch or other defect of the hair or head, postiche may be used for its decorative, interesting and varied effects in many dressings. The means of attachment is determined by the type of postiche; most are attached by combs, grips or pins. Large full postiche, e.g. wigs, are held in place by the shape and fitting of the piece, and postiche used to cover bald areas is fixed by special adhesives.

Types of postiche used for adding to a dressing may be made from weft, i.e. hair woven on to silks or thread, then sewn in a variety of ways, or foundational pieces, i.e. hair knotted on to foundation net, gauze or silk. Some of the decorative postiche commonly used are listed as follows:

Pin curls are small pieces of weft wound and sewn into various curl shapes and added to different parts of a dressing.

Ringlets are larger than pin curls but are made and used in a similar way.

Marteaux are folded pieces of weft, ranging in size from small, 25-mm pieces, to the larger, 150-mm pieces, and are attached to the hair by sewn loops or combs. These are flat pieces useful for the addition of a wave or waves.

Switches are longer lengths of hair, made from weft, twisted, coiled or plaited in a variety of ways.

Torsades may be made from marteaux and switches to form pieces of coiled hair which are both attractive and ornamental.

Swathes are made from two marteaux sewn end to end and worn encircling the head. Switches may be used in a similar way and are useful for securing long hair.

Chignons are wefted or knotted postiche, worn between the crown and the neck, useful for producing additional height, fullness and shape.

The modern cape wiglet, made from wefted or knotted postiche, is a long length of hair which fits on top of the head and drapes down into the neck. It is useful for converting a short head of hair into a long hair style. A simple-fitting, decorative band holds the piece in position; they are sometimes called bandeaux wigs or wiglets.

Fringes or frontal pieces are shapes of wefted or knotted postiche dressed in forward fringe movements.

Transformations are larger wefted or knotted pieces worn encircling the head or hairline. They are usually worn to disguise thinning front or side areas, and are the same size as a full wig but without the crown part.

Semi-transformations are wefted or knotted postiche, worn on the front, top and sides of the head, from ear to ear. They do not encircle the head, and are secured by a length of elastic or tension spring, which fastens in the nape of the neck.

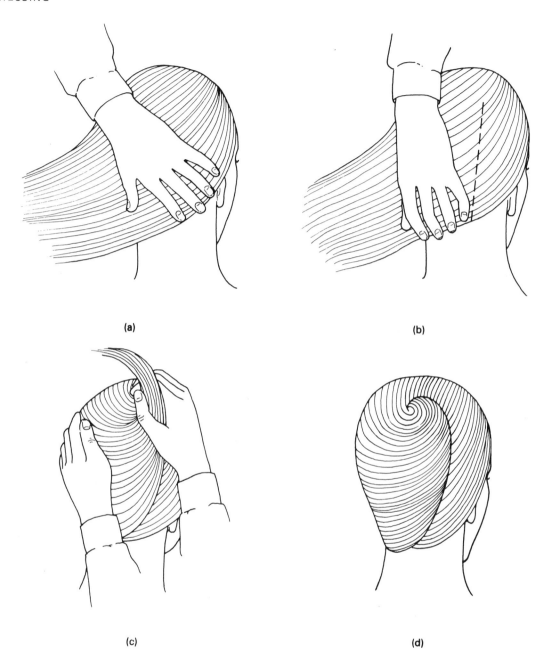

(a)

(b)

(c)

(d)

Fig. 9.6(a) — (d)   Dressing a pleat, showing correct hair/hand/head positions

Double loop clusters are wefted postiche formed by winding and sewing on a centrally placed cord, and finished with loops at each end. They are attached by combs or grips and are useful where an extra group or cluster of curls is required.

Diamond mesh foundations are commonly wefted pieces, but they may be knotted on a net foundation. The weft is made on two silks and a wire, which when folded and sewn forms an adaptable and pliable foundation piece worn in a variety of ways. Popular top knots of curls are made with them. They are sometimes called Cache Peigne, i.e. a bunch of curls on a hidden comb.

Toupée and Scalpette are pieces of postiche, usually knotted, and worn on the top and front of the head. They are used to cover bald areas rather than for added decoration. Wigs, periwigs and perukes are full pieces of postiche, i.e. complete scalp coverings, made from wefted or knotted hair on suitable foundations of silk, net or gauze. They offer a variety of shapes and styles and are dressed similarly to growing hair. Fashion and decorative wigs are made in many colours.

5. **Postiche** can be made in many shapes and given a variety of names; those which are decorative, popular and added to any part of a dressing are, e.g., all types of pin curls, ringlets and curl clusters. Those worn on top of the head, e.g. diamond mesh foundations and chignons, and those worn encircling the head, e.g. bandeaux, wiglets, switches and swathes, offer a wide range of style variation.

The hairdresser, dressing out a client's hair, may be required to discuss and offer advice regarding suitable postiche, and a number of details need consideration, e.g. measurements, shape, type of postiche and reasons for use.

Measurements and patterns are necessary for making or ordering postiche, and from the full head measurements for a wig, smaller pieces may be made from them, e.g. semi-transformations, or frontal pieces.

Measurements for a wig, male or female, are:

(*a*) *The circumference* of the head is measured from the middle of the forehead, round and above the ears, around the back of the head just above the neck, and round the other ear to the centre forehead.

(*b*) *Forehead to nape* measures from the middle of the front hairline, over the top of the head centrally, to the nape of the neck or neck hairline.

(*c*) *Temple to temple* round the back measures from the peak of the right temple above the right ear, around the back of the head, above the left ear to the left temple peak.

(*d*) *Ear to ear over top* measures from the top of the right ear, across the top of the head, to the top of the left ear.

(*e*) *Ear to ear round front hairline* measures from the top of the right ear to the front top of the left ear, along the edge of the front hairline.

(*f*) *Nape* measures from the back of the right ear, at the hairline, across the nape of the neck, to the back of the left ear at the hairline.

Other measurements required for smaller pieces, e.g. chignons and diamond mesh foundations, are taken from the size of the areas of the head on which the pieces are to be worn, e.g. the length and breadth of the area to be covered or in which the piece is to be positioned. These measurements vary according to the size of piece required.

Patterns are taken and made of all hairlines and scalp areas to be covered. For all close-fitting postiche, e.g. wigs and transformations, patterns of the natural skull shape should be taken. This may be done by transferring the head measurements to a piece of paper which is then cut and shaped. The paper pattern may then be placed in the appropriate position on the head, checked for size and shape, and if necessary adjusted.

Alternatively, to cover a large bald patch, the area should be covered with a transparent material, e.g. tissue, greaseproof paper, plastic or polythene, and the outline of the area traced with a felt-tipped pen.

The pattern may then be pinned to a block and used to form the shape of the foundation, on which the hair is knotted or the weft sewn. For this the pattern is outlined with galloon, i.e. a type of silk ribbon, and various types of foundation net may be sewn on the outlining galloon to form the shaped foundation for the attachment of the hair.

Details of postiche required should accompany the order for making, and are as follows: (*a*) The name, address and telephone number of the client. (*b*) The type of postiche required, e.g. frontal piece or chignon. (*c*) The shape or hair style for dressing the postiche. (*d*) The type of hair to be used, e.g. straight, wavy or curled. (*e*) The length and colour of the hair. If the client's natural colour is to be matched, a sample should accompany the order. (*f*) Details of type and length of parting, if required. (*g*) Details of any abnormalities. (*h*) The price quoted. (*i*) Dates of any fittings and when the piece is to be completed or collected.

Partings are made in wigs or postiche to simulate natural partings or divisions of hair. They consist of areas of foundation net, the length and width outlined with stitches as a guide to the centre and direction of knotting. The hair is knotted so that it covers the crown and centrally divides to appear natural. If they are Pompadour knotted, i.e two knots placed at each hole, this enables the hair to lift and be parted in any position. Knotted partings, often used as an exercise for directional knotting, i.e. knotting in different directions, may be made separate from the mount, and inserted in the foundational net of the mount. Often an area of the mount itself is used for knotting a parting. The inserted parting is protected and held flat by positional springs, i.e. flat, covered watch springs, one placed at each side.

A drawn-through parting is the finest and most natural of postiche partings. It is usually made separately and inserted when complete into the specially prepared parting area in the mount. The parting may be made of hair lace, i.e. a fine, diamond mesh net of real hair, or light-coloured foundation net. The underside may be protected with parting skin or fish skin.

There are two main methods in use for making a drawn-through parting. The English method consists of knotting all the hair required for the parting and then drawing the knotted hair through a light-coloured or flesh-coloured parting silk. The French method consists of knotting and drawing through the parting silk in one operation. When drawing through, a fine drawing needle or hook should be used, or a fine knotting hook may be used.

A record card is best used for the details and measurements of clients' postiche requirements.

6. Science and dressing. The tools, materials and chemicals used in the process of dressing will each have their effect on hair, e.g. dressing and control lacquers and creams, and the dressing result.

Lacquer is made from many natural and synthetic resins dissolved in alcohol. Shellac was a common ingredient and was used for dressing postiche. Newer synthetic resins, e.g. polyvinylpyrrolidone (PVP), and other types of plastic are now commonly used. Lacquers may be used in polythene or glass spray bottles, or aerosol propellant sprays, and when sprayed on to the hair the surface covering adds more 'body' to it. This helps to resist the effects of moisture and enables the hair to remain in the dressed shape for a longer time.

Most lacquers are easily removed by washing, but some resist removal and tend to build up on the hair. This may be removed by special lacquer solvent, or toilet spirit, usually applied to the hair before washing.

Lacquer should be sprayed on the hair from a distance of 300 mm from the head; most sprays are designed to distribute evenly at this distance. If the spray is tilted when used, a stream of lacquer is ejected; if sprays are held too close, too much lacquer is deposited on the hair. This causes beads of lacquer to form, the hair becomes wet, the set loosens and the dressing is spoilt. The lacquer and spray should be carefully used and sufficient lacquer to hold the hair in position, without overloading, should be applied.

Lacquer may be used to control hair for dressing, by lightly applying it to the hair and allowing it to dry, and it will be found that further dressing is made easier. This may be used on small areas of hair that prove difficult to control.

Precautions when using lacquers: (a) Do not use or store lacquers near a naked flame; they are inflammable and fire may be easily started. (b) Ensure that eyes are carefully shielded to prevent lacquer from being sprayed into them; discomfort, stinging and irritation is thus avoided. (c) Clients' clothes should be suitably covered. (d) Always clean the spray surface and do not allow the lacquer to dry and block the fine aperture. (e) Do not attempt to remove any blockage of an aerosol spray with a pin or the tail of a tailcomb. The lacquer is packed in these containers under pressure and if anything is poked into the aperture it could explode and cause damage to the eyes and face. A little spirit may be used to soften and remove a dried lacquer blockage.

Control creams and oils are used to add gloss, to bind the hair, reduce the effects of static electricity, and enable the hair to be smoothly positioned. They are made from a variety of fats and waxes, e.g. lanolin and beeswax; vegetable oils, e.g. almond, castor and olive; mineral oils, e.g. paraffin and petroleum jelly; and the essential oils, e.g. lavender, citrus, bay, jasmin, etc., with various gums and emulsifiers. Brilliantine, usually made from mineral oils, is a common dressing but dries out the hair surface. Almond oil is a more suitable dressing, but like most vegetable oils regular washing from the hair is necessary to avoid rancidity and odour.

Various kinds of control dressings are now available, some in aerosol propellant sprays, and should all be carefully and minimally applied; too much causes the hair to become lank and greasy.

Static electricity is produced by the friction movements of combing and brushing which causes the hair to fluff and fly away. The friction electrically charges the comb or brush which attracts the oppositely charged hair. This causes the hair to lift, by the mutual attraction to the comb, and sudden movements must be restricted or the dressing may be spoilt. Gently stroking the hair with the hand, the back of the comb or the use of another type of comb helps to remove the electrical charge and the hair fluffing, but control creams, oils or dressings are best used.

Natural gloss or shine on the hair is due to natural oil secreted from the glands of the scalp. This oil is called sebum and is formed in the sebaceous glands surrounding the hair follicles from which it passes to the hair and skin. If the hair surface, i.e. the cuticle, is smooth, light will reflect from the oily surface to give gloss or shine. The rougher the surface, e.g. if the cuticle is roughened or damaged, the duller the hair will appear.

7. Dressing and aesthetics. The beauty of a well-dressed head of hair is dependent on the cutting, the condition and the final position of the distributed hair, or the style shape produced. The dressing should combine the lines and movements within the shape so that they flow throughout. The forms produced should lighten the face and head and remove flat, odd shapes which are dull and uninteresting.

Each dressing technique is finally dependent on the aesthetic placing of the hair which should fit the artistic pattern imagined or created by the dresser. The final dressed shape will reflect aesthetic appreciation. This may be acquired and based on art-room work and exercises, from the sketching of simple lines and production of colour patterns to the moulding of many kinds of three-dimensional forms created with shape, colour, movement, balanced line and life.

The dressed head of hair is itself a three-dimensional form, which becomes artistic when a degree of both technical hairdressing ability and aesthetic appreciation is applied.

Dressing and hairstyling (see Chapter 10) are very closely interlinked, and the aesthetic aspects of both are so essential for the production of good work that one relies very much on the other.

Revision test 1

Q. 1   What is 'dressing the hair'?
Q. 2   How are the hands, mirrors and tools used in dressing?
Q. 3   Describe the addition of three suitable pieces of decorative postiche to dressings.
Q. 4   Name four chemical materials used in making lacquer or control dressings.
Q. 5   What is static electricity and how may this be dealt with when dressing?
Q. 6   Describe five means of hair or style ornamentation and how they may be used.
Q. 7   What is 'backdressing' and how is it used?
Q. 8   What is meant by 'overdressing'?
Q. 9   What are the measurements and details required for making decorative postiche?
Q.10   What are control dressings and what do they do?

Revision test 2

Complete the following sentences:

1   A completed dressing may be referred to as a .... or ....
2   Two backdressing methods are .... and ....
3   Long hair may be secured with ...., ... or ....
4   Five types of hair ornament are: ...., ..., ..., ... and ....
5   Two reasons for the need or use of postiche are:
    (a)..
    (b)..
6   The names given to full head postiche are ...., ... or ....
7   Hair lacquer may be made from .... or .... dissolved in ....
8   Three oils used in control dressings are ...., ... and ....
9   Natural hair gloss is due to .... which is produced by the .... in the skin.

Revision test 3

Complete the following sentences with the word or words listed below:

Weft. Control dressing. Knotted. Lacquer. Vegetable oil. Mineral oil. Essential oil. Pleat. Plait. Ornaments.

1   Hair .... on to net foundation is called foundational postiche.
2   PVP or shellac may be used to make hair ....
3   Almond oil is a ...., lavender oil is an ...., and brilliantines are made from ....
4   A variety of oils may be used to make a ....
5   A three-stem switch makes a suitable ....
6   Long hair is often dressed into a roll or ....
7   Flowers or jewels may be used as .... in dressings.
8   Hair intertwined between two or three silks or threads is called ....

Vocabulary

Backcombing	Pushing the hair back with comb or brush to bind or lift the hair.
Backbrushing	
Backdressing	Backcombing or backbrushing.
Beeswax	Wax derived from the bee's honeycomb and used in cosmetics and control creams.
Control dressings	Oils or creams used to control hair for dressing.
Dressing	The process of combing and brushing hair into a style, shape or dressing.
Dressing	Names given to completed hair shapes.
Coiffure	
Hair-do	
Essential oils	Volatile oils of vegetable origin used for perfuming cosmetics and control dressings.
Foundational postiche	Hair knotted on to foundation net or silk, or postiche made from weft and sewn on to a foundation of net, silk or gauze.
Hair ornament	Any thing or shape used to enhance a style.
Lanolin	A wax derived from the skin of sheep and used in cosmetics.
Mineral oils	Oils from petroleum or rock oil, e.g. liquid paraffin, soft paraffin or paraffin jelly, used in cosmetics.
Overdressing	Continually dressing hair until shape, balance and style is lost.
Plait	Hair interwoven or interlaced into a coil twist or other shape.
Pleat	Folding the hair into a roll or shape.
Sebaceous gland	A gland in the human skin which produces sebum.
Sebum	The natural oil secretion of human skin.
Shellac, PVP	Ingredients of hair lacquer. PVP is a synthetic resin, polyvinylpyrrolidone.
Static electricity	Due to the friction of combing and brushing; causes flyaway hair.
Teasing	Lifting, separating or placing small pieces of hair into position.
Vegetable oils	Oils derived from vegetable matter, e.g. olive, almond, castor and palm oils.
Weft postiche	Postiche made from hair weft.
Wig	Names given to full head postiche which completely covers the head.
Peruke	
Periwig	

Hairstyling

1. Hairstyling is the process of designing or creating hair arrangements which conform to basic patterns based on good cutting, setting and dressing.

A hair style is an expression of form or shape achieved by arranging hair into suitable balanced lines which complement the underlying head and face structure. Hair that does not follow this pattern is either a mess, or a bad style.

The purpose or main aim of the hair style is to enhance the appearance of the wearer. This boosts morale and confidence and should fit the hair for the occasion for which it is to be worn, e.g. working, playing, special dates, events or meetings. It should be part of the complete ensemble, i.e. clothes, make-up and accessories.

2. Hair-style design is dependent on: (*a*) the shape of the face and head; (*b*) the features of the face, head and body; (*c*) the dress and occasion for the style; (*d*) the quality and quantity of hair; (*e*) the age of the client; (*f*) the hair position, proportion and form in relation to other styling considerations.

(*a*) *The shape of the face and head* is the basis on which the dressed hair shape and form will rest. The proportions, balance and distribution should bear some relation to the underlying features, e.g. eyes, nose, chin, etc., which should be used as a guide to the finished hair shape.

The face forms an *inner shape* on which the hair style is placed. This outline of the lower part of the head, across the front hairline, round and in front of the ears, to the point of the chin, describes a distinct shape which is an individual characteristic. When the hair fits the inner face shape it should be an individual style shape.

Inner face shapes vary; some are round, oval, oblong and heart-shaped, others are square, triangular and diamond-shaped, but many are a mixture of shapes. The length, breadth and depth varies the shape considerably. The oval face shape is considered ideal because most hair styles will fit it. The length of square or oblong faces is accentuated by sleek, flat dressings, but diminished by full side shapes. The large, round face looks rounder when even, framing shapes are dressed, but dressings that elongate, e.g. high front, asymmetrical or one-sided dressings, are more suitable. Hard-looking face shapes, e.g. square and triangular, with prominent jawbones, appear harder when the hair is dressed back from the face, but softer when forward hair movements are used. (Figs. 10.1 & 10.2)

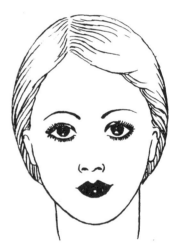

Fig. 10.1   Oval face shape

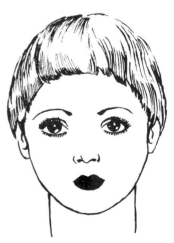

Fig. 10.2   Round face shape

The shape of the head, the outline of the skull, and the proportion of the head above the face is another individual hairstyling consideration, particularly when dressing the top and front of the hair. The roundness or flatness of the back of the head and the profile, which features the prominence or otherwise of the chin, mouth, nose, eyes and forehead, affects the style. (Fig. 10.3).

The neck, its length, fullness and width, directly affects the fall or hang of the back and nape hair. If the head is held erect the hair will fall naturally, but if drooping forward it will tend to lift the nape hair. Different head positions affect both the hair and the style. (Fig. 10.4).

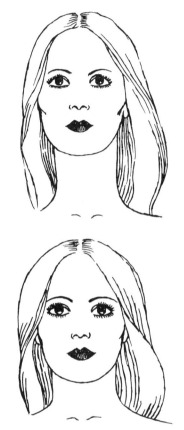

Fig. 10.4   Neck shapes — swan and short

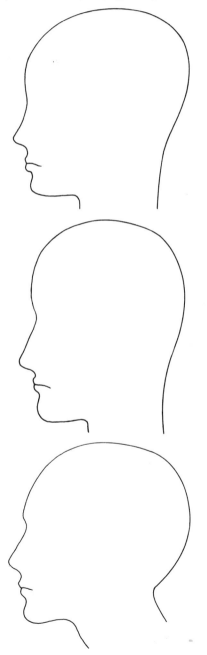

Fig. 10.3   Variation of head and face shape

(*b*) *The features* of the head and body help to determine the hair style. A prominent, large or badly placed nose may be 'diminished' by dressing the front hair angled, or by avoiding a central parting. A square jawline may be softened by full side dressings, and protruding ears are best covered. Heavily wrinkled eyes are made more obvious when straight, hard-lined fringes are dressed, but diminished by softly angling the hair away. Low, high, wide or narrow foreheads may be disguised by angling the hair and varying fringe positions. A common fault when disguising a defect is to make it more obvious by the amount of hair used to hide it. (Fig. 10.5 a & b).

Hollow or sunken cheeks may be diminished by dressing reasonably full side hair, but prominent ones require fullness above and below to achieve balance. Chin shapes are softened by longer hair, hardened by

Fig. 10.5(a)   Profile showing accentuated nose

Fig. 10.5(b)   Nose accentuated by style line

directing the hair in line with or towards them, and diminished by directing the hair softly away.

The shape of facial features, and the lines and shadows cast by them, should be used and correctly balanced with the hair bulk to determine, enhance or soften overall style effects.

The body. A large and fussy hair style on a large, big-built person can be most unsightly, and a small, flat, head-hugging style may be completely out of proportion. Consideration is necessary for the body shape and hair proportion to be balanced. A high style on a tall person accentuates height and a flat style on a short person makes the lack of height more noticeable. Extreme (e.g. high or low) shapes on a tall or short person accentuate the obvious, and the 'right look' is attained only after very careful consideration.

It is important to note the size, shape and characteristics of the person, e.g. whether there is stooping, whether the body is held erect, whether the movements are quick or slow, etc., and these are best observed when receiving the client or before hairstyling is commenced.

(c) *The dress and occasion* for which the style is to be worn helps to determine the style to dress. Styles vary with clothes worn and work undertaken, e.g. receptionist, office worker or busy housewife, which should influence the designs. There are many other occasions, e.g. working, playing, dates, interviews, visits to theatres and places of interest, which require varied shapes and styles to be dressed. Styles featured in demonstrations, displays or photography may require special styling.

A style for a special evening at the theatre will differ from one worn at work during the day which is part of the whole 'dressing-up' process. A beautiful evening gown will require an elegant hair style and most normal working clothes require smart, suitable and practical styles. Hairdressing assistants should always wear styles which appeal to clients for their suitability, practicability and good choice.

Many clients will require styles that are suitable and easy to manage, but for the special event practicability becomes inessential and the style need be suited to that particular event only. Generally the smart, unexaggerated, suitable and practical styles are best used for everyday occasions, and the more elaborate ones reserved for special events.

Usually the lower the necklines of dresses, the lower the hair style, and the higher the dress neckline the higher the style may be dressed. There are exceptions for which variations are imposed by the nature of the occasion, e.g. dancing competitors require balanced dressings which will show the complete ensemble to advantage, and ice-skaters will not want loose flowing styles that will impede movement or vision.

(d) *The quality and quantity of hair* is reflected in all hair styles. Bad texture and condition of hair does not look attractive and shining healthy hair is an essential of good hairstyling. Poor hair condition may be corrected by simple hair care, e.g. correct combing, brushing and shampooing, or medical attention and treatment. Usually good hair condition is affected by normal client care, or lack of it, and client use of many different materials.

Thin scanty hair is difficult to dress and needs a great deal of attention, particularly good cutting, setting and careful handling. Styles which make this type of hair look thicker and fuller are successful. Fine, thin hair presents problems as regards practical styling, which is soon affected by damp or moisture. Setting aids and dressings which add to the texture and elasticity are best used.

Dry, thick hair requires sleeker, smooth styles to contain it. This type of hair soon fluffs, spreads out, and loses shape, unless suitable control dressings, and full hair styles achieved with the minimum of backdressing, are used.

(e) *The age of the client* for whom the style is to be designed is an important consideration, and each age group requires special effects or styles.

The young teenager can 'take' most styles, and good or bad style effects are often becoming to this group. Hair dressed with straight or curled, long or short, hard or soft effects, may be used to advantage. Styles suitable for this group are often opposite to current fashion trends, and usually have their own teenage 'fashion' pattern. Styles associated with the older woman are not wanted.

The young married woman requires suitable, practical and stylish shapes which do not involve a lot of time to dress. She is more inclined to recent fashion trends and at an age when they are best used. Often the 'fun' shapes, e.g. gimmicky, 'way out', extreme styles, and the glamorous ones, are requested perhaps from this more than from any other age group.

Career women have a large range of smart, fashionable and attractive shapes and styles which they may wear as part of their everyday dress.

The older woman requires greater consideration for styling to be acceptable and suitable, and styles need to soften facial features and diminish the effects of the years. Lines and wrinkles need to be 'styled out', i.e. diminished by the positions of the hair, and the styles require more movement and correctly planned lines. The elegance of the older well-dressed and styled woman is much admired and reflects good hairstyling probably more than any other age.

(f) *Positioning of the hair* or dressing cannot be complete without consideration of other aspects of styling, and the dressing techniques used are an important part of the process (see Chapter 9).

The outer shape of a style is determined by the outline of the hair which surrounds the inner shape of the face and the effect of one on the other. Dressing varies the outer shape and its effect, e.g. dressing the hair in a hard square shape will not soften a square-shaped face. An oval face, with a low hairline, may be correctly styled by dressing the hair directly back and up from the face. The balance of the dressed outer shape is important and should be viewed from each side, in profile, to be fully seen. The back view of the shape is as important as the front.

3. Styling requirements. The positions and forms produced by the dressed hair require an understanding of suitability, balance, line, movement, softness and hardness of shape and appearance, and originality, which need to be defined for styling requirements to be met.

Suitability is the effect of the outer hair shape on the inner face shape and features and the proportion of the one to the other. A hair style is usually suitable when it looks right, and is achieved when the moulded hair form fits the other shapes of the head. The line of face or feature is accentuated or made more noticeable when the line of the hair is continuous or blended with it. A softness or diminishing effect may be achieved when the hair is angled, or curved, from the point or feature on the head.

A young hair style, i.e. one associated with the young, dressed on the older woman can be most unattractive because the lines of the face, eyes and forehead are accentuated by its sharper, sometimes harder lines. An 'older' style, i.e. one which produces an old effect, dressed on the younger client is perhaps more tolerable but similar contrasts exist. The moving lines of the older style do not always become or enhance the fuller shapes of young faces, and may be too much and cause an 'overdone' appearance.

Most fashion effects are designed for the young woman but may be suitably adapted for the older. The straight-down, forward fringe shape is becoming and effective on a teenager but unsuitable for the older woman.

The most suitable style is the one individually designed with all fashion and other style effects modified and adapted to fit and suit the individual. It is rarely suitable to use fashion effects simply because they are fashionable.

Balance is the effect produced by the amount, fullness and distribution of the hair throughout the shape. If too much hair is lumped together on one side of the head, leaving too little too flat on the other, an unbalanced effect results. This will not look right because the proportions and shapes of the hair will not fit the face shapes below. Symmetrical effects, i.e. harmonious hair balance arrangements, are achieved by the even, similarly placed arrangements of hair on both sides of the head. Long hair may be effectively placed on one side of the head and balanced by one earring on the other. This produces an asymmetrical effect, i.e. the irregular imbalance of hair arrangement, and may be achieved by varying the direction or directions of the hair in different parts of the head. (Fig. 10.6).

Balance is not achieved if the hair is dressed flat on a squat, round head, but it may become so if the hair is dressed higher on the top with slightly fuller sides, without exaggeration. A hair shape or style should look balanced from all sides of the head.

The line of a style is the direction or directions in which the hair is positioned which should follow throughout the shape. If the line suddenly ends, the style varies, the balance may be affected, and the wrong effect produced. The line of a style is determined by the effect of the various lines of the features and contours. A style line is the line of the hair in a shape. A figure S may be used as a style line

Fig. 10.6   Balance

Fig. 10.7   Style line or line of style

and all the hair should be positioned to describe it, both within the style and the outline. A complimentary style line is usually one that produces a suitable style.

The line of a style will carry the eye of the viewer along the directions in which the hair is placed. Many style lines produce illusionary effects and successfully accentuate or diminish different parts of the head. The well-executed dressings of well-known hairstylists are instances of the good use of complimentary style line. (Fig. 10.7).

Use of partings. Different effects may be created by the careful and considered use of partings in the hair. A long straight central parting elongates and accentuates a large prominent nose, but if a shorter, slanting parting is used it becomes less noticeable. A round fat face may be made to appear fatter with a centre parting, but thinner with the hair parted on the side. (Fig. 10.8 a & b).

Movement is the variation of the direction of the line in a hair style. The more varied the line the more movement there will be which adds a fluid effect to the shape. Hair dressed in curl and wave shape displays movement of line. The line of the style should continuously move, to a greater or lesser extent, from one point of the head to the ends of the hair.

Styles with movement are usually complimentary, particularly to the older woman. The contrasting straight-line styles, without movement, are not suitable for older clients but effective on the young for their sharp line, hardness and impact.

Soft and hard effects of a style are dependent on suitably balanced lines and movements. If the hair is dressed into a board-like packed shape or if it lacks complimentary line, a hard look is produced. If the hair is dressed without hard divisions, sudden

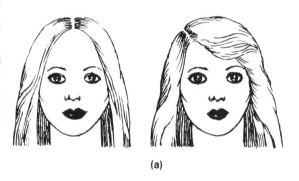

(a)

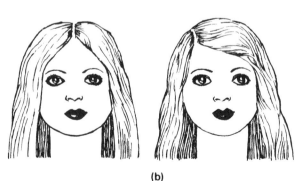

(b)

Fig. 10.8   Balance and partings

variations of line, abrupt finish of movement and the harshness of some contrasting shapes, then the style may be soft to look at and have a more pleasing and natural effect. Good suitable colourings help to produce soft style effects, but bad colouring easily produces hard unwanted effects.

Rhythmical movement and balance is softening but lack of movement and irregular, unbalanced shape produces hard style effects. The average salon dressing does not need to be packed down to look solid and hard; the smooth composed finish should never be at the expense of naturalness. (Figs. 10.9 & 10.10).

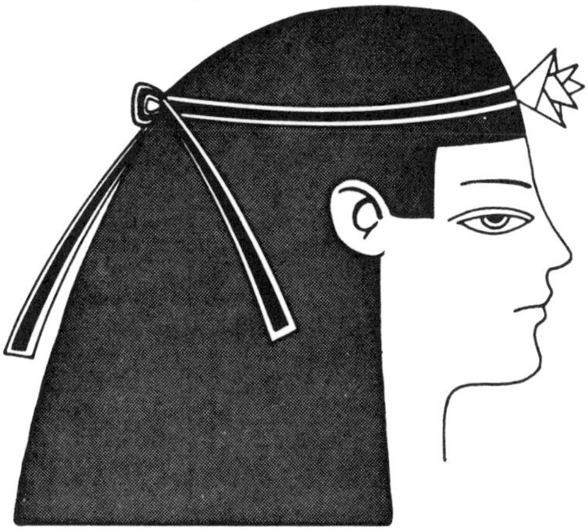

Fig. 10.9   Hard line — Egyptian

Fig. 10.10   Soft line — classic Greek

Originality in salon styling is restricted to individual styling. Creating a style or line not used before requires a great deal of thought and work. It is possible to be original by adapting style or fashion lines which create interesting variations. Each client is different to start with and a little effort and thought should enable style lines that are 'hers' to be created. Slavishly copying styles may result in repetition and client dissatisfaction.

Freedom to produce original styles presents itself elsewhere than in the salon. Displays, demonstrations and hairdressing competitions offer a greater range of possibilities for original creative styling. Despite the restrictions of the salon, always try to be as original as possible by varying the effects of styles.

4. Personal choice in styling plays a large part in the selection and application of hair styles, and liking or disliking them restricts the use of many. Restricting a range of styles purely to those the hairdresser likes or dislikes may result in only the older, out-of-date styles being attempted.

New styles are often disliked because they are new and not understood. Often there is reluctance to adapt new lines, and though personal choice may be against them they may, on adaptation, be perfectly correct and pleasing. Personal preference of styles is justified but not when it results in limiting the range. Dislike of a style because it is at fault is another matter; some styles are so called yet do not comply with the basic requirements of a style.

A varied clientele requires a large range of styles, and different lines, shapes, effects and variations are requested by the different types of client. A stylist may become known for his particular form of styling, others become known for their extensive range and adaptability. A few individual hairstylists or designers work to their own original lines or patterns and invariably deserve the acclaim they receive. The successful stylist's personal choice of hairstyling is usually based on hard work, technical ability and aesthetic appreciation.

The personality of the client may be reflected in her hair style, and is a styling aspect often overlooked by the hairdresser, but it should be used to create individual differences of shape. Each client has her own mannerisms, appeal or attractiveness; some are smiling, vital and alive, and may wear hair styles that are more adventuresome. The smart, mature client requires sleeker, sophisticated hair styles and the older client requires elegant, simple, graceful shapes to enhance their personalities.

5. Salon styling requires a range of styles which depend on the clientele in existence, or to be attracted. Some salons cater for one type of client, e.g. young or old, but most cater for many types and ages. The older the clientele the more the 'bread and butter' type of styling will be in demand, i.e. practical, uncluttered, easy-to-manage styles. Other older clients may demand fashion trends to be adapted to suit them, and these will test the stylist's abilities and skills. The more varied and competent the techniques and abilities of the stylist, the more varied and larger the clientele becomes; the good stylist is nearly always appreciated and in demand.

(Hairstyling relies on other aspects of hairdressing, and reference should be made to Chapters 8 and 9, on cutting and dressing.)

Revision test 1

Q. 1   What is a hair style and its purpose or aim?
Q. 2   Describe the factors which should be considered when designing a hair style.
Q. 3   What effect does the outer hair shape have on the inner face shape when styling hair?
Q. 4   What are soft and hard style effects?
Q. 5   What is meant by the line or lines of a style? Give examples.
Q. 6   How does the shape of face and head and its features affect hairstyling?
Q. 7   How do clothes, and the event for which they are to be worn, affect the styling of hair?
Q. 8   The quality and quantity and condition of the hair are reflected in the style. Give reasons and examples.
Q. 9   How does the size and shape of the body, and age of client, affect choice of a style?
Q.10   Briefly describe each of the following terms:
         (a) Movement. (b) Personality. (c) Balance. (d) Partings. (e) Suitability.

Revision test 2

Complete the following sentences:

1   Designing hair arrangements is called ....
2   The following points should be considered when designing a style:
      (a) ....
      (b) ....
      (c) ....
3   The face forms the .... shape and the hair forms the .... shape and the effect of one on the other is an important aspect of hairstyling.
4   A correct style should be based on the following:
      (a) ...., (b) ...., (c) ...., (d) ....
5   Movement is the varied direction of the hair or ....
6   Salon styling requires to be ...., ... and ....
7   The effects of styling will .... or .... the bad or prominent features of the head.
8   A good hair style reflects good hair .... and the .... of the client.
9   Original hairstyling may be used more in ...., ... and ....
10   Good hair-care techniques, e.g. ...., ... and ...., help to maintain good hair condition.
11   Older clients require .... styling effects.

Revision test 3

Complete the following sentences with the word or words listed below:

Soft. Hard. Asymmetrical. Symmetrical. Line. Oval. Movement. Originality. Square. Round.

1   Hair styles with .... are more likely to suit the older woman and produce .... effects.
2   Hair dressed flat, packed down, produces .... effects.
3   Styling hair to one side produces .... effects.
4   Evenly styled hair with similar sides and regular balance is called .... styling.
5   The direction in which the hair is dressed is called the .... of the style.
6   Styles individually designed, not copied, are more likely to have ....
7   .... face shapes are not softened by swept-back styles, and .... faces are exaggerated by flat styles. The ideal face shape for styling is an .... shape.

Vocabulary

Accentuates	Makes more definite or noticeable.
Adapt	Change or alter to make it fit or suit.
Asymmetrical	Irregular balance effects of a style.
Balance	The effect of hair shape on the features of the face and head; even proportions.
Creation	Original hair style design.
Diminish	To make less marked or noticeable or with less emphasis.
Ensemble	The total effect of hair style, make-up, clothes, shoes and accessories.
Face shapes	The inner shapes of the head, e.g. round, oval, oblong, square, triangular, etc.
Hair style	The dressing or arrangement of hair in shapes or forms of a particular pattern.
Hairstyling	The process of designing, creating or dressing a hair style.
Hairstylist	A hairdresser capable of creating hair styles.
Hardness	The heavy, dull and thick parts of style.
Head features	Contours of the head, face, its size, position, neck and nape aspects.
Head shapes	Outer shape of head varied by dressing.
Illusionary effect	The line of a style which accentuates or diminishes features or points on the head.
Inner and outer shapes	The face forms an inner shape, and the hair and head an outer shape, in outline.
Line	The line of a style is the direction or directions of the positions of the hair.
Movement	The variation of line, e.g. waves.
Originality	New or created for the first time; the ability to be original, inventiveness.
Parting	A separating division in the hair.
Personality	Mannerisms, habits, ways and characteristics of a person.
Practical	Easy to manage, longer-lasting styles.
Rhythmic movement	Soft, repeating fluid lines or undulations.
Softness	A hair style without abrupt, sharply defined edges, light and fluffy.
Suitability	Pleasing effects of hair shape on face.
Symmetrical	Even, regular, balanced style effects.

Hairstyling

6. Types of hair style vary according to the occasion for which they are worn, and each may have a large number of individual patterns. To describe all named styles is pointless, and almost endless, but a general outline may be of use.

A day style is usually a simple, suitable and practical style wearable during the daytime. Day styles should be attractive, uncluttered, easy to manage, without ornamentation, extreme colour or elaboration, There are exceptions, e.g. a chiffon scarf or wrap may be worn on the head, and some ornaments are used, e.g. slides, combs, grips, and bands of different types and colour. Generally the day style is not highly elaborate or ornamented.

Cocktail style or dressing is the name given to a more exaggerated day style. It should be suitable for wear at a special meeting or date during the daytime or early evening; ornaments and variations of colour may be used. Many wear cocktail styles as day dressings; the style is usually determined by the position held at work and personal preference.

Evening styles are more elaborate shapes, not necessarily practical, and are suitable for wear in the evening, e.g. for dances, parties or other special occasions. The line of the style is usually augmented with colour or ornamentation. They are usually simple high dressings, or extreme exaggerated shapes. The occasion, and the boldness of the wearer, helps to determine the elaboration required.

High fashion or *haute coiffure* styles are the latest trends in hair fashion styling. They may at first appear extreme, and are often disliked, but are usually accepted as the fashion becomes understood, worn and seen. High fashion styling requires originality, good technique and experience, and is rarely achieved by the inexperienced. High fashion styles are wearable by a type of model only, or a few types of head, and are not suitable wear for the majority without adaptation.

Fashion styles are adapted high fashion or special fashion lines created for suitable adaptation for different types of head, hair or clients. These are favoured by the smart, well-dressed or trendy type of client. The new, different, sometimes a return to the old, ideas are aspects of fashion styles and shapes.

The constant demand for change of fashion is stimulated by an endless variety of events, mood and habit, and the wish always to be different.

Children's styling requires uncluttered, natural, never artificial, suitable dressings; the hair rarely needs the degree of finish required by women. The simple shapes and styles are usually the best used. Occasionally there is a need for a more sophisticated shape.

Men's styling is based on the same principles as styling for women, e.g. the shapes dressed should fit, balance, suit, be practical and well finished. The natural, uncut look is favoured by many men and is a feature of men's fashion. Men's styles are not usually as elaborate as women's, but if the wheel of fashion turns a little more, elaborate styling for men may once more return.

7. Competition styling requires experience in all techniques of hairdressing and styling. There are specific techniques, lines, styles, colours and ornaments used in competition work not intended for salon use without adaptation. There are, however, many techniques evolved on the competition floor that may be usefully applied in the salon. Generally some of the finest examples of hair artistry are to be seen in hairstyling competitions, and the hair-style designer or creator of original hair styles, with the ability to dress hair, is the successful competition worker.

Types of hairstyling competitions vary according to local, regional, national and international requirements. International events are usually the ultimate in standards of styling variations. Each type of competition is designed for a particular kind of styling, e.g. day, cocktail, evening or free style, i.e. any choice of style. There are other events for specific aspects of hairdressing, e.g. cutting, colouring, perming, the use of postiche and children's styling.

Future competitors need to know the requirements before entering a competition which has a set of rules listing qualifications for entry. These must be strictly followed and adhered to; failure to do so could result in disqualification.

Competitions vary to allow for the variety of

experience, from the junior beginner to the successful stylist. First entries are usually made for junior events, gradually working through different types until competence and experience allow entry to the senior ones.

The different competitions should be visited to see what is done and how they are conducted; this is a good way for the future competitor to start. By watching competitors working, and by listening to experienced viewers, a great deal may be learnt. Disregard the adverse criticism heard at most events, usually made by those who could not do better. All those working on the competition floor deserve credit for their enthusiasm and endeavour. Closely observe the styles created, and remember, if viewing from a distance, that movements and details may be obscured. A closer look may be attained when the models leave the floor, after being judged, and mingle with the audience.

The competitors work to a particular style, to be dressed in a fixed amount of time, often under great tension. Not only is self-control required, but the model, who may be suffering from nerves, may also need attention.

When the dressing and work is completed, the competitors leave the floor, and the judges are introduced. The job of the jury, composed of experienced hairdressers and stylists, is to select the most competently designed and dressed head of hair. Points are awarded for all aspects of the style, which are collected, counted and checked. The competitors receiving the highest numbers are placed in the winning positions accordingly and announced to the audience.

There is usually a long lapse of time between viewing the first competition and winning one, and a lot of hard work must be fitted in between for success to be attained. The application of patience and practice is necessary for competition preparation.

The model for entry to a competition will ideally need good-texture hair and skin, neither too coarse nor too fine. The hairlines, the hair length, the colour or colours to be achieved, and general shape and appearance, should be carefully considered when selecting her. A beautiful girl with perfect features, good hair and colour, with good deportment and personality, helps considerably, but if the competitor does not have the necessary styling ability she may be wasted as a model. The style to be entered should be practised regularly, the timing of dressing should be accurate, and the style finish correct and well rehearsed.

The style chosen should conform to the competition rules, e.g. if a day style is required do not over-elaborate, if a free style then a wider choice is allowed. Always read, follow and apply the rules; any exceptions must be determined by the competition director or secretary.

8. **Fantasy dressings** are extreme styles dressed, with or without added postiche, in any shape or form almost to perfection and never intended for normal day wear. There are fantasy competitions which allow additions of hair, glass, plastic and other materials in many shapes and forms, but the work of the true hair artist is to be seen in this field. Fantasy work is the result of creative design and dressing, with specially made postiche, in a widely imaginative variety of shapes, and is used for displays or exhibitions of hair artistry. (Fig. 10.11 a & b).

Allegorical hair styles are dressings depicting a story or theme, and though not necessarily fantastic, many are. Special events, things or shapes are woven around, or in, the hair style, e.g. the bird in a cage is a common one: the hair is dressed in a cage shape, or a light cage is made and the hair dressed around it, and small model or live birds are placed inside. Competitions for this type of work are not as popular as they were and little is now seen of this kind of dressing. (Fig. 10.12).

Historical dressings or styles depict an event, a famous person or a particular period in time. Repeatedly the finer points, lines and shapes of historical dressings have been interpreted into modern lines. The intricacy and patience required for this work involves time and devotion, not to mention hairdressing ability. (Fig. 10.13).

Powder dressings are historical styles that require varying amounts of coloured, perfumed powder, an essential part of the dressing. Tallow, lard and other types of grease were used on which flour or powder was blown with bellows, and the dressing was completed with a heavy shellac lacquer. These styles proved to be most unhygienic and declined in popularity when a tax was placed on the imported powder in 1795. Modern versions of these and other historical dressings are to be seen occasionally at some demonstrations and displays.

Famous historical dressings include: Princesse de Lamballe, of Louis XVI's reign (about 1780); Marquise de Pompadour (about 1725); Marie Antoinette (1777); La Frégate la Junon, of Louis XVI's reign (about 1790); and Croisat's (1830) coiffure.

9. **The science of hairstyling** is that of hairdressing and the products applied to the hair. Over the years all manner of preparations have been made and used to enhance the looks of the wearer. Today products are made which aid the aesthetic styling of hair in which science plays such an important part. (The relevant scientific parts of each chapter should be read and applied to hairstyling.)

10. **Aesthetics and hairstyling.** Hairstyling beauty is composed of shapes, forms, proportions, rhythm of line or movement, balance, symmetry and asymmetry, words equally part of the artist's and hairstylist's vocabulary, with similar meanings and

Fig. 10.11   A fantasy style

Fig. 10.12   An allegorical style

effects. The shape produced by one form super-imposed on another and the effects of related lines are the basis of works of art and of hairstyling.

Sketching or drawing may be applied in several ways in the salon and, like hairstyling, relies on the illusionary effects produced by the influence of one line on another.

Impressions and sketches may be made of styles to be dressed, which can be used to give clients some idea of their finished appearance. Sketched style records may be compiled which may be altered or added to, and used at a later date. Other attractive styles, lines and movements may be noted or sketched, in outline or detail, in a variety of places, e.g. theatres, museums, while viewing television, etc.

Designing styles for salon, displays or competitions, and adapting current fashion or historical lines, may be more easily carried out with pencil and paper first before attempting them in practice. This also applies to designing window or showcase displays and arrangements. Used in this way, sketching becomes a valuable styling aid and helps to retain useful ideas.

Aesthetic appreciation and understanding are encouraged throughout the training and education of many young hairstylists and play an important part in the realm of hairstyling. Without this appreciation, which may be learnt in one way or another, inside or outside the art room, many styles are disliked and

never copied or adapted, simply because they are not 'seen' or 'understood'. With aesthetic appreciation the choice and possibilities of hairstyling are immeasurably increased. The successful stylist has learnt to see, feel and interpret into hair shapes.

Art exercises, if only learning to see and observe, are a series of experiences which help develop feeling and understanding. It is, or seems, a long way from the first art exercises to the first purposeful hair style. There cannot be a direct, quick transfer of art to hairdressing; it is an indirect, gradual process of learning, often unknowingly, which arrives at the stage of hairstyling.

11. Postiche and styling involves similar hairdressing techniques. Postiche may be used in many kinds of dressing, and historical, allegorical and fantasy dressings require a high standard and variation. The addition of postiche to other types of style may drastically alter its appearance.

The popular top knot is used to add height and fullness, particularly on fine sparse hair, and ringlets, plaits and curl clusters enable more varied and interesting dressings to be achieved. Simple day styles may be quickly converted to elegant evening dressings by postiche of matching or contrasting colour. Small pieces of postiche may be used to correct unbalanced styles simply by their positioning. (Fig. 10.14).

The client's use of postiche should be considered

Fig. 10.13   A historical dressing

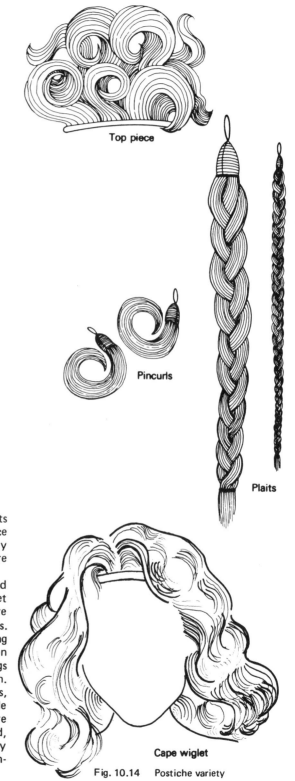

Top piece

Pincurls

Plaits

Cape wiglet

Fig. 10.14   Postiche variety

and a few words of advice given her on its positioning, securing and removal. Client reassurance that only simple management of postiche is necessary overcomes restricted use of it, and style variations are increased.

Postiche used in hairstyling may be dressed and prepared before the client enters the salon. Quiet salon periods may be used by the staff to prepare postiche and reduce time taken for final adjustments.

It is unhygienic for postiche to be worn too long without cleaning. Frequency of cleaning depends on its use. Suitable boxes should be used to protect wigs and postiche from dirt and dust and to store them in.

Hair ornaments may be made, in various shapes, from small pieces of postiche, e.g. small flowers made from real hair make useful additions. These are intricate to make, and are now rarely seen or used, but usually justify the time and effort required by their making and, as with other hairstyling techniques, add interest and variety.

Revision test 1

Q. 1   Name and describe five different types of hair style.
Q. 2   Describe what is meant by a good competition model, and list the points and reasons for choosing her.
Q. 3   What is *haute coiffure*? Briefly explain the difference between other fashion styles.
Q. 4   What are the differences between a modern day and a cocktail dressing or style?
Q. 5   What is meant by the 'illusionary effects' in styling?
Q. 6   What is a fantasy dressing? Give a brief description.
Q. 7   What is a historical dressing? Name four.
Q. 8   What is the difference between an evening and a fantasy dressing?
Q. 9   What is competition hairstyling? Briefly explain competitions generally.
Q.10   Briefly describe each of the following terms:
        (a) Allegorical dressing. (b) Cocktail dressing. (c) Competition jury. (d) Men's styling. (e) Fashion styling.

Revision test 2

Complete the following sentences:

1   A dressing that depicts a story or theme is called an .... style.
2   In some competitions the choice of style is open and they are called .... competitions.
3   Name three different types of hair style:
     (a)...
     (b) ....
     (c)...
4   Name three styles which need not be practical, and one which should always be practical:
     (a) .... (b) .... (c) .... (d) ....
5   Name three items of importance to the young hairstyling competitor:
     (a) .... (b) .... (c) ....
6   Name four aspects of style for which a competition jury will award points:
     (a) .... (b) .... (c) .... (d) ....
7   List four materials that may be used in powder dressing:
     (a) .... (b) .... (c) .... (d) ....
8   Name three suitable pieces of postiche that may be added to a style:
     (a) .... (b) .... (c) ....
9   Name two aspects of artwork important in hairstyling:
     (a) .... (b) ....

Revision test 3

Complete the following sentences with the word or words listed below:

Day. Evening. Cocktail. Allegorical. Model. Practical. High fashion. Not elaborated. Elaborate. Client.

1   The new and latest style worn by a few is called .... A style depicting a story or theme is called ....
2   Dressings suitable for daytime wear are called .... styles and should be .... for wearing.
3   Fantasy styles are very .... and should be dressed on a .... rather than a ....
4   Day styles are .... but .... dressings may well be.
5   A style with more elaboration than a day style but not as elaborate as an evening dressing is called a .... style.

Vocabulary

Allegorical dressings	Shapes or styles depicting a story or a theme.
Cocktail dressings	More elaborate styles suitable for wear at a special daytime event, similar to many modern day dressings.
Competition styling	Styling to a specific type of dressing required by the competition rules.
Day style	Day styles should be practical, suitable shapes for wear at work or play during the daytime.
Evening styles	More elaborate shapes or styles, not necessarily practical.
Fantasy dressings	Extreme shapes or styles, not necessarily worn other than for displays.
Free styling	The choice of any shape or style, usually for certain types of competition.
Hair ornaments	Ornaments worn in the hair and made of hair into flowers and many other shapes.
Haute coiffure	High fashion, the latest and newest fashion shapes and trends.
Historical dressings	Styles or shapes of a particular period of time other than the present or the recent past.
Powder dressing	A type of historic dressing greased and sprayed with white or coloured powder.
Practical dressings	Usually the type which are long-lasting and easy to manage.
Style	The shape described by the hair and the line, movement, suitability, balance, etc., in relation to other parts of the head.

Hair Colouring—Categories and Application

1. Hair colouring is the process of adding or altering the natural hair colour. It is used to disguise or cover grey and white hair, to enhance or completely change the natural shade. For centuries hair colourings have been used, in one form or another, to produce different effects for various reasons. In recent times it has become popular for both men and women to use hair-colouring cosmetics for fashion and style effects.

The field of modern hair colouring is wide, and may be separated into two main divisions: (A) The addition of hair colouring, e.g. tinting. (B) The removal of natural and synthetic hair colouring, e.g. bleaching and decolouring.

(A) Artificial and synthetic colourings added to the hair are grouped according to the length of time they remain on the hair. These are: (A1) temporary colourings; (A2) semi-permanent colours; (A3) quasi-permanents; (A4) permanent tints or colours.

(A1) *Temporary colourings* are obtained in several forms: rinses in concentrated solutions, setting agents, and hair colour lacquer, sprays, crayons, paint and glitterdust. These remain on the hair until washed or shampooed. They do not usually penetrate the hair or directly affect the natural colour but coat the surface of the hair cuticle only. Some may be absorbed by very porous and poor-condition hair. (Fig. 11.1).

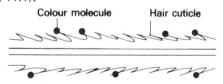

Colour molecule   **Hair cuticle**

Fig. 11.1   Temporary colouring
(effect of molecules on hair surface)

Temporary rinses consist of dilutions of the colour concentrate, i.e. a few drops are added to a measured quantity of water. The mixtures vary according to instructions and colour depth required. The liquid rinse produced is applied with a brush, sponge, or by repeatedly pouring through. Hot water should be used to dilute and ensure that it will cling to the hair. For sponge or brush applications the hair should be subdivided into 6–8 mm sections, and the rinse evenly and repeatedly distributed.

Advantages of temporary rinses are: the temporary colouring effect, ease of removal, the conditioning properties, the subtle toning effects on grey, white and normal hair, and the fashion effects on bleached hair.

Hair colour setting lotions are one of the most popular forms of temporary colouring. The shades are incorporated in suitable setting agents, e.g. plasticizers or hair conditioners, with which the hair may be set. No mixing or dilution is required and they may be applied with a sponge, brush, or poured directly from the bottle and distributed by frictioning with the fingertips. It is important to towel dry the hair before the application or the excess water will dilute the colour.

The advantages of the coloured setting lotion are its range of colours and the variety of setting agents available for different types of hair. They are a good 'colour introducer' for clients hesitant to have their hair coloured, and the colourings are easily removed by washing.

Coloured hair lacquers are temporary colourings which are sprayed on the dried, dressed hair. This product has a restricted colour range but there are several suitable colourings available.

Hair colour sprays are made in liquid and powder form, in various colours, for use on the dried dressed hair. They coat the hair cuticle from which they are easily removed by brushing or washing. Some of these colourings are metallic, e.g. gold, silver, bronze, and other metallic colours are popularly used. Care should be taken when using them on blonde, white and bleached hair or discoloration may result.

Hair colour crayons and paints are mainly used for their theatrical effects. Periodically they become popular and generally used, and are particularly useful for highlighting a dressing.

Glitterdust is made of glittering or shining coloured metal dust which when sprinkled on the hair produces a twinkling, sparkling effect. Gold and silver are most commonly used, and though temporary colour effects are attained glitterdust is strictly an ornamentation.

(A2) *Semi-permanent colourings* are made in liquid and cream forms, and need no mixing; the addition of water or hydrogen peroxide is not required. They are deposited in the hair cuticle where they remain longer than temporary colours. The colour gradually lifts each time the hair is washed, though some last through six to eight shampoos. Although not intended to cover a large percentage of white hair, they do so to a greater extent than temporary colourings. (Fig. 11.2)

Deeper penetration of colour

Fig. 11.2   Semi-permanent colouring

The colour range is varied, but careful choice is necessary, e.g. a black rinse on white hair will not produce pleasing results, and subtle effects will not be achieved. Timing and development are affected by the salon temperature and the texture and porosity of the hair, e.g. heat and poor hair condition may speed absorption.

Preparation for semi-permanent applications is as follows. The hair should be shampooed with a suitable shampoo, e.g. one specially made for pre-colouring, and thoroughly dried to prevent dilution of the colour. The scalp should always be checked for cuts, sores or abnormalities which may be aggravated by the colourings. Suitable protective coverings should be used for both client and operator.

Application may be made with a sponge, brush, application bottle, or poured direct from the container on to the hair. The colouring should be evenly applied and the hair left loose on the head to allow for air circulation and even development. Steamers or accelerators may be used to speed processing. Heat should not be used without covering the hair, preferably with a plastic cap, or the colouring will dry out, which prevents it reaching the depth and evenness required.

Skin stains may be caused on dry skin and may be removed with toilet spirit or specially made removers. Barrier creams or vaseline can be applied to the hairline before application to prevent bright, noticeable staining.

Advantages of semi-permanent colourings. They are more effective and longer lasting then most temporary colourings, and a larger colour range and choice is available. Root regrowth is not noticeable since the colour will have lifted by the time the contrasting hair has grown. Natural hair colour is not affected and skin tests are not required since most skin tolerates this type of colouring. Some contain foaming agents which prevent the liquid running off the hair. Various types of semi-permanent rinses and shampoos are made and it is important that instructions for their use are followed for good results.

Some permanent colourings may be diluted or mixed to produce semi-permanent effects. These products may contain substances which are known skin irritants and should not be used without testing skin reaction first; mixtures of this type of rinse should only be made on the manufacturer's recommendation.

(A3) *Quasi-permanents* is the name given to newer forms of colouring which last longer than semi-permanent, but not as long as permanent, colourings. They are made in semi-viscous or cream form often with an oily base and are applied to the hair like a tint. The colours produced are effective, with a translucent sheen, and a large range is available. (Fig. 11.3).

Fig. 11.3   Quasi-permanent colouring

(A4) *Permanent colourings* are numerous and varied. The modern oxidation colourings are made in cream, semi-viscous and liquid forms. Most colourings used for tinting require to be mixed with hydrogen peroxide, without which they would be completely ineffective. These products are used to cover white, grey and most natural hair colour to produce other natural, fantasy or exotic, and fashion shades.

Tinting consists of the synthetic colouring being made to penetrate the hair cuticle and be absorbed in the cortex, i.e. part of the internal hair structure, where it is oxidized and remains permanently fixed. The natural hair colour may be affected by the lightening action of the oxidation process. Although the colour effects are permanent, the choice of product, weather effects, and growth of hair all affects its lasting qualities. (Fig. 11.4).

Fig. 11.4   Permanent colouring

2. Colour choice is determined by the texture, porosity and condition of the hair (the amount of natural colouring present often being called the natural base colour), the client's requirements and her skin colouring, the type of colouring used, and the shade of colour desired.

Hair texture or the various thicknesses of hair affects the degree of tint absorption. Generally fine hair takes a tint quicker and more readily than thick coarse hair, and the texture variations between very fine and very coarse hair will affect the degree of tint absorption accordingly.

Porosity and condition. The condition of hair affects its porosity. Poor-condition hair, e.g. cuticle torn and lifted, quickly absorbs larger amounts of tint which may cause unevenness of colour. Other states or conditions of hair may resist tint absorption, e.g. closely packed cuticle cells resist the colour and loosely packed ones allow penetration. (Fig. 11.5).

Natural hair colour is mainly contained in the cortex and is composed of colour pigments in the form of granules called melanin. Four basic colours are contained in varying amounts in each shade, i.e. black, brown, red and yellow. Pheomelanin is the name given to the red and yellow pigments, which are smaller than the black and brown melanin cells.

Varied quantities of colour pigment produce the

Closed cuticle

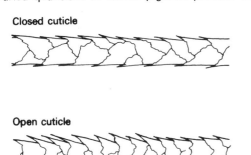

Open cuticle

Fig. 11.5   Cuticle — closed and open

different hair shades, e.g. dark-brown hair contains more melanin and less pheomelanin. Light ash blonde contains less black and brown pigment with a greater amount of yellow than red colour pigment. Ash or drab shades are determined by the quantity of red pigment present and contain less than the gold or warm shades. (Fig. 11.6).

Grey or white hair contains little or no melanin. The less melanin the whiter the hair. The amount of white or grey hairs in a head of hair is usually expressed as a percentage, e.g. if every other hair is white or grey it is said that there is 50 per cent grey present. Approximate percentages may be arrived at and used to determine the choice of colour, e.g. a red tint applied to 70 per cent grey hair could produce a gaudy, unnatural colour.

Albino hair is completely white owing to the absence of melanin. This is usually due to the body being unable to make and distribute the melanin which may also be absent from the skin and eyes, a condition known as albinism. Partial albinism is similar but with some colour pigment present in the hair, eyes and skin.

The client's choice of colour shade should not be ignored; it may be necessary to use clashing colours for a particular reason or event, e.g. a theatrical stage part, but for normal colouring the natural blending shades are best used.

Skin colour helps to determine the choice of a suitable synthetic one, e.g. a deep-red tint will clash with a red or ruddy skin complexion. The colour of

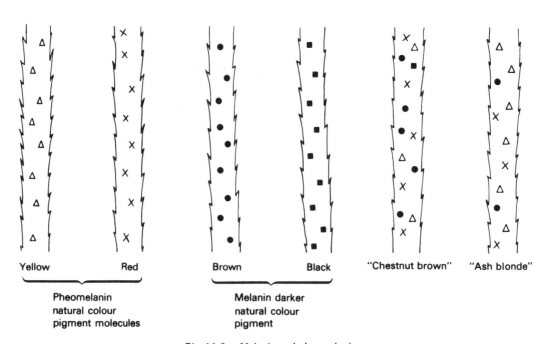

Yellow   Red   Brown   Black   "Chestnut brown"   "Ash blonde"

Pheomelanin natural colour pigment molecules

Melanin darker natural colour pigment

Fig. 11.6   Melanin and pheomelanin

skin is determined by the amount of melanin present, e.g. the darker the skin the more melanin is contained. Sunlight will vary the amount of melanin, particularly in lighter skin colours, e.g. white skin becomes 'tanned' in sunny weather, which is nature's way of ensuring added protection of the underlying skin tissues against the ultra-violet rays in sunlight. (Fig. 11.7).

Sunning   **Suntanned**

Fig. 11.7   Skin tan - ultra-violet rays

The type of colouring used may vary considerably. Modern colourings are comparatively simple to apply and good results are achieved if correctly chosen, mixed and timed. The choice of a light temporary colouring on dark hair would be wrong because the colour would be absorbed, an example of incorrect colour choice and type.

The shade of colour desired often determines the type and choice of colour. A white-haired client may require a slightly toned colour effect, without heaviness, and the temporary and semi-permanent colourings may be suitable. Newer additions to quasi-permanent and permanent colour ranges may be used to produce, e.g., silver, pewter, blue and violet tone effects. Emphasis should be placed on the use of lighter, rather than heavy and dark, colourings for white hair on the older type of skin, lacking in colour, in order to avoid clash.

3. Skin reaction. Most permanent and quasi-permanent colourings contain substances that will irritate some types of skin. Before the application of this type of colourant the skin should be tested, 24 to 48 hours beforehand, to determine skin reaction to the colourant intended to be used. A skin test may be made periodically to assess tolerance to the colourant. It is possible for clients regularly having colour treatments to react to the materials used, and their skin should be tested before each tint is applied.

A client is more likely, to though will not necessarily, react to tinting products if they are allergic to other substances, e.g. washing-up detergents, lipsticks or some types of food. Colourings containing irritating substances should clearly state on the label and instructions the possibility of skin reaction.

Skin test, alternatively called predisposition test, Sabouraud—Rousseau test and patch test, is carried out as follows: A small amount of tint intended for use should be mixed, with the correct strength of hydrogen peroxide, and applied to an area approximately 10 mm^2 to the skin behind the ear, or in the fold of the arm, after cleansing the area with spirit. The patch should be covered with collodion which forms a protective film when dry, and the client asked to report any discomfort or irritation in the following 24 to 48 hours. The client should be seen during this period so that signs of reaction are not missed.

If there is skin reaction, i.e. inflammation, swelling, irritation or discomfort, in the area of the skin test, then no colouring treatment should be carried out. If this positive skin reaction is ignored, a more serious reaction could result if tinting treatment is given, and under these circumstances no colourings containing these irritants should be applied. If there is no skin reaction (a negative test reaction), i.e. no itching, soreness or inflammation, then colouring treatment may be carried out.

4. Preparation of the hair for tinting is made more efficient if all material and equipment is placed in readiness for use, e.g. towels, protective coverings for client and operator, glass measures, dishes, applicator brush or dispenser, combs, cotton wool and rubber gloves. The colourants are selected and checked after colour choice has been made, i.e. checked that the correct tube is in the correct box, etc.

Sectioning the hair from centre forehead to nape, and from ear to ear across the crown, should be done before mixing the colouring. Sub-sections approximately 6 mm wide are taken when the material is applied, starting in the nape. Hair in the lower parts of the head and beneath the top layers is usually darker and more resistant than the upper layer, owing to the effects of brushing, combing and sunlight which lighten or lift the cuticle and make the hair porous.

Mixing the colouring should not be guesswork. It should be prepared as directed, with the correct quantities accurately measured, as the wrong proportions may produce unwanted colour effects. Prepare the tint immediately before use and do not allow it to stand for any length of time or the material loses its effectiveness.

Application of the tint should be evenly distributed and each sub-section well covered. Too little material used produces varying colour effects, and too much results in waste. Good coverage is essential for good results.

Cream tints, usually applied with a brush, should be placed on, not scraped off, with the brush. The tint container should be placed near the client to prevent any of the tint from dripping on to the client or floor, etc. Semi-viscous and liquid tints may be applied with a sponge, applicator bottle, or dispenser. The application of tints is varied by the viscosity of the material, but for controlled effects the brush is most commonly used.

Processing or development begins when the application is complete. This must be accurately timed; if too little time is given to development the result will be underprocessed, i.e. not complete, and the wrong colour will be produced. Too much time given to development may, with some colouring products, result in overprocessing, i.e. too dark shades being produced. Steamers and accelerators may be used to speed processing which, when complete, should be tested for colour result. This is done by testing a strand of hair.

Hair colour or strand test consists of removing tint from a strand of hair by lightly rubbing with a paper tissue or removing with the back of a comb, and comparing with any untinted part or the colour shade required for evenness and similarity. If the result is even throughout the strand length the tint may be removed. If there is unevenness a further development period, or the need to reapply more tint, is indicated. It is important to allow most colouring products the recommended processing or development time for good colour to be attained.

Removing the tint depends on the type of tint used. Some require the addition of a little water, light massage and rinsing, others require shampooing. Skin stains may be removed by the addition of some of the tint direct to the stain. This softens the tint stain which is then easily removed with water, but do not allow this to remain too long or deepening of the stain will result. The hair should not be roughened at this stage or hair tangling will result.

Colour result should be checked when the hair is dry. The colour of hair in a wet state appears darker owing to the water on the hair. By rubbing the hair with a towel the colour result may be seen.

5. Tinting in practice will vary for a first-time application and a regrowth tint, and commencement of application will vary according to the natural base shade, the resultant colour required and hair porosity.

Virgin hair is hair that has not been previously tinted or chemically treated. A first-time application on virgin hair requires a specific method. Regrowth tinting, often called a retouch, consists of applying the tint to the regrowth of hair, or hair grown since the previous tint.

Tinting a virgin head of hair requires the application to be made first to the mid-lengths, i.e. the main part of the hair, then to the points, i.e. the last 25 mm of the hair tips, and finally to the roots, i.e. 12—25 mm from the head. This allows for the varying degree of porosity throughout the hair length. The hair points are naturally lighter, particularly on long hair, owing to wear and weather. The roots are closest to the head and heat from the head activates the tint more quickly. The mid-lengths are usually the most resistant and will absorb tint more slowly. (Fig. 11.8).

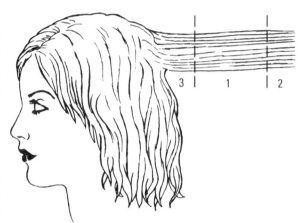

Fig. 11.8   Application of tint to virgin hair

With the use of steamers and accelerators it is possible to level out development by causing the hair to absorb the colouring at an even rate, which reduces development time by half.

Regrowth tinting is the application of tint to hair grown since the last processing. By retouching, i.e. retinting root regrowth (the newly grown hair), the colour is maintained. The tint application is made to the regrowth only, allowed to process and then removed from the hair. The mid-lengths and points should not be processed each time the regrowth is retouched; this can only result in overprocessed and poor-condition hair.

Combing through after a regrowth tint is permissible with some colouring products. The tint is diluted with water, or water is added to the hair, and combed through the hair. This maintains an even colour and allows for any colour lifting from the hair since the last tint. Repeatedly combing undiluted tint through the hair affects the hair and resultant colour.

Tinting darker or lighter is possible with modern oxidation tints, by adding to, or lightening, the natural shade. The difference between the two is the natural base shade to be treated, the synthetic colour chosen, and the hydrogen peroxide strength used.

A client with light-brown hair may require a darker shade. The colour choice is made, i.e.

considering texture porosity, condition, percentage of grey, etc., and a brown or dark-brown colour may be used. Since the natural colour shade is to be darkened it will not be necessary to use a high-strength oxidant.

If the client requires a lighter shade than her own natural colour a stronger oxidant will be necessary to lighten the natural darker pigments and oxidize the lighter synthetic colour in the hair. If the degree of lightening is to be too many shades below the natural colour, e.g. lightening from black to light blonde, then pre-bleaching should be carried out first.

Resistant hair is hair that does not readily absorb tint. It is usually better to apply to any known resistant parts first so that they receive a longer processing time. White hair may be resistant, but usually it is more porous and needs to be applied to last of all, particularly if warm or red shades are being used. It may be necessary to pre-soften resistant hair, i.e. make it more porous by causing the cuticle to lift with diluted hydrogen peroxide and ammonium hydroxide.

The resistance or porosity of the hair may be determined by developing a 'feel' for the hair. Touching the hair should tell an experienced hairdresser its condition, from which its porosity may be assessed, e.g. rough hair is more likely to be porous.

Other factors help to determine resistance or porosity. Hair which takes perm quickly or has been permed recently, hair which curls easily and tightly, previously coloured hair, and dry hair, are indications of porosity. Hair more likely to be resistant is hair which soon drops out of set or shape, takes perms slowly, greasy hair, and smoothly surfaced hair. Occasionally fine hair is highly resistant, but it usually takes colour quickly.

6. Competition and fantasy colouring is the application of all kinds of colour to produce special effects. The result is not always meant to be natural or suitable for normal wear. Some are excellent examples of good, wearable colour, but others are strong, harsh and garish effects as a fashion or styling requirement. The fantasy colourings are usually more extreme in vivid and startling colour blends. Lighting plays an important part on the resultant colour effects and requires consideration.

Lighting has its effect on salon as well as competition colourings. Blue light produced by many fluorescent tubes will neutralize the warm or red effects of hair colour. The yellow light of bare electric bulbs adds warmth to hair colour, and neutralizes blue or ash colour effects. 'Whiter' lights

show truer hair colour than that viewed in other artificial light. Sodium street lighting will show red colours as brown.

It is necessary to consider the kind of light in which the colour of the hair is to be viewed in, e.g. account should be taken of the typist working under fluorescent light for most of the day.

7. Precautions which should be taken when using colour or colouring products are listed as follows:

(*a*) Always examine the scalp thoroughly for spots, cuts, inflammation or any signs of abnormality, before the application of colourings, to prevent reaction or aggravation.

(*b*) Choose colours wisely; the application of wrong colours undermines the confidence of the client.

(*c*) Use colour carefully, and do not allow the materials to be spread over the client or equipment.

(*d*) Clean and replace all tools and materials after use, and check colour applicators before use; any dark colour remaining in an applicator brush could discolour light or bleached hair.

(*e*) Do not try to make temporary colourings do the work of the permanent types but use products in the manner for which they are intended.

(*f*) Remove stains from clothes immediately with clean water; if allowed to remain they become difficult to remove.

(*g*) Use reliable products and materials which should always be correctly stored and maintained. Poor-quality products result in loss of time, effort, money and clients.

(*h*) Measure quantities accurately; do not rely on guesswork.

(*i*) Test for skin reactions before colour applications, and strand test for resultant colour after applications.

(*j*) Avoid the use of metal containers, or discoloration of the hair may result.

(*k*) Do not roughen the hair when pre-shampooing or when removing colourants.

(*l*) Protect the hands and skin by using rubber or plastic gloves or suitable barrier creams.

(*m*) Remove surplus water from the hair before colour applications to prevent dilution of the colour.

(*n*) Keep colourings away from the eyes, and do not use hair colourings on eyebrows or eyelashes. Special, non-irritating, preparations are made for eyebrows and lashes.

(*o*) Check and use the correct volume strengths of hydrogen peroxide.

(*p*) Always work methodically and efficiently to produce confidence and good results.

8. Summary of hair colourings:

Product	Uses	Duration	Development time	Other factors
Temporary				
Rinses	Tones grey and bleached hair	One shampoo	Immediate	Colour introducer
Setting lotion	Colour tones	One shampoo	Immediate	Colouring and setting aid
Sprays and lacquers	Colour dressing aid	One shampoo	None	Dressing aid and colour introducer
Crayons	Theatrical effects	One shampoo	None	Special effects
Glitterdust	Dressing highlights	One shampoo	None	Colour, dressing aid, ornamental
Semi-permanent				
Rinses and shampoos	Colours and cleans	6—8 washes	5—15 mins	Longer-lasting full colour, not always suitable for bleached hair
Quasi-permanents				
Cream, liquid	Lightens, colours, tones	Grows out	20—45 mins	Fashion effects
Permanent				
Cream, liquid, oil-based, oxidation	Adds colour and lightens, tones bleached hair	Grows out	30 mins approx.	Permanent, fashion, special and a variety of effects

Revision test 1

Q. 1   What is hair colouring?
Q. 2   Describe the types and uses of temporary colouring.
Q. 3   What is the difference between quasi-permanent and permanent hair colouring?
Q. 4   What determines the choice of a permanent colouring?
Q. 5   What is 'skin reaction' and why is a skin test necessary before tint applications?
Q. 6   What is semi-permanent hair colouring and what is the difference between this and permanent colourings?
Q. 7   List six precautions to be taken when using hair colourings.
Q. 8   How does competition and fantasy colouring differ from that carried out in the salon?
Q. 9   What is the difference between tinting virgin hair and retouching a regrowth?
Q.10   Briefly describe each of the following terms:
        (*a*) Strand test. (*b*) Combing through. (*c*) Resistant hair. (*d*) Natural pigment. (*e*) Longer-lasting tints.

Revision test 2

Complete the following sentences:

1   Hair colouring is the process of .... to or .... the natural hair.
2   The removal of natural and synthetic colour is called .... and ....

3 Artificial or synthetic colourings are divided into ...., ..., ... and
   ....
4 A type of colour which penetrates the hair shaft is .... One that remains on the surface is
   ....
5 Another name for the process of adding synthetic to natural hair colour is ....
6 Colour choice is determined by ...., ... and ....
7 Hair colour pigment is called ...., and is composed of the following colours: ....,
   ...., ... and .... The lighter are called ....
8 A skin test should be given at least .... before the application of a ....
9 Tint application to regrowth is called a ...., and the tint should always be ....
   before .... through the lengths of the hair.

Revision test 3

Complete the following sentences with the word or words listed below:

Surface. Penetrating. Temporary. Semi-permanent. Quasi-permanent. Permanent. Skin test. Strand test. Colour choice. Base shade.

1 Rinses which wash out of the hair are called .... Those that last through several washes are
   called .... Colours which remain in the hair but gradually lift are called ...., and
   colours which remain fixed in the hair are called ....
2 Permanent colourings are .... colours and semi-permanent colourings are ....
   colours.
3 A .... should always be made before, and a .... should be made after, a colour
   application.
4 Selection of a suitable colour is called ...., and one of the considerations is the
   .... of the hair.

Vocabulary

Albinism	Congenital absence of skin and hair colour.
Albino	One suffering from albinism.
Application	The process of applying colour.
Base shade	The natural or base colour of hair.
Colourant	Name given to all colourings, sometimes used specifically for quasi-permanents.
Colour choice	Determined by texture, porosity, base colour and condition of hair and skin.
Colour shampoo	Colour in a shampoo base; cleans and colours.
Combing through	Combing the tint through after retouch, diluted to prevent overprocessing.
Competition colour	A variety of strong colours for use in competitions and displays only.
Development Processing Timing	Terms given to the 'taking time' of a tint process or application.
Discoloration	Unwanted colours produced by chemicals.
Fashion colour	A colour in popular demand.
Hair colouring	The addition of artificial or synthetic colour to the hair.
Lightening	Term used for bleaching or lifting colour.
Melanin	Natural colour pigment, e.g. black and brown.
Overprocessing	Overdevelopment of colour which causes darkening, poor condition and porosity.
Penetrating colour	Colour which penetrates cuticle and is absorbed in the cortex, e.g. permanents.
Pheomelanin	The lighter natural pigments, red and yellow.
Quasi-permanent	Apparently or nearly permanent.
Regrowth	Hair grown since the last tint.
Resistant hair	Hair which resists colour penetration.
Retouch	Colour application to regrowth.

Rinsing	Pouring colour through the hair.
Skin test	Skin reaction assessment to tint.
Strand test	Used to assess the resultant colour, or suitability of colour, of hair.
Surface colouring	Colour deposited on cuticle, temporary.
Tinting	The application of colour, mainly permanent.
Tinting lighter	Reducing natural colour and adding colour.
Virgin hair	Hair not previously coloured or processed.
Viscosity	The quality of being viscous, i.e. having a glutinous character intermediate between liquid and solid.

Hair Colouring—Varieties of Colourings

9. The chemistry of colour involves a large number of materials to produce a range of colouring products with a variety of effects. The earlier products were limited in colour but led to the discovery of more complicated and extensive varieties.

Colouring products may be divided into the following groups: (A) vegetable; (B) vegetable and mineral; (C) mineral.

(A) *Vegetable dyes,* or colourings, are made from the flowers, stems and barks of various plants. Some of the earliest known, used for colouring hair, were extracted from common growing plants. *Henna* was produced from the powdered leaves of the Egyptian privet or *Lawsonia inermis, alba* or *spinosa.* It was commonly used for 'henna packs' or applications to add red colour to the hair. This is a harmless colouring which penetrates the hair and is often called Lawsone.

Camomile or chamomile, from the flower of the camomile plant, produces a yellow-coloured pigment used for brightening the hair. It is still used in some hair-brightening shampoos. It is not a penetrating but a surface colourant.

Indigo, from the leaves of the indigo plant, gives a blue-black colour and when mixed with henna produces a variety of colours.

Walnut, from the pod shells of the ripening fruit, produces a yellow-brown dye of the surface, non-penetrating type.

Quassia, from the bark of the quassia tree, was used with camomile to brighten hair.

Other substances, e.g. sage, sumach, oak bark, cudbear, and logwood, have been used to produce a variety of colour shades and effects.

(B) *Vegetable and mineral* colourings are a mixture of vegetable extracts and substances of mineral origin. One of the commonest is a substance known as *compound henna,* i.e. the vegetable henna mixed with a metallic salt, which is a surface colourant. Compound henna is incompatible with modern colouring and perming materials and must not be confused with vegetable henna.

(C) *Mineral colourings* are divided into two groups: (i) metallic dyes, and (ii) the modern aniline derivatives.

(i) *Metallic colourings* are surface-coating dyes which are known as reduction, metallic, sulphide and progressive dyes. They consist of metal salts, e.g. lead acetate, silver nitrate, copper sulphate, bismuth citrate, and salts of iron, nickel, cobalt, cadmium and manganese, which are acted on by pyrogallol, sodium sulphide and various other chemicals, to produce metallic hair coatings. The colours range from red to black, usually dark, with a dull lustre. They are not now commonly used but occasionally found in 'hair colour restorers'.

Incompatibility is the inability to mix without reaction. Hair coloured with metallic dye is incompatible with hydrogen peroxide, an ingredient of modern colouring and perming materials. If metallic-dyed hair is treated with one of these, discoloration, intense heat and complete disintegration of the hair could result.

Tests for metallic salts and incompatibles. Hair coated with copper salts, when placed in a mixture of hydrogen peroxide and ammonium hydroxide, will boil and almost completely disintegrate. Compound henna on hair will react similarly, and lead deposits will lighten quickly. Silver deposits will not allow perming materials to penetrate and the result of perming hair so treated will be failure.

To test for metallic dyes on hair, place a small piece in a 'peroxide and ammonia' mixture, before attempting to apply colourings. If incompatible salts are present, discoloration, heat and breakage of the hair will result.

(ii) *Aniline derivatives* are substances used in many modern hair colourings. The distillation of coal and coal products produces many chemicals of medical and cosmetic use, and among these are the aniline derivative dyes. These produce the penetrating oxidation dyes in many permanent colourings, e.g. paraphenylenediamine, paratoluylenediamine, diaminophenol and ortho-aminophenol, which are used in a variety of ways.

Temporary colourings consist of large-molecule dye pigments and are not able to penetrate the hair shaft. These are made from para-hydroxyazobenzene, a yellow colouring, and phenylazo-2-naphthol, a red colouring, and are generally called 'azo' dyes or sulphonated azo dyes.

Semi-permanent colourings may be made from nitrodiamines, nitrated aminophenols and picramic acid, and are collectively called 'nitro' dyes. These have smaller pigment molecules and penetrate into the hair cuticle. They are not permanent and gradually wash from the hair.

Quasi-permanent colourings are made from toluene, diamine and diamino benzenes, which have smaller pigment molecules and penetrate into the cortex. Although they act, and should be treated, as permanent colourings, they are not permanent. The colour gradually lifts but over a longer period of time than that taken by the semi-permanents.

Permanent colourings are made from small-molecule 'para dyes', i.e. paraphenylenediamine, which are known as penetrating oxidation dyes. They are oxidized in the cortex by hydrogen peroxide and other oxidizing agents. Collectively the para dyes are called synthetic organic dyes. It is possible with these to lighten the natural pigment, melanin, and oxidize the synthetic dye, to produce a simultaneous lightening and tinting action.

Although these dyes penetrate the hair as small molecules, on oxidation they combine to form larger molecules which enable the hair to retain the colour throughout subsequent shampooing. These larger molecules are known as Bandrowski's base. The synthetic organic dyes are likely to cause skin reaction and skin tests should be made to assess the possibility of allergy to these substances.

The earlier metallic dyes, e.g. sulphide and reduction dyes, were known as double application dyes. The modern permanent oxidation tints, usually mixed with an oxidant, e.g. hydrogen peroxide, are known as single application dyes.

10. Hydrogen peroxide is one of the commonest oxidants used in modern colouring. It is mixed with the cream or liquid containing the colour pigment, which at first appears colourless, but darkens on exposure to air.

Lightening or darkening with modern permanent colourings and the use of hydrogen peroxide enables the colouring to penetrate the cuticle, the natural pigment to become oxidized or bleached, and the synthetic colouring activated and deposited in the hair shaft.

To lighten natural hair colour 'up' two or three shades, a higher volume strength hydrogen peroxide should be used. If the natural colour is to be taken 'down' to a darker shade, then lower volume strengths are used.

The volume strength to use is determined by the manufacturer's instructions, the colour the hair is to be lightened or darkened, and the porosity of the hair. (For dilutions of hydrogen peroxide, see Part 3.)

Pre-lightening the hair is necessary when the natural colour is to be lightened to a very light shade. A liquid mixture of hydrogen peroxide and ammonium hydroxide, or other bleaching agents, may be used. The modern colourings can lighten by several shades but cannot lighten to the very light tones.

Pre-softening is a technique used on resistant hair which involves the application of dilute hydrogen peroxide and ammonium hydroxide, not to lighten, but to soften the hair cuticle and allow penetration of colour pigment.

Activation of colouring processes is aided with steamers and accelerators which have similar actions; the heat from them causes the hair to swell and the cuticle cells to lift, which allows quicker penetration of colouring into the cortex, and a reduction of the processing time by half.

With the use of these activators, e.g. steamers and accelerators, tint applications can be made to the whole length of hair irrespective of varying porosities of the roots, mid-lengths and points. The distribution of heat allows even processing throughout the hair length, but applications must not be delayed or unevenness of colour could result.

11. Aesthetics and colouring. There are similarities between colourings used in the art room and the salon, and these are based on the use of colour in its primary, secondary, complementary and contrasting forms, and the line and design in which it is used.

Colour is recognized as a colour by its hue, e.g. blue, green, red. The brightness of the colour is its intensity, e.g. bright glowing red or dull brown red, and its lightness or darkness, e.g. light warm red or dark rich red. A colour is seen as colour by the eye which registers the reflection of light from a coloured surface and stimulates the nerves leading to the brain. A black surface absorbs most of the colour and no hue is registered. A white surface reflects a mixture of colours and is seen as white, and a red surface will absorb all colours other than red.

When mixing paints of primary colours, i.e. blue, yellow and red, the secondary colours, i.e. violet, green and orange, may be attained, and from a mixture of the primary and secondary most other colours may be achieved. When white and black are added a variety of shade and tone is produced.

Light illustrates a range of colour when the rays of the sun are bent or refracted as they enter raindrops, then reflected from the far surface of the drop and refracted again as they pass out. The result is that light rays are broken up into a spectrum of colours which are visible in the form of a rainbow. The colours as they pass through are bent at a different angle; violet has the greatest deviation and red the least.

The colours of the spectrum are violet, indigo, blue, green, yellow, orange and red. Outside the visible spectrum are other rays; at the violet end are ultra-violet rays which cause skin tanning and affect photographic film, and at the red end are infra-red and radiant rays with marked heating effects.

The spectrum may be demonstrated by passing white light through a prism so that it is refracted to form the colours of the rainbow. The different colours may be recombined to produce white light, and if a disc on which the spectral colours are painted is rotated they appear to blend and are seen as white.

12. Colouring hair. The colours used are divided into the different base shades, e.g. black, brown, red and yellow, and are toned with mixtures of other colours to produce a large variety. Most colour shade charts are arranged with a column of base shades on one side and in line with each a column of colour variations, e.g. the same depth of colour but with different tones. If ash, gold, red, purple or blue is added to light blonde a different colour shade is produced. The addition of warm colour (e.g. red, gold or yellow), or cold colour (e.g. green and blue), to base shades produces an almost endless variety. Ash shades may be produced with the addition of blue, and matt shades with the addition of green. Gold shades are produced with added yellow, warm shades with red, and purple or violet tones are produced with a mixture of red and blue. The shades produced by different colour mixtures are invaluable to the hair colourist.

13. Colouring boardwork and hair to be made into postiche is attained with normal hair colourings, e.g. the range of synthetic dyes, and a variety of food colourings, e.g. cochineal and other listed food dyes. At one time a variety of coloured inks and most metallic and vegetable colourings were used. A greater use is now made of materials compatible with other hairdressing processes.

The traditional method of colouring hair in boardwork was to boil the hair in water to which was added the dye. Catechu, tannin, Bismarck powder, nigrosin and other mordants, i.e. chemicals added to fix the colour, were commonly used.

Most colouring is carried out before hair is made into postiche so that the foundations are not affected. If the foundations of postiche are subjected to water or other chemicals, they may shrink, rot and tear. Modern colourings may be used to tint postiche but not without testing for incompatibles first. Newer postiche colourings are now being introduced which do not affect foundation materials.

The cheaper and coarser imported hair, e.g. Asian, Indian and Chinese, is specially treated, disinfected and coloured in bulk and may be purchased in a variety of colours. Before recolouring this type of hair it is usually necessary to test for incompatibility.

Colour matching, i.e. matching hair to be made into postiche with the client's natural shade, is best done before commencing work on the piece, by using different natural-coloured hair, rather than synthet-ically colouring afterwards. The same applies to lightening or bleaching the hair which is best achieved by repeated bleaching in low strengths of 'peroxide'. The old boardworkers used sulphur dioxide to produce bleached 'white hair'. Bleaching the hair over long periods with high volume strengths of hydrogen peroxide causes roughness and poor condition.

Colour mixing or mixing hair to colour is the blending of two or more shades of hair to produce another shade or colour and is a boardwork preparation process.

14. Tinting faults and corrections:
Patchy and uneven colour after tint application
  Insufficient coverage or application of tint.
  Sections too large.
  Overlapping, causing colour build-up in parts.
  Underprocessing, not allowing full colour to develop.
  Use of spirit setting lotions which may remove colour.
  Correct by spot tint, apply to light areas, and balance.
Resultant colour too light
  Too light or insufficient colour in shade chosen.
  Peroxide strength too low to allow full development.
  Underprocessed, or hair too porous to hold colour.
  Choose darker shade, check 'peroxide', pre-pigment.
Colour fade after two or three shampoos
  Bleaching effects of sun. Underprocessed.
  Poor condition, too porous, needs reconditioning.
  Harsh physical treatment, e.g. brushing, sand and salt.
Colour too dark after application
  Colour choice too dark. Overprocessing.
  Poor condition, porous hair.
  Possible incompatibles present, make tests.
  Use colour reducer as recommended.
Scalp stain
  Cream or oil very dry skin before application.
  Remove with spirit, special stain remover, or tint.
Hair too red
  Peroxide strength too high.
  If pre-bleached, wrong choice of neutralizing colour, or not bleached light enough.
  Apply matt or green colour to neutralize red effects.
Scalp irritation or skin reaction
  Not cleanly shampooed, tint still present.
  Result of too high volume peroxide being used.
  Bad combing and tint application, too harshly done.
  Possible reaction to tint chemicals, give no treatment, send to doctor and notify insurance company.
Discoloration of hair
  Poor condition, too porous, not holding colour.

Repeated combing of undiluted tint through the hair.

Possible reaction to incompatibles, test.

Green colour — possibly the effect of blue ash shades on yellow base. Possible reaction to metallic salts.

Correct with the use of warm or red colour but beware of producing dark brown.

Mauve colour — possible incompatible reaction.

Counteract with contrasting colour or remove with colour reducers.

Good colour coverage except for grey or white hair
Hair resistant, pre-soften or use lighter shade with higher volume peroxide.

Hair resistant to tint
Pre-soften, or use higher volume peroxide, and increase processing and development time as directed.

Revision test 1

Q. 1   How are varieties of colourings divided? Give examples of each classification.
Q. 2   What is incompatibility? Give examples and describe a test for incompatibles.
Q. 3   Name three types of colouring used in boardwork, and describe a method of colouring hair to be used in postiche.
Q. 4   Describe three possible faults, causes and corrections of tinting.
Q. 5   Name three vegetable, one vegetable and mineral, and three mineral dyes.
Q. 6   What is colour? What determines its variety and how is it seen as colour?
Q. 7   In which group, or groups, of modern colourings do temporary, semi-permanents and permanents belong?
Q. 8   What are the spectral colours? Describe a method by which white light may be shown to contain them.
Q. 9   What is pre-lightening and pre-softening? Briefly describe the uses of steamers and accelerators.
Q.10   Briefly describe each of the following terms:
         (a) Bandrowski's base. (b) Metallic salts. (c) Lawsone. (d) 'Para' dyes. (e) Allergy.

Revision test 2

Complete the following sentences:

1   Name three examples of vegetable colourings:
     (a) ...., (b) ...., (c) ....
2   Name three examples of metallic colourings:
     (a) ...., (b) ...., (c) ....
3   Name three primary and three secondary colours:
     (a) ...., (b) ...., (c) ...., (d) ...., (e) ....,
     (f) ....
4   Name a chemical group used in the following colourants:
     (a) Temporary — ....; (b) Semi-permanent — ....; (c) Permanent — ....
5   The reaction of incompatible colourings on hair may cause (a) ...., (b) ....,
     (c) ....
6   Name two surface and two penetrating dyes:
     (a) ...., (b) ...., (c) ...., (d) ....
7   A once commonly used vegetable and mineral dye was called ....
8   Name two oxidation processes: (a) ...., (b) ....

Revision test 3

Complete the following sentences with the word or words listed below:

Surface. Penetrating. Small. Large. Para. Nitro. Azo. Mordant. Breakage. Hydrogen peroxide.

1   Permanent colourings may be described as ...., and contain a chemical group called
     .... These contain .... molecules of pigment.

2   Temporary colourings may be described as .... and contain a chemical group called
     .... These have .... molecules of pigment.
3   Semi-permanent colourings contain chemicals belonging to the .... group.
4   Nigrosin is an example of a .... which was used in colouring hair to be made into postiche.
5   The result of an incompatible reaction on the hair could be discoloration and ....
6   An active ingredient of oxidation colouring is ....

Vocabulary

Aniline derivatives	Dyes made from coal derivatives.
Ash, drab and matt	Shades containing blue or violet, used for neutralizing warm reds.
'Azo' dyes	Used in temporary colourings.
Cold colours	Blue and green.
Colour	The hue, intensity and shade.
Compatible	Able to mix without violent reaction.
Compound colourings	Mixtures of vegetable and mineral dyes.
Hair colour restorers	Substances often containing metallic salts used to tint hair.
Incompatibility	Inability to mix without reaction.
Infra-red and radiant rays	Invisible rays emitted from the red end of the spectrum.
'Lightened up'	Reduction of colour, e.g. bleaching.
Listed food dyes	Recommended colourings for food used in some hair colourings.
Metallic colourings	Surface-coating, reduction, sulphide and progressive dyes of metal salts.
Mineral colourings	Metallic and aniline derivatives.
Mordant	Chemical used or added to colours to fix them in the hair.
'Nitro' dyes	Chemical group used in semi-permanents.
'Para' dye	Abbreviation of paraphenylenediamine.
Penetrating colourings	The aniline derivatives and those deposited in the hair cortex.
Primary colours	Blue, yellow, red.
Secondary colours	Violet, green, orange.
Spectral or rainbow colours	Violet, indigo, blue, green, yellow, orange and red.
Synthetic organic dyes	General term given to artificial colourings, e.g. aniline derivatives.
Ultra-violet rays	Invisible rays emitted from the violet end of the spectrum.
Vegetable colourings	Dyes made from plant leaves and stems.
Warm colours	Red, gold or yellow.
White light	Rays of the sun containing the spectral colours.

Chapter Eleven — Part Three

Hair Colouring—Bleaching, Toning and Decolouring

15. Bleaching is the process of lightening the natural colour pigment of hair. The effect of the chemical action is the alteration of melanin from a coloured to a colourless pigment. The process is one of oxidation, e.g. the addition of oxygen from an oxidant to the chemicals in hair.

Bleaches or lighteners are made in liquid, cream and powder form and are called liquid, oil or paste bleaches.

Oil bleach contains ammonium hydroxide and a sulphonated oil, e.g. sulphonated castor or Turkey red oil, as its main ingredient, which is mixed with hydrogen peroxide to form a viscous liquid. Several types are made, some intended for lightening only, others to lighten and add colour tone to the hair, e.g. warm, gold, silver or blue.

Liquid bleach may be a simple mixture of 1 ml of ammonium hydroxide to 20—50 ml of hydrogen peroxide. Too much 'ammonia' will redden the hair; the quantities needed depend on the shade required.

Powder bleaches or lighteners are made from magnesium and sodium carbonate powders which are mixed with oxidizers, e.g. hydrogen peroxide, sodium bromate or perborate, and stabilizers, e.g. sulphuric and phosphoric acids, glycerine and ethyl alcohol, together with alkaline ammonium hydroxide and sodium acetate.

The formulations vary but usually white or blue powder forms a creamy paste when mixed with oxidants. This was commonly called 'white henna' but has no relationship or comparison with vegetable henna. *The paste or cream bleaches* have the advantage of staying where placed on the hair and not running, which could cause overbleaching. Results are speedily achieved and with the many additives do not produce too red or warm a colour, or irritate the skin.

Hydrogen peroxide (H_2O_2) is one of the most commonly used chemicals for hair lightening. It has many of the properties of an acid, and is often listed as such, but it is not an acid, and is capable of releasing a large percentage of oxygen which is vital to the oxidation process of lightening. Its effectiveness is increased by the addition of an alkali, e.g. ammonium hydroxide.

Apart from bleaching, hydrogen peroxide is used in hair colourings, pre-lightening and softening treatments, the removal of some colourings, permanent waving normalizers, and in lightening shampoos and rinses.

It may be purchased in different volume strengths, e.g. 10, 20, 30 and higher volumes. The higher the volume strength the larger the amount of oxygen available, e.g. from 1 litre of hydrogen peroxide of 20 volume strength, 20 litres of free oxygen may be liberated. It is dangerous to use too high volume strengths on the hair or the head; severe burns and hair breakage could result.

Dilutions of hydrogen peroxide. The following volume strengths may be obtained from 100, 60, 40, 30 and 20 volumes by diluting with distilled water (see Appendix III for percentage strengths):

Volume (H_2O_2)	Parts H_2O_2		Parts water		Volume produced
100	3	+	2	=	60
100	2	+	3	=	40
100	3	+	7	=	30
100	1	+	4	=	20
100	1	+	9	=	10
60	2	+	1	=	40
60	1	+	1	=	30
60	1	+	2	=	20
60	1	+	5	=	10
60	1	+	11	=	5
40	3	+	1	=	30
40	1	+	1	=	20
40	1	+	3	=	10
40	1	+	7	=	5
30	2	+	1	=	20
30	1	+	2	=	10
30	1	+	5	=	5
20	1	+	1	=	10
20	1	+	3	=	5
20	1	+	7	=	2½

A peroxometer, i.e. a type of hydrometer, may be conveniently used to test the volume strength of hydrogen peroxide. Unstabilized hydrogen peroxide may lose its strength or efficiency if unstoppered and exposed to the air and dust, which could slow the lightening action.

Ammonium hydroxide (NH$_4$OH) is produced when ammonia gas is dissolved in water. This is a valuable alkali, used in conjunction with hydrogen peroxide to assist in lifting the hair cuticle and in the penetration of the bleaching agent. It dissolves grease and may be used in degreasing and hair-cleansing lotions, sometimes mixed with borax.

This may be purchased in various strengths, the strongest being 0·880, i.e. the specific gravity of the solution. This must be diluted before applying to hair or lightening mixtures, e.g. 1 ml to 20—50 ml hydrogen peroxide. Always store this chemical in a cool dark place to prevent decomposition, and make sure it is well stoppered to contain the dangerous gas or fumes.

16. Preparation for bleaching includes the following tools and materials to be placed in readiness for use: rubber gloves and other protective coverings, bleaching agents, glass or china containers, and applicators, e.g. soft-bristle brush, cotton wool wrapped around a tailcomb, or an applicator bottle. Metallic tools or containers should not be used with oxidizing agents or the metal becomes corroded and the hair discoloured.

Sectioning is similar to that required for tinting, but generally the thicker the bleaching agent the smaller the sections should be. Liquid bleach penetrates a larger hair section more easily than paste bleach and the largest sections, approximately 6—12 mm, should be taken; smaller sections are required for oil bleach, and the smallest for cream and paste bleach.

Application of a bleach will vary but generally the less porous parts are treated first. It is important not to overlap previously bleached and more porous parts of the hair. To prevent this, olive oil, cold creams or vaseline may be applied to the demarcation line, i.e. the line between regrowth and bleached hair. Uneven applications result in patchy colour, and should be made evenly and thoroughly. On completion of application check the hairline, particularly about the ears, to ensure full coverage.

Overbleaching is caused by using too high strengths of 'peroxide', processing too long, overlapping applications, combing bleach through lightened hair, and lightening too porous hair. This results in the hair becoming brittle or broken, spongy and very porous, and unevenly coloured, which makes further colouring, toning, perming and management difficult. (Fig. 11.9).

Overbleached hair when wet is almost like chewing gum, and the resultant shape of setting is soon lost. The keratin structure is so weakened that a little tension causes the hair to break. Bleached or lightened hair should be treated with conditioners

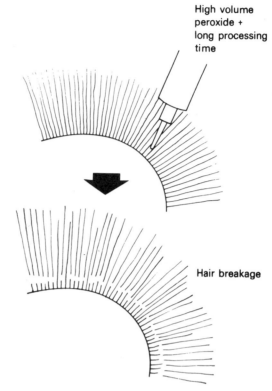

High volume
peroxide +
long processing
time

Hair breakage

Fig. 11.9   Effect of overbleaching

before further chemical processing takes place.

Removal of lighteners after bleaching should be gently carried out. The hair cuticle, particularly if overbleached, may be raised, roughened and easily tangled. The hair should be moved gently and rinsed carefully with cool, not hot, water to prevent further softening and tangling.

Special conditioners and anti-oxidants or anti-oxidizers, i.e. substances used to stop or prevent oxidation, should be used to neutralize the chemical action of oxidants. These contain cuticle-smoothing properties which enable the hair to be easily combed and managed. Quaternary ammonium compounds and some acids are used in these products, e.g. rinses and finishing lotions, and help to counteract the alkaline effects of bleaches and lighteners.

17. The bleaching action. When lighteners are mixed and applied, the ammonium hydroxide or sodium acetate content cancels out or neutralizes the effect of the stabilizers, e.g. sulphuric and phosphoric acids, and this allows the hair cuticle to swell and the chemicals to penetrate. The released oxygen is then free to act on the natural colour pigments. The darker pigments, black and brown, are acted on first and the hair becomes lightened. Further development and oxidation acts on the red and yellow pigments. It depends on how much dark and red pigment is initially present as to the degree of lightness attainable. (Fig. 11.10).

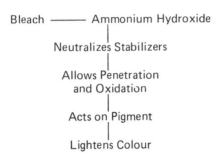

Fig. 11.10   Bleaching action

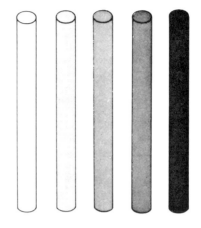

Light yellow–Gold–Darker bleached shades

Fig. 11.11   Light and dark peroxide effects

Very dark hair contains large amounts of dark pigment which may be lightened by low strengths of 'peroxide' to leave the warmer, red pigments unaffected, which will make the hair appear red. It may be necessary to use higher volume strength oxidants or repeated oxidizing processes to lighten the dominant red pigments.

To reduce black hair to a very light 'white' or platinum shade, the hair should be bleached as light as possible and the remaining light-yellow colour neutralized with a suitable toner, e.g. preferably a violet colour. Before this drastic lightening is attempted the hair should be tested, e.g. a strand of hair treated and processed to assess the lightness of colour attainable, to prevent a long-drawn-out process with unsatisfactory results.

Colour lift achieved by bleaching produces a range of shades from dark brown to very pale yellow. It is rarely possible to bleach white, silver or platinum, without toning. Some very light-brown and blonde hair is easily reduced to a light shade without toning, but the darker the hair the more difficult it is to produce the lighter shades. (Figs. 11.11 & 11.12).

18. Streaking or bleached streaks are names given to strands of bleached or lightened hair. Small pieces are usually more effective than large, chunky ones, and in prominent parts of the head may be used to highlight a dressing.

Methods of streaking. vary. Sectioned strands of hair may be pulled through holes, strategically placed, in a plastic cap, and the bleach applied with a brush, cotton wool or applicator. The cap prevents the bleach from running on to other parts of the hair. The process may be speeded by steamers and accelerators but the hair should not be allowed to dry or oxidation is reduced. (Fig. 11.13).

Alternatively, small strands may be wrapped in aluminium foil, which retains heat produced by the

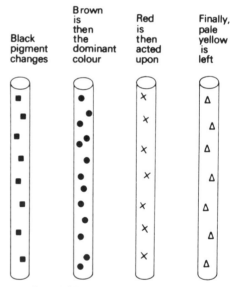

Fig. 11.12   Colour lift and change

oxidants, and quickly achieves the degree of lightness required. The root ends should be tightly enclosed to prevent bleaching the lower part of the strand. It is not necessary to apply heat to speed the process or the bleach will 'bubble' and run to produce unwanted yellow patches on the roots. (Fig. 11.14).

Tipping, frosting, brightening and blending are terms used to describe the effects of bleaching a part or parts of the hair. Toners are usually applied to produce various colour effects, either blending or contrasting with the client's natural colour.

19. Tinting bleached hair back to a natural colour

Fig. 11.13   Streaking hair through a cap

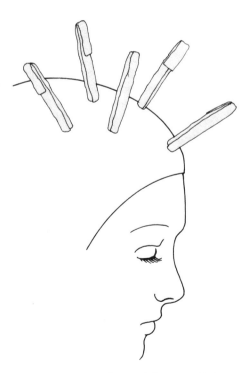

Fig. 11.14   Streaking — foil-wrapped hair

is easily achieved with modern colourings and it is easier to darken than lighten. As a client ages, skin and hair colour is reduced, and the request for the 'natural colour' of twenty years previous should be met with caution, or too dark results may be achieved. What was the natural colour is now probably too dark, and two or three shades lighter is more likely to be suitable. If the hair is in good condition the application may be made as for a virgin head. If there are very porous parts, colour filling or pre-pigmentation, i.e. putting base colour in the hair which enables other colouring materials to adhere evenly, may be required. Red colour is commonly used on which the final colour becomes attached.

It is usually better when tinting back to aim at a warm shade; the ashen, drab or matt shades may show a percentage of green. Pre-pigmentation colour filler should be used as recommended by the manufacturers, and very porous ends should be cut to allow for a normal application.

20. Brightening shampoos and rinses consist of shampoos and liquids with small amounts of bleaching agent and are used to lighten hair colour slightly. A useful lightener may be made by mixing 28 ml of hydrogen peroxide with 28 ml of warm water and 14 ml of soapless shampoo. The quantity of 'peroxide' may be increased if a lighter shade is required. (For brightening rinses and shampoos, see Chapter 4.)

When to bleach. With the ability to tint lighter with modern colourings there is often hesitation about bleaching. Generally, if the natural colour of the hair to be lightened is dark, and very light shades are required, then it should be pre-bleached or lightened with a bleach product first. A tint should not be made to do the work of a bleach; although tints are able to lift one or two shades, lightening several shades is more satisfactorily attained by bleaching.

The effects of sun, sand and sea or chlorinated water on the hair are similar to further bleaching or oxidation processes. The sun tends to dry and lift the cuticle, brushing and the abrasive action of sand roughens, and sun and salt water will slightly bleach. Hair previously lightened or coloured is particularly prone to these elements and is best covered in strong sunlight; sand, sea or chlorinated water should be rinsed out as soon as possible.

Testing. Where doubt exists as to the colour or porosity of the hair, always test first by applying the intended materials to a small strand of hair. Any variation of colour on the test strand may be adjusted in the final application.

Precautions to be taken with bleaches and bleaching:

(*a*) Apply bleaching materials evenly and use the correct volume strengths.

(*b*) Do not overbleach by overlapping or

processing too long.

(*c*) Do not bleach hair previously treated with metallic or compound hair colourings.

(*d*) Do not allow the bleach to dry out; oxidation almost ceases when the bleach is dry.

(*e*) Any red colour left in the hair after bleaching from dark shades should be counteracted with neutralizing shades.

(*f*) Bleach in stages, preferably with low volume strengths rather than one high one, to produce very light shades.

(*g*) Blue colourings or toners used on a yellow base may produce green; test first.

(*h*) Metallic containers and tools are soon spoilt if bleaching materials are spilt over them; use glass or china containers.

(*i*) Do not bleach hair in poor condition or in a porous state; overlapping applications on this type of hair result in breakage.

(*j*) Avoid mixing or using lighteners or colourings without checking the manufacturer's instructions.

21. Toning is the process of adding colour, usually to lightened hair. A variety of light or pastel shades may be used on very light shades of bleached hair. The lightest toners can only be used on the lightest bleached base; if used on dark hair the colour would be completely absorbed, and all effects lost.

Toners may be temporary, semi-permanent, or quasi-permanent and permanent colourings used in a diluted form. Specially made toners for use on lightened hair, usually aniline derivatives, are used similarly to permanent colourings, i.e. the skin reaction is assessed by patch testing before applications are made.

Mixing toners depends on the type used. Those mixed with 'peroxide' require low strengths only; the use of higher strengths may produce patchy results and porous hair.

Application of toners is similar to the application of permanent colourings, but some are used by pouring on the hair and lightly massaging in. All need to be evenly applied and account made for any porous areas.

Development and timing of processing will vary according to the type of product used, e.g. aniline derivatives require 20–45 minutes. Other toners require several applications for the colour to be built up in the hair.

The *toner colour range,* e.g. beige, silver, rose and other pastel shades, is used for its subtle toned effects. It is important to remember that colour added to colour produces a slightly darker shade and that differing colours mixed together produce a wide range of varieties. The following list gives examples and may be used as a guide:

Red on green makes brown.
Red on yellow makes orange.
Blue on yellow produces green.

Green may be cancelled out by violet and orange.
Violet may be reduced by orange and green.
Blue on red produces violet.

The colour finally produced will depend on the depth of colour in the hair to be toned and the shade of toner used.

22. Decolouring is the removal of synthetic colourings from the hair by special colour reducers or strippers.

Oxidation tints may be removed by reducing agents, e.g. sodium bisulphite or sodium formaldehyde sulphoxylate. Most manufacturers make special colour reducers for their products and it is to be preferred that the same make of colour and stripper are used. An oxidant should not be used in any form as it will help the colour to penetrate rather than remove it.

Compound henna, vegetable and mineral dyes may be removed by special colour reducers only. Hydrogen peroxide must not be used to remove these colourings, as the chemicals are not compatible.

Temporary and semi-permanent colourings may be reduced by repeated shampooing and the application of spirit.

Method of decolouring or colour reducing. The removal of oxidation and 'para' aniline derivative dyes from the hair may be carried out as follows: First wash and dry the hair. Mix the correct colour remover, after checking the manufacturer's instructions. Apply the decolourant to the parts of the hair where colour is to be removed, e.g. where colour build-up has occurred, or to the whole of the hair. Allow the reducer to act, preferably uncovered and without heat; processing time is usually 10–30 minutes. Where necessary, and if in accord with manufacturer's instructions, speed the process by covering hair with a plastic cap and placing under a warm dryer, steamer or accelerator.

Thorough shampooing is necessary when development is completed, to remove excess chemicals and neutralize their actions. If not thorough the decolouring process may need to be repeated.

The 'peroxide' test should be used when the decolouring chemicals have been removed from the hair. A weak solution of hydrogen peroxide, i.e. 3 volume strength, is applied to the decoloured hair. If any synthetic pigment remains it will become oxidized by this solution and darken again. Without this test the hair could darken over the following day or two owing to the oxidizing effects of the atmosphere. The use of the 'peroxide' test indicates any ineffectiveness of the decolouring process. If the hair darkens after testing, reapply the decolourant after removing the 'peroxide' solution; several applications may be needed to strip the unwanted colour.

Recolouring after decolouring treatments will vary according to the products used. Generally no other chemical processing should follow immediately, but with some products recolouring may be recommended. Perming may be carried out successfully, preferably at least a week after decolouring. Where possible perming treatments should be applied before decolouring, and the lightening action of some normalizers should be taken into account.

New products are constantly being introduced which may vary the methods, conditions and aspects of colouring, lightening, toning and decolouring. What was a standing rule for many years may be repeatedly altered by the introduction of products containing modern chemicals, by new ideas, and by the research of cosmetic chemists and scientists. Many manufacturers of these products, old and new, supply instruction, advice and courses for their use.

23. Colour correcting — lightening and toning:

Fault	*Cause*	*Correction*
Uneven colour	Poor application. Section too large. Mixing incorrectly.	Spot bleach or recolour.
Dark ends	Underbleached or overbleached porous ends. Toner too dark. Overprocessed toner. Remains of dark tint.	Rebleach. Lessen porosity with oil. Remove, use lightener. Time accurately. Remove and tone.
Too yellow	Underbleached. Base too dark. Wrong toner. Wrong bleach.	Bleach lighter. Try stronger bleach. Use violet or matt. Use other than oil.
Too red	Underbleached. Too much alkali. Wrong toner.	Bleach again. Use blue bleach not oil. Use matt, green or olive.
Dark roots or patches	Poor bleach application. Toners too dark.	Rebleach evenly. Remove, use lightener.
Roots not coloured	Underbleached. Undertimed. 'Drippy' toner. Temperature of toner not hot enough.	Bleach down again. Apply full timing. Apply cream not liquid. Reapply as directed.
Colour fade	Overporous. Harsh treatment. Exposure.	Correct condition. Advise on hair care. Keep hair covered. Comb dilute toner through.
Hair breakage	Overprocessed. Incompatibles. Harsh treatment. Sleeping in rollers, etc.	Recondition. Test. Advise. Demonstrate effects.
Discoloration	Underprocessed. Exposure. Home treatments.	Correct development. Condition and cover hair. Test and advise.
Tangle	Overbleached. Bad shampoo. Overrubbing. Overbackcombing.	Use anti-oxidants. Use correct movements. Use gentle actions. Reduce and demonstrate.

Fault	Cause	Correction
Green tones	Incompatibles.	Test.
	Blue on yellow.	Use red or warm shades.
	Too blue ash.	Use violet.
Inflammation	Skin reaction.	Doctor's advice.
	Torn scalp.	Advise.
	Disease.	Doctor's diagnosis.
Irritation	Skin reaction.	Doctor's advice.
	Harsh treatment.	Advise.
	Disease.	Diagnosis.
Colour not taking	Overporous.	Recondition.
	Poor condition.	
	Lacks pigment.	Pre-pigment.
	Lacquer build-up.	Remove excess.
Colour build-up	Overporous.	Recondition.
	Poor condition.	

Revision test 1

Q. 1   What is bleaching or lightening? Describe the types of bleach used.
Q. 2   What is 'overbleaching' and what precautions should be taken to avoid it?
Q. 3   List the precautions which should be taken when bleaching or toning.
Q. 4   What is toning and how should toners be used?
Q. 5   What effects do sun, sea and salt have on tinted or bleached hair?
Q. 6   What is decolouring and how is this carried out? List the precautions which should be taken.
Q. 7   Describe four lightening or toning faults and how they may be corrected.
Q. 8   Describe the chemical action of bleaching.
Q. 9   List four colours which may be used to neutralize other, unwanted, shades or colours.
Q.10   Briefly describe each of the following terms:
        (a) Stripper. (b) Stabilizer. (c) Peroxometer. (d) Demarcation line. (e) Colour lift.

Revision test 2

Complete the following sentences:

1   Two chemicals which may be used in decolouring products are (a) .... and (b) ....

2   The following strengths may be diluted to produce 20 volume 'peroxide':
     40 volume 1 part + ... parts water.
     100 volume .... part + ... parts water.
     60 volume .... parts + ... parts water.

3   Name three different kinds of lighteners: (a) ...., (b) ...., (c) ....

4   Two terms used to describe the removal of natural and synthetic colourings from the hair are (a) .... and (b) ....

5   Name the possible causes for hair that is
     Too red — ....
     Too yellow —..
     Too green —..

6   A skin test is required before the application of .... and ....

7   Name three chemicals that may be used in bleaches or lightening products:
     (a) ...., (b) ...., (c) ....

8   Which colours may be produced by mixtures of the following:
     Red + yellow = ... Red + green = ... Blue + red = ... Blue + yellow ....

9   Hair in an overbleached state should be .... before the application of a tint or toner.

Revision test 3

Complete the following sentences with the word or words listed below:

Overlapping. Overbleaching. Conditioning. Porous. Pre-pigmentation. Resistant. Incompatibles. Acid. Compatible. Alkali.

1   Hydrogen peroxide is .... with modern colourings but .... with compound henna and metallic salts.
2   By .... the application of bleach to hair that has been previously treated it could be made more ....
3   When tinting hair back after the hair has been bleached the hair should be subjected to .... and ....
4   Ammonium hydroxide is an .... and its effect may be counteracted afterwards with .... conditioners.
5   The result of .... is poor hair condition and hair breakage.
6   Oils and creams may be applied to overbleached hair to prevent breakage, but pre-softening should be applied to .... hair.

Vocabulary

Ammonium hydroxide	An alkali added to some bleaching agents to neutralize the stabilizers.
Anti-oxidant *Anti-oxidizer*	Substances used to prevent oxidation.
Bleaching	The process of removing natural hair colour.
Blending	Hair lightened or coloured to blend with natural colour or, e.g., highlighting.
Brightening shampoos and rinses	Used to lighten the hair slightly.
Chlorinated water	Water with chlorine, e.g. swimming-pools, which tends to lighten hair.
Colour lift	Lightness produced by bleaching and tinting.
Decolourants *Strippers* *Colour reducers*	Substances used to remove synthetic colour.
Decolouring	The process of reducing or stripping synthetic colourings.
Demarcation	The line between coloured and regrown hair.
Frosting *Tipping*	Small parts of lightened hair, hair ends or tips.
Hydrogen peroxide	H_2O_2 — one of the commonest oxidants used in hair lightening and tinting processes.
Lightening	Alternative term to bleaching.
Oil bleach	Viscous liquid, ammoniated and sulphonated castor oil, Turkey red oil, used in bleach.
Oxidation	The process of the addition of oxygen.
Oxidants *Oxidizers*	Substances which produce oxidation.
Paste or powder bleach	A white or blue powder, mixed with H_2O_2, to produce a creamy, paste bleach.
Peroxometer	A type of hydrometer used for measuring the volume strength of 'peroxide'.
Pre-pigmentation	The addition of colour to porous hair so that further colour will adhere. Sometimes called *colour filling.*
Stabilizer	A chemical used in bleaches to prevent deterioration of the materials.
Streaking	Lightening or colouring strands of hair.
Toners	Colourings used for toning.
Toning	The process of adding tint or colour after lightening.

The Hair and Skin—The Hair

1. Hair is an outgrowth of the skin and is sometimes described as a threadlike filament growing from the skin. It is part of the natural body covering, and human hair is distinctive, in structure and growth, from that found in any other group of living creatures. (Fig. 12.1)

The hair of animals is referred to as a coat. When it is fine and thickly placed it is called *fur,* e.g. the coat of the beaver. When the hair is fine and kinky, with a rough surface, and a tendency to felt or mat together, it is called *wool,* e.g. the coat of the sheep. Very stiff hairs are called *bristles,* and if stiff and sharp are called *spines,* e.g. the coat of the hedgehog.

Human hair, the material with which the hairdresser works and on which most processes act, is a physical characteristic of man that remains constant. It is classified and recognized as three distinct groups, Negroid, Mongoloid and Caucasian, into which most other hair groups may be placed. This difference between hair groups is used by the criminologist just as he uses other means of classification, e.g. fingerprints.

Negroid hair is woolly, kinky, tight curly or wavy hair. *Mongoloid hair* is straight and lank, similar to that of the American Indian. *Caucasian and European hair* is the loosely waved or straight type. There are other types and groups of hair which make an interesting study. The scientific study of the structure, function and diseases of human hair is called 'trichology', and one learned in these subjects is called a 'trichologist'.

2. Functions. Hair may be compared with the nail, horn, hoof, claw and feather of animals and birds, and its main function is that of protection. Hair protects in three ways: (*a*) by acting as a *buffer,* to soften knocks and blows; (*b*) by forming an *insulating* layer round the head; (*c*) by acting, with skin, as a *warning system,* when anything nears the surface of the body.

Hair's protective function as a *buffer* is well known to those with little or no hair. A light blow on a bald head may prove severe or damaging to the underlying tissues, and at least painful. The thicker the layers of the hair the more a knock or blow is cushioned, and relatively 'hard knocks' may be shrugged off with a rub.

As an *insulator* against cold and heat the hair is able to form a layer of air between the skin and the outside of the hair. This prevents rapid heat loss and assists the skin in maintaining the normal body temperature, i.e. 37°C., (98.4°F.), in cold conditions. In hot conditions the insulating effects of the hair operate by retaining the moist perspiration, which evaporates slowly, and cools the surface of the skin.

The sensitivity of the hair and skin to touch and pressure enables it to act as an excellent *warning system,* by which the movements or presence of foreign bodies or insects may be detected. The hairs of the ears, eyes and nose are particularly adapted to this function. As an insect nears these hairs there is an automatic response which results in it being brushed off. Vibrations of movements of these hairs quickly detect the possibility of attack from without.

Adornment may be described as another function of hair. Hair beauty concerns itself with the aesthetic arrangement of the hair and it is popularly known that a well-dressed person, with a good hair-do, feels good. The psychological aspects of hairdressing are therapeutically of value in the treatment of some mental conditions. Hairdressing may simply help to boost the confidence of the individual whose appearance affects the response of others. An untidy, unkempt head of hair does not encourage attraction or favourable encounter. On the other hand, a well-dressed head of hair is attractive and does something for the person and others around. Fortunately for hairdressing, young, old, sick and healthy people respond favourably to good hairdressing, and hair's function of adornment may well be another protective one.

3. Types of hair on the human body are: (*a*) the long, terminal hair of the scalp and face; (*b*) the short, bristle hairs of the nose, ears, eyebrows, eyelashes, and the hairs of the axillae, thorax, pubis, arms and legs; (*c*) the lanugo type of vellus hair which covers most other areas of the skin.

The largest amounts of hair are to be seen in the areas covering delicate underlying organs: the scalp hair which covers and protects the head and brain; the beard protecting the glands of the neck; the

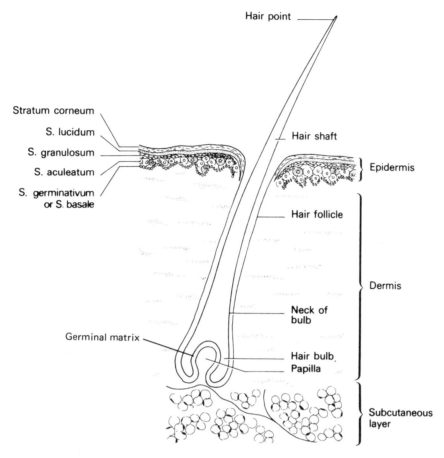

Fig. 12.1   Hair in skin

axillae hair of the armpits which protects the upper lobes of the lungs and the pubic hair covering the reproductive organs; the eyelashes or cilia, and the eyebrows or supercilia, protecting the eyes; the nostril hairs or vibrissae, and the hairs of the ears, protecting these entrances.

By the presence of hair in these particular areas, dust particles, small insects and water are prevented from entering the skin or body openings.

The absence of the fine downy covering of vellus or lanugo-type hair, from parts of the body without long hair, e.g. the female face, makes for a very harsh appearance. The softness afforded the contours of the face by vellus hair is an essential aspect of beauty.

4.   The parts of the hair (see p. 162). The conical shape of the bottom of the hair, growing in the skin, is called the *hair bulb,* and as this thins, the term *neck of the bulb* is used. The hair length is described as the *hair shaft,* which continues above skin level and terminates in the *hair point* or tip. The hair point of a new hair tapers, but when mature is made blunt by cutting. The root end of the hair should not be confused with the root of a plant. There are no fibrous roots on the conical rounding of the hair bulb. (Fig. 12.2).

The surface of the hair is called the *hair cuticle.* It is composed of flattened, squamous or epithelium cells, of hardened keratinous tissue. The cells are arranged in an overlapping, imbricated way like the tiles of a roof or the scales of a fish. The free ends of these cells are directed towards the hair point. This fact is used when determining the roots from the points of hair in boardwork. (Fig. 12.3).

The condition of the hair affects the positions of the cuticle cells, e.g. when the hair is very dry the cells lift or curl at the edges. This may cause interlocking and hair tangle when the hair is roughly treated or disturbed. The hair cuticle cell arrangement should be remembered when considering the hair follicle lining (see p. 163).

The cortex lies beneath the surface of the hair cuticle. The cortex cells are elongated, spindle- or cigar-shaped, and comprise the largest section of the hair. Melanin, the natural colour pigment of the hair,

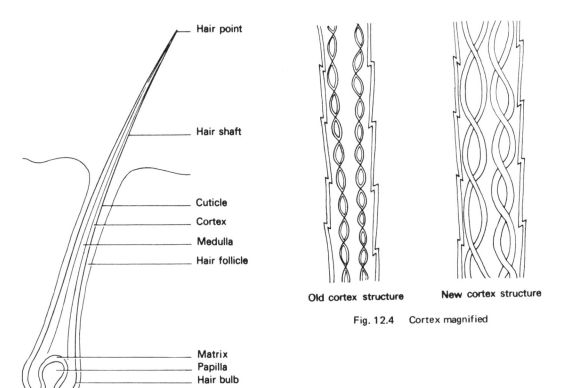

Fig. 12.2   Hair section showing cuticle, cortex and medulla

Fig. 12.4   Cortex magnified

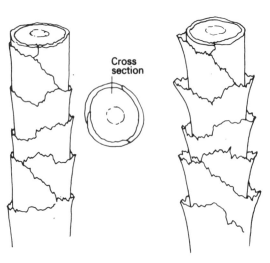

Fig. 12.3   Cuticle magnified

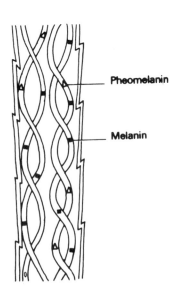

Fig. 12.5   Cortex — cell and colour arrangement

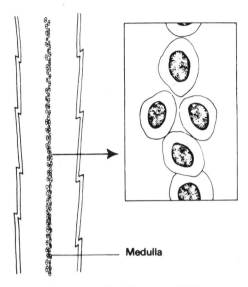

Medulla

Fig. 12.6   Medulla — magnified

is found in large quantities in the form of granules, both in and around the cortex cells. A colourless or white hair with little or no pigment may have a large number of air spaces in place of colour granules. The cortex is composed from the chemical protein keratin, which is formed from long chains of amino acids, on which perming reagents act. (Figs. 12.4 & 12.5).

The medulla is the central portion of the hair. It is composed of a number of small soft cells, interspersed with air spaces. The medulla is not always present in all hairs. The reason for this is not clear, but it seems that in human hair the medulla is thinner, and more often absent, than the thicker medulla, nearly always present in other mammalian or animal hair, and the lower the order of the animal, the more dominant the medulla becomes. In the absence of the medulla the cortex is enlarged and takes its place. When viewed under the microscope the medulla may appear as a thin line, continuous, broken or intermittent, and the colour pigment is clearly seen through the transparent cuticle. (Fig. 12.6).

The hair follicle is a tube-like indentation or elongated depression in the skin. It extends downwards, at an oblique angle, and is embedded in the dermis. The follicle contains that part of the hair below the surface of the skin. The follicle lining is structurally similar to the hair cuticle. It is composed of flattened, overlapping cells, with the free edges pointing towards the root, opposite to that of the hair cuticle. The imbricated lining of the follicle interlocks with the cuticle cells of the hair surface. It is by this means that the hair is firmly held in the follicle. This interlocking occurs in the lower part of the follicle only. Further up the follicle the walls part from the cuticle in the area where the sebaceous gland duct enters. (Fig. 12.7).

The follicle lining is composed of a surface which is in close and direct contact with the hair, Huxley's layer, and Henle's layer, i.e. distinct layers of cells, which together comprise the *inner root sheath.* Surrounding the inner root sheath is the *outer dermic root sheath,* i.e. layers of cells which correspond with the basal and papillary layers of the skin. These are enveloped with a glassy or *vitreous membrane.* The final layer of the outer root sheath is composed of elastic connective tissue which corresponds with the reticular layer of the dermis. The entire inner root sheath disappears further up the follicle. (Figs. 12.8 & 12.9).

The hair papilla, at the base of the hair follicle, is a cone-like bud which protrudes or extends upwards into the follicle. The hair papilla and *germinal matrix* are the growing points of the hair. It is from the papilla that the cells of the hair are produced and pushed upwards through the follicle. The lower part of the papilla produces hair cuticle cells, the sides produce

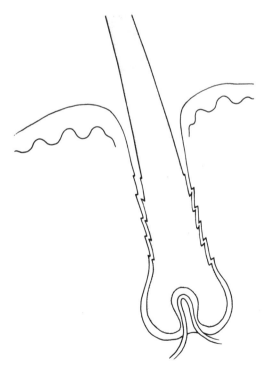

Fig. 12.7   Interlocking cuticle and follicle surfaces

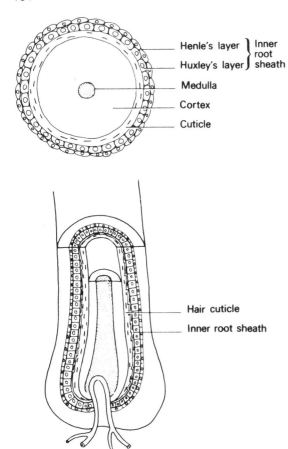

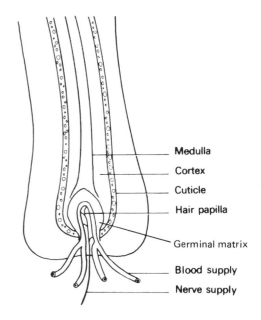

Fig. 12.10   Hair papilla

Fig. 12.8   Follicle holding hair below skin

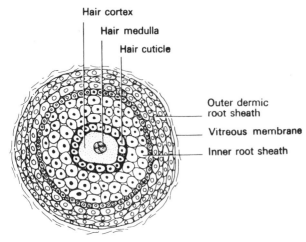

Fig. 12.9   Cuticle surface and follicle lining cell arrangement

the cortex, and the tip or top of the papilla produces the medullary cells. (Fig. 12.10).

The blood supply, both venous and arterial, enters the base of the papilla and supplies the necessary nutrients, removes waste products, and helps to maintain the chemical and cellular activities. The papilla is supplied with a network of nerves which, together with a band of nerves surrounding the follicle, constitutes the nerve supply to the hair and follicle.

The soft cells produced at the papilla are moulded by the follicle and become hardened or keratinized as they near the surface of the skin. Growth continues and the hardened pliable hair lengthens until development is complete. At this stage it remains only for the hair to fulfil its functions of protection and adornment, and then fall away.

The activity at the papilla and matrix, i.e. layers of cells surrounding the papilla, produces the colour pigment of hair. The melanocytes, i.e. cells containing melanin, are formed in this area and are interspersed between the cortex cells. When there are few or no melanocytes, grey or white hair results. This may occur after prolonged illness or disruption of the papillary workings. Although a sign of age, grey and white hair is present in very young people, and the reason for its presence is not fully understood. It is probably due to malfunctioning of the melanin-producing mechanism or chemical changes in the body of the papilla.

Colour change is produced as melanocytes enter the cortex at its formation stage and grow above the level of the skin. This accounts for the gradual darkening, or greying, of hair as the old is replaced by a different-coloured new hair. Colour change often occurs about the age of puberty when blonde hair changes to a darker shade. Since the growth and colour change of the hair is a gradual process, sudden blanching or 'going white overnight' is not possible. No doubt in cases of sudden shock, e.g. chemical explosions or bomb blast, the possibility of bleaching may occur.

5. **Follicle appendages** apart from the hair are: the sebaceous and sudoriferous glands, the hair muscle, the blood and lymph vessels, and the nerves supplying the follicle. (Fig. 12.11).

The sebaceous gland is situated in the dermis of the skin, adjoining the hair follicle. The gland is lobulated, resembling a bunch of grapes, and the opening of the gland, or the mouth of the gland duct, i.e. the tube carrying the gland's secretions, is at the middle of the upper third of the follicle. *Sebum,* the natural oil of the skin and hair, is produced in the gland body. It is contained in the lobules or sacs of the gland, and when secreted passes into the duct and follicle, and out on to the skin and hair. (Fig. 12.12).

The gloss and sheen associated with good hair condition is partly due to sebum, which lubricates the skin, makes the hair pliable and flexible, prevents dryness, splitting or cracking, and prevents water from entering the skin. Sebum, under normal conditions, has a slightly antiseptic action. It helps to prevent the growth of some bacteria and possible infection. This is thought to be due to the acid reaction of sebum. The term 'acid mantle of the skin' refers to this healthy covering of the skin and hair. Sebum has a *p*H value of less than 7, i.e. acid. Wax or cerumen of the ears is similar to the sebum of the skin. Wool fat is the sebum of sheep, i.e. lanolin.

If too much sebum is secreted the hair becomes lank and greasy. If allowed to accumulate and decompose, spots, pimples and blackheads may result, due to bacterial infection of the sebum, which could finally result in skin infection and breakdown. Too little sebum secreted results in dry, sore, cracked and possibly infected skin. This may occur when degreasing chemicals, e.g. some washing detergents, are repeatedly used. Poor personal hygiene, e.g. not washing regularly, causes bad odour due to decomposing sebum.

The sudoriferous or sweat gland is a coiled ball of tubes or ducts, called the *glomerulus,* situated in the dermis. The gland duct, through which the sweat travels, is a long spiralling tube which opens at the surface of the skin. This surface opening is called a *skin pore.* Sweat is mainly composed of water, but salt and other materials, e.g. urea and mineral salts, may be present. In normal circumstances the amount of mineral salts and waste matter in sweat is small, and normal secretions assist the skin's function of

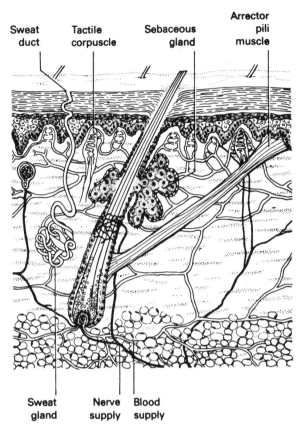

Fig. 12.11   General skin and hair diagram

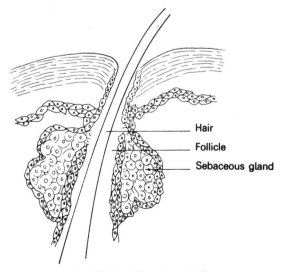

Fig. 12.12   Sebaceous gland

maintaining the correct body temperature. In abnormal circumstances the content of sweat is high with waste products, e.g. in times of stress or sickness, when the body's excretory organs are not able to cope. (Fig. 12.13).

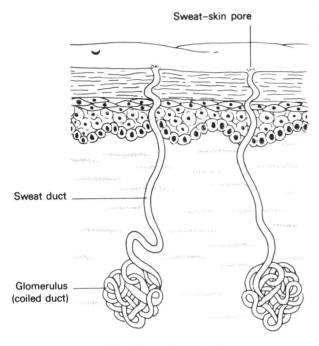

Fig. 12.13   Sweat glands

Sweat glands are both *secretory,* i.e. they produce substances within the body of the gland which are passed out, and *excretory,* i.e. waste products from the body pass through the gland and out on to the skin.

There are two types of sweat glands: the *eccrine,* which are small and secretory, are found all over the body, but the larger *apocrine* secretory and excretory glands are found mainly associated with hair follicles.

Sweat fulfils its cooling effect by the principle of evaporation. Sweat is formed in beads of water and as the liquid evaporates the temperature of the skin and body is lowered. If allowed to accumulate and decompose, bad odour and possible disease result.

The hair muscle is called the *arrectores pilorum* or *arrector pili.* It is attached to the hair follicle and the underlying surface of the epidermis. It is a small involuntary muscle, i.e. not purposefully moved at will, which on contraction raises the follicle and hair to an upright position. The muscle lies at the same oblique angle in the skin as the hair follicle. In cold weather the muscles contract which causes the characteristic 'goose pimple or flesh' on the skin. The elevation of the hair helps to contain an insulating layer of warm air around the skin, preventing heat

loss from the body. In times of stress or danger the arrector pili muscles are stimulated and the hairs stand upright, a protective function more commonly seen in animals than humans, e.g. the coat of a cat will rise to form a protective barrier when threatened by another animal.

'Hair ache'. If the hair is not combed or stimulated, the blood flow and tissue around the arrector pili muscle becomes restricted or 'cramped'. This causes discomfort and pain, particularly in the fine skin of an older person. Anything that restricts the hair in one position for a length of time, e.g. lacquer, hair fixatives, or rigid hair styles, may cause hair ache. This may occur when the hair has been parted and worn in one position and then changed; the hair is said to 'hurt' when moved. Light stimulation or massage should ease the discomfort of hair ache.

6. The blood supply to and from the hair follicle is via small vessels situated at the base of the hair follicle. There is no direct supply to the hair other than through the papilla. The blood carries to the papilla the nutrient supply for hair and follicle growth, and the transfer of these nutrients takes place in the papilla, where they are utilized by the cellular activity within.

Waste products are transferred back to the blood stream through small venous capillaries. If the nutrient supply is interfered with by abnormality, e.g. illness, starvation or radioactivity, a variation in hair structure, cessation of growth or papillary activity could result. Variation of the hair in thickness, texture and natural colour can only arise from changes occurring during the formation stage of hair growth.

The main *blood vessel of the head* is the common carotid artery, which subdivides into the internal and external carotid arteries. The internal lies deep in the tissues of the neck, and supplies the brain, eyes and other parts of the head with blood. The external subdivides into the facial, temporal and occipital branches. The facial branch supplies blood to tissues of the face. The temporal and occipital branches, after further subdivisions, reach the capillary stage, e.g. minute hairlike vessels, and supply the dermis, hair follicles and hair papillae with blood.

The blood is returned to the heart by means of small venules, i.e. minute vessels or veins, which lead to the external and internal branches of the jugular veins. The internal branch carries blood from the deeper parts of the head, and the external branch carries blood from the scalp and hair follicles. The main jugular veins are situated in the sides of the neck; they receive the blood from the head and carry it back to the heart. (Fig. 12.14 a & b).

7. The nerve supply of the hair and follicle is situated at the papilla and above the hair bulb surrounding the follicle. Each of the follicle

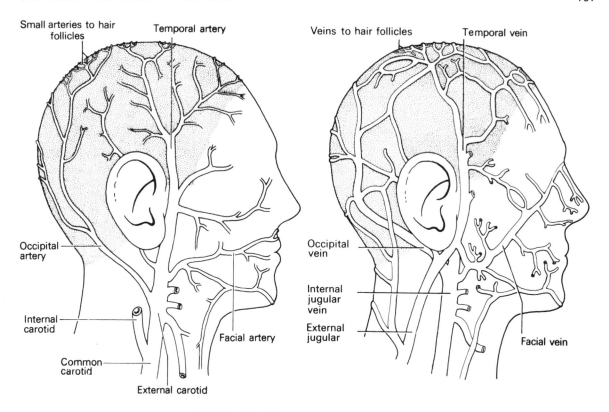

Fig. 12.14(a) — (b)   Blood supply to the head

appendages, except the hair itself, has its own nerve supply.

The main nerves of the scalp and head originate in the brain and the cervical region, i.e. the neck, and the spinal column. There are twelve pairs of cranial nerves, i.e. nerves from the brain, and eight pairs of cervical nerves. The fifth, seventh and eleventh pairs of cranial nerves are the most important as far as the head and scalp are concerned.

The fifth cranial nerve, called the trigeminal, is a mixed, i.e. motor and sensory, nerve which conveys impulses to and from the brain and body tissues. It divides into three main branches, the *ophthalmic* which supplies the eyes, eyelids and tear glands, the *maxillary* which supplies the forehead, temples and sides of the face, and the *mandibular* which serves the muscles of the lower jaw and cheek.

The seventh cranial nerve, called the facial nerve, is a mixed motor and sensory nerve which supplies the face, tongue and palate.

The eleventh cranial nerve, called the spinal accessory, is a motor nerve which supplies the neck muscles and deeper structures of the head.

The cervical nerves, mainly parts of the second and third, supply the scalp, back of the head, ears and neck with motor and sensory nerve endings. Branching out from these main nerves are sub-divisions of very fine nerve fibres which branch out to form junctions in the subcutaneous tissue of the skin. These supply the hair papilla and the lower part of the hair follicle. Other similar junctions supply the upper parts of the hair follicle and the dermis. (Fig. 12.15).

8. Hair structure — new theory. Recent advances in photo-micrography, i.e. the art of producing large pictures of microscopic objects, have begun to reveal another version of the structure of hair. It is not generally known just how this affects existing theories of perming, colouring and other aspects of hairdressing.

The hair cuticle is now thought to comprise curved scales which overlap one another. There are approximately three to the complete circle, or circumference of the hair, and there appears to be a series of cuticle layers.

The cortex consists of long 'cable bundles', i.e. long lengths of cables intertwined to form bundle units. Each of these cables are themselves bundles of smaller cables, which in turn divide yet again to form even smaller units of cable bundles. These are

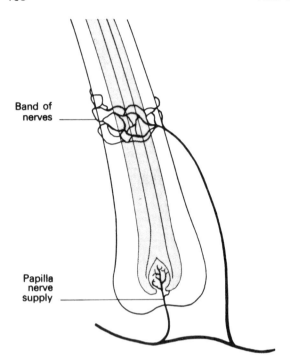

Fig. 12.15   Nerve supply of hair and follicle

respectively referred to as micro-cables, photo-cables, and the smallest units as proto-cables, which are composed of amino acids. The cable system within the cortex is continuous, branching and sub-branching from the larger to the smaller cables. The pigment appears to be distributed as was originally thought.

The medulla appears to be a soft mass of cables resembling spaghetti. The loops of the soft cables appear to form air spaces.

Throughout each section of the hair, generally composed of hard and soft keratin, there now appears an inter-tissue malleable material called 'hair putty'. This apparently forms a large part of the weight of hair. When the putty is destroyed the hair disintegrates and falls apart.

It now seems that the chain-link system, the conversion of cystine to cysteine, and the cigar-shaped cells of the cortex, will be reconsidered in the light of this and no doubt further research.

Revision test 1

Q. 1   Describe the purpose, function, classifications and uses of hair.
Q. 2   List the appendages of the hair follicle and fully describe two of them.
Q. 3   Fully describe the muscle attachment to the hair and its functions.
Q. 4   How does the hair grow?
Q. 5   How and where are the colour pigment cells produced? Describe how hair receives its colour.
Q. 6   Describe the blood and nerve supply to and from the follicle.
Q. 7   What are the sebaceous glands? Where are they situated and what do they do?
Q. 8   What is the relation between the hair cuticle and the follicle lining of the inner root sheath?
Q. 9   Name and describe the functions of the sweat glands.
Q.10   Briefly describe each of the following terms:
        (a) Hair ache. (b) Vibrissae. (c) 'Acid mantle'. (d) Melanin. (e) Glomerulus.

Revision test 2

Complete the following sentences:

1   Name three main classifications of hair found in the different races of the world: (a) ...., (b) ...., (c) ....
2   The follicle lining is composed of the surface and .... and .... layers which together comprise the .... root sheath. Surrounding this is the ....
3   The growing point of the hair is called the ....
4   The cells which contain colour are called ...., and are interspersed between the cells of the ....
5   The .... gland secretes sweat, and the gland which produces natural oil is called the .... gland.

6   Two types of sweat glands are called .... and ....
7   The hair muscle is called the .... and its contraction may cause the hair to ....
8   Name two main blood vessels and two main nerves supplying the scalp or head:
     (a) ...., (b) ...., (c)........................, (d) ....
9   The sweat duct opening at the skin surface is called a ...., and the main contents of sweat
     are .... and ....
10   The bottom of the hair is called the .... which surrounds the ....

Revision test 3

Complete each of the following sentences with the word or words listed below:

Cortex. Cuticle. Medulla. Papilla. Hair bulb. Lanolin. Cerumen. Sweat gland. Oil gland. Arrector pili.

1   The hair surface is called the ...., and the central portion of the hair is called the
     ....
2   The hair grows from the .... which is situated at the base of the hair and protrudes into the
     ....
3   Sebum is the secretion of the .... gland. Wool fat, the sebum of sheep, is called
     .... The wax of the ears is called ....
4   When there is no medulla its place is taken by the ....
5   The sudoriferous gland is the name given to the .... gland.
6   'Hair ache' may be caused when there is restriction of the blood flow and the ....

Vocabulary

Adornment	Ornamentative or decorative.
Arrectores pilorum	Names given to the hair muscle.
Arrector pili	
Capillaries	Very small arterial vessels.
Carotid artery	A main artery of the head.
Caucasian hair	Wavy or straight European hair.
Cerumen	Wax secreted by ceruminous glands in ears.
Cervical nerves	Eight pairs, from neck portion of spine.
Cranial nerves	Twelve pairs, from the underside of brain.
Eccrine	Names given to the sweat glands.
Apocrine	
Sudoriferous	
Epithelium	Cellular tissue.
Glomerulus	The main body of the sweat gland.
Hair papilla	The growing point at the bottom of the follicle.
Inner root sheath	Follicle lining, follicle surface cuticle composed of Huxley's and Henle's layers.
Jugular vein	The main vein of the head or neck.
Keratin	Elastic tissue composed of polypeptide amino acids; allows hair stretch.
Keratinous	Containing keratin.
Lanolin	Wool fat or sebum of sheep.
Lanugo hair	The soft, downy hair of the unborn child.
Mammalian	Pertaining to mammals which carry, feed and nurture their young.
Matrix	The upper part of the papilla.
Melanocytes	Cells containing melanin, natural pigment.
Mongoloid hair	Straight lank hair of the American Indian.
Negroid hair	Tight kinky hair.
Outer dermic root sheath	Basal, papillary and vitreous membrane layers of outer follicle lining.

Sebum	Secretion of sebaceous gland, natural oil.
Squamous	Layered.
Terminal hair	Long hairs of the scalp and face.
Trichology	The science and study of hair.
Vellus hair	Lanugo-type hair present on parts of the body, e.g. the female face.
Venules	Very small subdivisions of veins.

The Hair and Skin—The Skin

8. The skin is the external or outer covering of the body and one of the largest and most important organs. It contains a number of appendages, i.e. things part of or near to it, and protects the delicate organs and tissues below. Contained in the skin are the hairs, hair follicles, the sebaceous and sudoriferous glands, muscles, blood and lymph vessels, nerves and sensory organs. (Fig. 12.16)

The *functions* of skin are: protection, heat control, secretion and excretion, sensation and absorption.

The skin protects the body by producing extra colour pigment to prevent harmful rays of the sun damaging or burning underlying tissue, e.g. sun tanning. It forms a bacterial barrier and prevents infection, and a resilient tough covering, which even when cut or torn repairs itself.

The extremes of heat and cold are regulated by the normal hair function, the arrectores pilorum and sudoriferous glands, which help to maintain the body temperature.

Secretion and excretion is maintained by the sebaceous and sudoriferous glands through which the secretions and waste products are conveyed when passing through the skin.

The sense organs are the dermal papillae or touch tactile corpuscles which lie immediately under the top layer of the skin. Dermal papillae are well supplied with many nerve endings which enable the stimuli and responses of the body to take place. Separate touch corpuscles convey the sensations of heat, cold, pain and touch.

The skin absorbs little except that of a greasy or oily nature. The depth of absorption is limited but newer chemicals have deeper, penetrating qualities. Moisture or water is rejected by the waterproofing effects of sebum.

9. Parts of the skin. The skin is composed of several layers of cells; the lower the layer the more active the cells, and the top layer of the skin is the final result of the cellular activity below.

The epidermis is the surface, outermost or external, covering of the skin, and is divided into several layers or strata. The top skin surface is called the *stratum corneum* and is composed of hard, horny

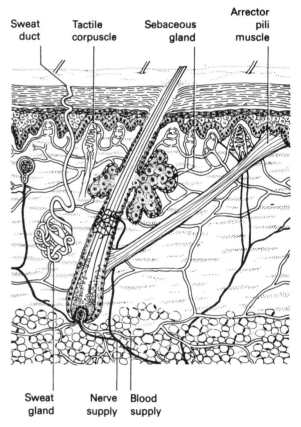

Sweat duct · Tactile corpuscle · Sebaceous gland · Arrector pili muscle

Sweat gland · Nerve supply · Blood supply

Fig. 12.16   Skin section, magnified

or cornified, non-nucleated cells arranged in an overlapping manner. There is little elasticity or colour in these cells, and the uppermost are in the process of falling from the skin. When the skin is wrapped in plaster or bandage for a long time the dead cells may be clearly seen on its removal as white flakes or strips of dead tissue. It is this part of the skin that is constantly being washed, rubbed or worn away.

The next discernable layer, below the corneum, is the *stratum lucidum,* which consists of layers of clear colourless cells. Sunlight penetrates through to the layers below and activates temporary skin colouring.

The *stratum granulosum* lies beneath the lucidum, and is composed of layers of granulated cells which are softer than the hard cells above.

The *stratum aculeatum* is an accumulation of cells undergoing change in structure and activity. It is known as the stratum spinosum, stratum mucosum, the rete mucosum, the prickle cell layer and the Malpighian layer. The upper cells of this layer are similar to the granule cells above, which they eventually become as they grow upwards. Below these are the prickle, spiny cells, which are nucleated and part of the growing area of the epidermis. Beneath the prickle cell layer is the stratum mucosum or Malpighian layer where colour pigment or skin colouring is found.

The *stratum germinativum* is the germinating layer of the epidermis. It is composed of larger, nucleated, keratinous cells, columnar in shape, which form a clearly shaped line along the undulating bottom of the epidermis. It is sometimes called the stratum basale, i.e. the base layer, or the growth layer, and together with the stratum Malpighii, the Malpighian layer. The cells of this germinating layer are living and active and form the varying layers and cell structures above. The stratum germinativum is the underlying growth sector surrounding the hair follicle and appendages.

There is no blood or nerve supply to the epidermis and all nutriment supplies are from the dermis below. The epidermis is formed of epithelium or epithelial tissue which is composed of flattened, cylindrical, columnar and squamous cells in one or more layers.

The dermis is the largest layer in the skin and abundantly supplied with blood and nerve vessels from which the epidermis receives its supply. The dermis, sometimes called the true skin, corium or cutis, contains the lymphatics, i.e. vessels of the lymphatic system which work closely with the blood system, and in the upper region the nerve endings of the tactile cells or papillae, i.e. those responsible for sensations of touch, heat, cold and pain.

The dermis is composed of fibrous connective tissue, i.e. the binding tissue of the body. The upper layers of the dermis are called the *papillary layer,* and the lower are called the *reticular layer,* i.e. an open, loose network of cells.

Underlying the dermis is the *subcutaneous tissue,* sometimes called the sub-cutis, which is composed of loose cellular and fatty or adipose tissue. This part of the skin serves as a storehouse for fat and gives firmness and roundness to the body contours, as well as assisting in temperature regulation and acting as a protective cushion.

The different layers of the skin tend to merge into one another but there are distinct differences between the epithelium of the epidermis, the connective tissue of the dermis, and the adipose tissue of the sub-cutis. The skin, in a normally healthy state, will resist poisonous substances, but if broken it may readily absorb them into the blood stream, resulting in body infections.

10. The scalp is the hairy covering of the upper part of the head, and extends from the forehead, above the ears, to the nape. It is composed of the epidermis, dermis, sub-cutis, and the *epicranial aponeurosis,* i.e. a sheet of tendon covering the head, which together form the movable or flexible part of the head covering. The muscle part of the scalp is called the epicranius or the occipito frontalis, which originates from the occiput and frontal bones of the skull, with its insertion in the aponeurosis. Between the epicranial aponeurosis and the bones of the cranium is a sheet of connective tissue.

11. The skull is the bony case or shape of the head, or cranium. It is composed of eight bones: the occipital, the frontal, two parietal, two temporal, an ethmoid and a sphenoid, which articulate to form sutures, i.e. bony seams or junctions. The two soft spots on a newly born baby's head are due to the spaces between the bones, called fontanelles, which close up to form sutures as the baby grows. These are called the anterior fontanelle which takes the longest to close, and the posterior fontanelle which closes within the first two or three months of birth.

The lower part of the head, the face, is composed of fourteen facial bones: two maxillae, a mandible, two turbinal, two malar, two palatal, two nasal, two lachrymal and a vomer. (Fig. 12.17).

12. Hair growth. In the unborn child the formation of hair in the skin initially takes place by the downgrowth of epidermis and an upgrowth and cellular activity in the area to become the papilla. The epidermis continues to grow down and the cells from the papilla move up until the first follicle is complete. The first hair is then formed, which is a lanugo or vellus type, and soon discarded, before or soon after birth. The following hair takes the clearly recognized form it is to retain throughout life, and is replaced time and time again, until no more can be produced by the follicle.

Replacement of hair takes place periodically; as one hair is formed it grows, develops, remains in the skin up to six or seven years, and then falls, normally to be replaced by another. The life of an individual hair varies, subject to variations in the body and the mechanical activities and external factors inflicted on it.

The growing stage of hair is called the *anagen* stage of growth and varies from a few months to several years; it is during these stages that the length, thickness and texture of hair are determined. (Fig. 12.18).

The next stage is called the *catogen* period in which no further growth of hair takes place but cellular activity continues at the papilla. The bulb

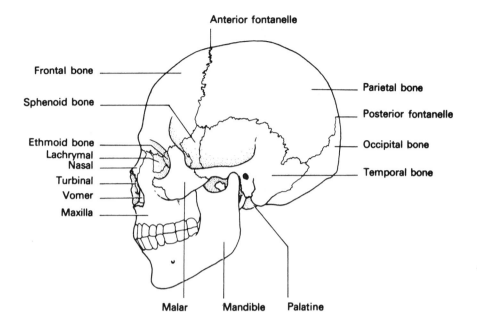

Fig. 12.17   Skull and face bones

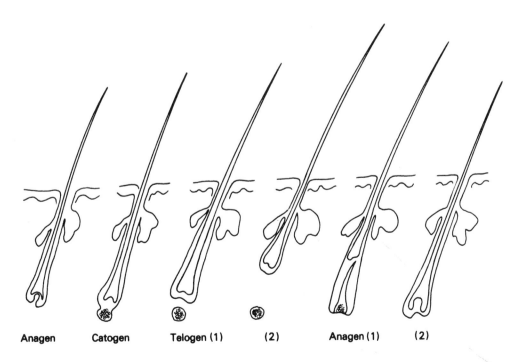

Fig. 12.18   Anagen, catogen and telogen growth stages

gradually separates from the papilla and a mass of tissue surrounds the brushlike bulb. If the hair is pulled out at this stage it appears clubbed with an irregular rounding of the bulb. The hair remains but slowly moves up the follicle.

The final stage is called the *telogen* or resting stage in which there is no further hair or papilla growth. The follicle begins to shrink, becomes smaller and separates from the papilla area. This resting stage does not last long and towards the end of the telogen period the follicle begins to grow down again. At the same time the papilla becomes more active, the old hair is moved further up the follicle towards the surface, and a new hair is formed at the new or regenerated papilla. This begins the next anagen stage, and either the new hair pushes up alongside the old, or the two remain in the same follicle for a short period.

The *activation* for the growth of new hair is not as yet entirely clear. It is thought that germinating cells are passed down from the old hair to the papilla which activates the growth of new hair. There appears to be a simultaneous growth of the follicle and the new papilla as in the beginning of first growth in the unborn child.

After the telogen or resting stage a new growth takes place and, at an uneven rate, replaces the old. In some animals there is a more even rate of development; they moult or lose a large part of their hair which is then replaced. In humans this does not happen, or there would be a stage where everyone would be bald, or partly bald, for a period.

The growth of hair is influenced or determined by: good health and diet, age and sex, hormone balance, heredity factors, climate, physical conditions and disease.

Health and diet. In normal health hair will form, grow, develop, finally fall out and be replaced, and to maintain good health a balanced diet is necessary. Deviation from a normal diet affects the supply of necessary nutrients to the papilla and the growth of hair. If any of the essential vitamins or food materials required for normal metabolism are absent, then normal hair development will be affected.

A normal, balanced diet consists of the following: *Protein,* a source of energy found in lean meat, fish, cheese, eggs and milk. *Fats,* both animal and vegetable, which may be stored in the body as fuel and are derived from meat, eggs, fish oil and nuts. *Carbohydrates,* in the form of starch and sugars, are derived from bread, potatoes, beans, cereals, honey, glucose and fruits. *Minerals* which form part of the body fluids and assist regulation of cellular activity are chloride, sodium, phosphorous, potassium, iodine, sulphur, magnesium, as well as other trace elements. These are derived from table salt, milk, eggs, cheese, herrings, edible seaweed, fish, liver, sprats, figs and red meats. *Vitamins* are derived from animal fats,

fruit, vegetables and fish, e.g. vitamin C or ascorbic acid in fresh fruits, and assist body functions, development and maintenance.

Age and sex. As the body ages the essential functions tend to slow down and skin loses its elasticity and becomes drier. This causes the characteristic 'crow's feet' wrinkles at the corners of the eyes. There is a pattern of hair fall or baldness which comes with old age, but this is not necessarily a symptom. The chemical secretions of the body which help to determine and maintain the sex of a person are associated with the growth of hair and skin cells.

These chemicals, known as *hormones,* are produced by a system of *ductless glands,* i.e. the endocrine or glands of internal secretion. These glands do not have ducts but pass their secretions directly into the blood stream, e.g. the thyroid and parathyroids, the thymus, pituitary, adrenals and gonads. The hormones produced by these glands are likened to chemical messengers or regulators. In contrast the *duct glands,* e.g. the sebaceous, sudoriferous and salivary glands, have tubes, canals or ducts through which the secretions are passed out of the skin.

Heredity effects on hair growth are varied and interesting; parents with good hair may have offspring with poor hair and vice versa. There appears to be no direct set pattern, yet parents pass on their own inherited factors, derived from their parents and so on, which allows a great variation of possible inherited factors. A person of good health may be inclined towards a particular pattern of baldness because father, grandfather or great-grandfather displayed it, but this does not mean that it will develop or that it has been passed on with all the other factors concerned, e.g. environment, type of diet, general attitude, knowledge, etc. Provided inherited aspects of good physical and mental health are assured, any abnormal tendencies may be corrected or prevented.

Climate and seasons, particularly extremes of climate, affect the normal working of the body and hair growth. There appears to be a seasonal change in hair growth, and spring and/or autumn are times when there may be greater hair fall. During the summer there is a faster growth rate which slows down during the winter. In many people there is no noticeable change. Some skin diseases display a noticeable difference in symptoms in summer and winter. The greatest effects of climatic and seasonal factors are probably the changes in environment and diet which result from them.

Some of the effects of *physical conditions* or treatment, e.g. combing, brushing, etc., have been discussed, but the restrictions of tight caps or hats, or any other abnormal restriction of the blood vessels, will prevent satisfactory functioning for hair growth. When this is accompanied by excessive sweating, tension, possibly fear, then other factors of major importance are involved. If postiche is too heavy, worn too long, or not cleaned regularly, the results of wear, tear and poor hygiene are soon noticed.

Disease has a direct effect on the skin and hair, e.g. fevers, blood and stomach disorders, and the results of prolonged illness affect normal body functioning. The after-effects of some illnesses and diseases may be permanent on the hair and skin, but generally once the body returns to normal health the hair will function and regenerate normally.

The effects of disease or ill health on the hair are not noticeable until months after, since variations of the hair shaft above the skin surface occur during the growing or development stage below the skin, e.g. the effect of present illness may affect hair now being produced at the papilla which will take time to grow and appear above the surface of the skin.

13. Hair shape is determined in the anagen stage of hair growth by the shape of the follicle and papilla and the effects on it when forming. (Fig. 12.19).

The follicle, normally slanting in the skin, may turn, bend or twist and the hair growing through may be formed to fit these convolutions, and instead of a straight length of hair a twisted shape may be produced.

The shape of the budlike papilla produces the cells which form hair, and if this shape is more rounded on one side than the other, the resultant hair will be elongated on one side more than the other. When hair is set it is stretched on the outer and contracted on the inner side, which produces the bend or curl. If hair naturally forms with the longitudinal lengths of the sides differing, then it will bend to the shorter side to produce natural curl.

The cross-section or diameter of hair may be round, oval or kidney-shaped. The hair will curl more easily if its diameter is oval or kidney-shaped, and is more likely to be straight if the diameter is round, but this is not the determining factor; it is determined by the formation of the hair when growing.

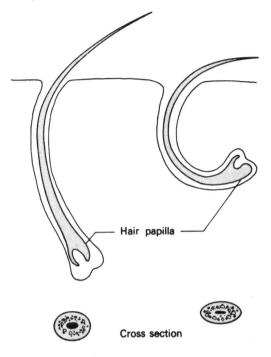

Fig. 12.19   Hair shape — curly hair

The effects of internal and external factors on the hair are many and complicated. Effects of radio-activity are marked on hair shape and formation, and the psychological effects on hair in health and disease are too numerous for consideration here.

A more complete understanding of the structure and growth of hair and skin, which are part of the general functions of the body, may be achieved by a detailed study of the systems of the body, e.g. the skeletal, muscular, nerve, lymph and blood, digestive, respiratory, reproductive and endocrine systems, in addition to that of hair and skin.

Revision test 1

Q. 1   Describe the skin, its appendages, functions and uses.
Q. 2   Describe the differences between the scalp and skull.
Q. 3   How does hair grow? Name the stages of hair growth.
Q. 4   What influences or determines the growth of hair?
Q. 5   How is the shape of hair determined?
Q. 6   Describe the different layers of the skin.
Q. 7   What should a balanced diet contain and why?
Q. 8   Name the bones of the skull and face.
Q. 9   What are the glands of internal secretion?
Q.10   Briefly describe each of the following terms:
(*a*) Tactile corpuscles. (*b*) Curly hair. (*c*) Diet. (*d*) Trichology. (*e*) Fontanelles.

Revision test 2

Complete the following sentences:

1   Name six bones of the skull:
    (a) ...., (b) ...., (c) ...., (d) ...., (e) ....,
    (f) ....
2   Name the five layers of the epidermis:
    (a) ...., (b) ...., (c) ...., (d) ...., (e) ....
3   The different stages of hair growth are called:
    (a) ...., (b) ...., (c) ....
4   The upper layers of the dermis are called ...., and the lower layers are called ....
5   Name the different sections or layers of the scalp:
    (a) ...., (b) ...., (c) ...., (d) ...., (e) ....
6   Articulating edges of skull bones form .... The 'soft spots' on a baby's head are called
    ....
7   The appendages of the skin are:
    (a) ...., (b) ...., (c) ....

Revision test 3

Complete the following sentences with the word or words listed below:

Connective tissue. Epithelial. Adipose tissue. Malpighian layer. Touch organs. Hair. Anagen. Arrector pili.
Sweat glands. Telogen.

1   The epidermis is composed of ...., the dermis is mainly composed of ...., and
    the sub-cutis layer is composed of ....
2   The tactile corpuscles or .... lie beneath the epidermis, and detect heat, cold and pain.
3   The natural colour pigment of the skin is formed in the ....
4   Three appendages of the skin are ...., ... and ....
5   The active growing stage of hair is called ...., and the resting period is called ....

Vocabulary

Adipose tissue	Tissue containing fatty globules and fat cells, found in the sub-cutis.
Fatty tissue	
Anagen	The active growing stage of hair growth.
Aponeurosis	A tendon underlying the scalp.
Catagen	A stage of hair growth when cellular activity ceases or slows down.
Connective tissue	The binding tissue of the body.
Convolutions	Twisting or coiling together.
Dermis	The true skin below the epidermis.
Corium	
Cutis	
Duct glands	Glands with ducts or tubes through which secretions pass.
Ductless glands	Secretions pass directly into the blood.
Endocrine	Internally secreting, a ductless gland.
Epidermis	Top part or surface of the skin.
Epithelial tissue	Tissue or cells covering cutaneous or mucous membranes or surfaces.
Hormone	Secretion of an endocrine gland.
Lymphatics	Part of the blood system. Fluid lymph is carried by lymphatics or vessels to lymph glands and into the blood.
Papillary layer	Tightly packed cells of upper dermis, containing tactile corpuscles.
Reticular layer	Loosely packed lower dermis layers.

Scalp	Flexible, movable covering of the head.
Skull	The bony case or cranium.
Squamous	Terms of epithelial cells or tissue.
Columnar	
Stratum	Layer, often abbreviated to S.
S. corneum	
S. lucidum	
S. granulosum	Layers of the epidermis.
S. aculeatum	
S. germinativum	
Subcutaneous	Tissue below the dermis.
Sub-cutis	
Tactile corpuscles	Nerve endings in the dermis, responsible for feelings of heat, cold, pain, touch.
Organs of touch	
Dermal papillae	
Telogen	Resting stage of hair growth.
Trichologist	One learned and practised in trichology.
Trichology	The science and study of the hair.

Chapter Thirteen

Hair Care

1. Hair care, conditioning or reconditioning are commonly used terms which refer to methods of caring for the hair so that it reflects a normal, healthy appearance. Hair care is a fundamental aspect of hairdressing; if the state of hair is poor, good hairdressing will not be shown to advantage. The beauty of healthy hair, in suitable style and shape, is pleasing to wear and be seen.

2. The condition or state of the hair is affected by external physical treatment and atmospheric influences, chemical effects of hairdressing processes, and the internal functions of the body, in particular the aspects of hair growth.

External factors. In normal health the hair is subjected to many 'normal' treatments, e.g. hair management, which will, if not correctly carried out, adversely affect the hair (see Chapter 2). Unless the client, who deals with her hair several times a day, is informed of correct hair management techniques, this alone could be the main cause for poor hair condition. Good hair grooming is a continuous application of correct techniques.

Atmospheric influences. The normal wear and tear and effects of the sun and wind may dry out the surface of the hair and skin. This may cause hair conditions which are neither manageable nor pleasing to look at. Extremes of climate, e.g. hot dry or humid, and cold dry or wet, have their effects. Slightly wavy hair in dry warm climates may become straight and limp in colder wet climates and may require perming. The moisture content of the atmosphere is one of the main reasons for this and will affect the pliability and elasticity of the hair.

The chemical and physical processes of hair-dressing, e.g. perming, bleaching, tinting, rely on the penetration of the hair structure and alteration of the natural state of hair, which affects it externally and internally. This may result in chemical imbalance or physical disruption which affects both its condition and appearance. Overprocessing, e.g. overbleaching, overtinting or overperming, will in some cases break the hair cuticle and cause the hair to become porous, dry, and difficult to manage or process further.

Internal functions of the body, e.g. factors of hair growth, in health and disease, will affect hair condition. A poor, unbalanced diet affects the health of the body just as it produces varying conditions of the hair and skin. Abnormal functioning of the organs or systems of the body may ultimately affect the hair and skin. Drugs or treatment of disease or illness may have their effects on the hair and its reaction to further processing. The hair of women in pregnancy, which is often at its best, may deteriorate in condition after the birth of the baby. There are many reasons for this, and the initial stress and strain of adapting to the caring of the child are among them.

Psychological factors which may affect the internal functions of the body may arise, for many reasons, to affect normal hair state. These may be concerned with aesthetic aspects of appearance, e.g. worrying about one's looks, arising from poor hair condition, or for reasons of insecurity which may affect hair condition.

Ill-health and disease or internal cause of poor hair condition should not be overlooked, and may be recognized by the thoughtful hairdresser. The treatment of abnormal hair states due to internal causes, by those unqualified to do so, may result in aggravating the condition, and possibly the spread of infection. It is for the medical practitioner or doctor to assess the cause of abnormal body states and not for the hairdresser to diagnose or treat.

The scalp should be examined for any rash, spots, sores, breaks in the skin or other signs of disease which prohibit the use of conditioners or conditioning treatments. Any client displaying signs or symptoms of disease should be referred to the doctor. This must always be done tactfully, and if first noticed by a junior or young hairdresser, the senior, manager or manageress should be immediately informed, before any comment is made to the client.

3. Determining the condition of the hair is not always a simple matter. It may be dry, broken, and greasy at the roots. This could be due to harsh brushing with hard bristles, which has torn the cuticle causing it to dry, at the same time stimulating the sebaceous glands. It may have been chemically overprocessed recently, causing the hair lengths to become dry and porous.

The scalp may suggest possible reasons for the hair

state. By feeling the skin surface, particularly on the hairlines and above the ears, greasiness or dryness may be noted, which may be due to natural secretions or other products. The hair lengths and points, if closely examined, may suggest poor treatments and processes that it may have been subjected to. The hair type should be noted and its lank, greasy, dry, spongy or springy resilience considered.

The client should be asked what difficulties she has encountered when dealing with her hair. She may have recently returned from holiday where the hair had been exposed to the effects of sun, salt and sand. It may be that the client has been sick and not had the time to attend to her hair.

After the scalp has been thoroughly examined, the absence or presence of any abnormal signs noted, and the state of the hair determined, then consideration may be given to rectifying the condition of the hair.

4. Conditioners are chemically composed substances designed to improve some conditions of the hair. They may be in liquid or cream form, or incorporated in shampoos, setting agents or other products. Some are designed to be used alone or with other agents, and to deal with a certain special condition, e.g. dry or greasy hair. Most will add shine and gloss to the hair, and enable it to be more pliable and hold wave and curl, or become easier to manage and process.

The type of conditioner to use is determined by the hair condition, e.g. brittle, limp, frizzed or overprocessed, etc., and in such a condition that the hair appears dull, does not retain a set or colourings and is generally difficult to manage.

5. Types of conditioners may be of the surface or penetrating kind, or with the properties of both.

Surface or external conditioners usually add gloss and ease hair management. They do not penetrate the hair but achieve their purpose by smoothing or coating the hair surface, or chemically neutralizing the effects of previously used chemicals, e.g. shampoos, tints, bleaches.

Those commonly used are: dressing creams and oils, reconditioning lotions or creams, and acid or rehabilitating rinses, which may be applied to the hair before, during or after treatments. These substances may contain lanolin, cholesterol, vegetable and mineral oils, fats, waxes, lecithin, citric, acetic and lactic acids.

Penetrating or internal conditioners enter the hair shaft by capillary action, i.e. passage of materials through the cellular spaces of the hair structure. These are designed to replace chemically, repair or form chemical attachments where the cross-links of the keratin structure in the cortex have been destroyed or left unconnected through normal or excessive chemical or physical actions of previous processes. These conditioners smooth the cuticle and

add resilience to the whole structure and may contain sulphur compounds, quaternary ammonium products, alcohol, and may be mixed with other surface-acting conditioners. (Fig. 13.1).

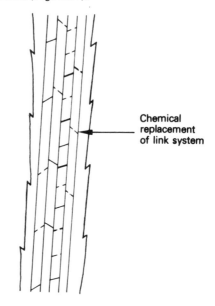

Chemical replacement of link system

Fig. 13.1   Penetrating conditioners — capillary action

Both the surface and penetrating conditioners may be combined with bactericides and fungicides to prevent the growth of or kill bacteria and fungi present on the hair and skin. These include tar derivatives, formalin, hexachlorophene and other suitable disinfectants.

Most modern conditioners contain carefully blended substances which achieve their effects by chemically balancing the hair structure, and the effects on it, particularly the acidity or alkalinity of its surface, i.e. its pH. The anionic, cationic, non-ionic and amphoteric properties of chemical combinations, and their actions on the surface of the hair and skin, are important, particularly after other, different chemicals have been used, e.g. the anionic hair-fluffing effect of some shampoos may be neutralized by the cationic effects of some cream rinse conditioners.

These conditioners do not rely on their physical properties remaining on the hair after washing. Their effectiveness is achieved by electrochemical action which invariably remains after the vehicle, i.e. the liquid or cream base, and the chemical contained, have been removed. This should be taken into consideration when a shampoo is followed by a conditioner, then a setting agent, possibly a dressing, and finally a hair-holding lacquer. Some conditioners may be allowed to remain on the hair, but others should be rinsed or washed from the hair.

6. Conditioning or reconditioning may be applied to correct some hair states, the effects of processing, as 'before or after' treatments, or to maintain healthy hair.

Dry, brittle, broken, split or porous hair may be due to, e.g. bad brushing or combing, sleeping in rollers, wearing heavy postiche too long, tearing and breaking hair with cheap combs, overbleaching or overprocessing tints or perms and hair straighteners, or exposure to heat, sun or wind. These conditions may be corrected with surface or penetrating types of conditioner. *Rehabilitating rinses,* e.g. acid rinses in liquid or cream form, and *reconditioning creams* or lotions, e.g. containing oils, fats, waxes or lanolin, may be helpful. Cutting removes broken or split ends but it will not remove the cause of the breakage.

Greasy hair or lank, resistant, lifeless hair, due to excessive brushing or stimulation, overaction of the sebaceous glands, or the continued use of greasy or oily products, may be corrected with alkaline rinses, e.g. ammonium hydroxide, borax and astringent lotions. Newer conditioners containing fungicides are particularly helpful.

Before and after processing, conditioners may be required to counteract a porous hair state so that it may successfully take a perm or colour. The alkaline effects of many processes require acid conditioners to return hair back to its normal acid state. Some contain penetrating chemicals which are applied by pouring through the hair.

Corrective conditioners, of which there are many proprietary brands, should always be used as directed by the manufacturer. One application rarely corrects and several are usually necessary over a period of time.

Maintaining a healthy condition requires the periodic use of products which counteract harsh effects and prevent bacterial growth. Many poor states are due to these factors being ignored in the first place. Rinsing the hair correctly, carrying out processes as recommended, and physically treating the hair gently, and with common sense, will help.

7. Treatments with conditioners, or corrective treatments, have been specifically designed to correct the effects of poor hair care and processes. Applied carefully, with appreciation and consideration of the hair state, successful results may be achieved. Used incorrectly, the conditions will be aggravated rather than corrected.

The following treatments, with or without conditioners, may be usefully applied: hand massage, hot towels, steamers, accelerators, radiant heat, thermal caps, mechanical vibratory massage, oil treatments, shampoos and applications, and high frequency.

Massage is a method of manipulating the skin and muscles and may be applied to different parts of the body, by hand or machine. Massage used in the salon is applied to the scalp, neck and face only. Body massage and treatments may be applied in the beauty salon by qualified beauty culturists or therapists.

The uses and effects of massage are: (*a*) improved blood flow and supply to the skin; (*b*) stimulation and soothing of the nerve endings; (*c*) toning of the muscles, i.e. assisting normal contraction and relaxation; (*d*) removal of congestions or fatty adhesions in the skin; (*e*) removal of waste matter from the surface of the skin; (*f*) stimulation of the skin and appendages; (*g*) improvement of local secretions, diffusion and nutrition.

There are many *hand massage movements* which may be applied to different parts of the body, but the ones of special use to hairdressers are: (*a*) effleurage; (*b*) petrissage; (*c*) tapotement; (*d*) vibration.

(*a*) *Effleurage* is a smoothing or soothing, stroking action, performed with firm but gentle movements of the hands and fingertips. It is used before and after most stimulating treatments. It improves the skin functions, soothes and stimulates nerves, and relaxes tensed muscles. (Fig. 13.2a).

(*b*) *Petrissage* is a deeper, kneading movement used to break down adhesions or fatty congestions, and assist elimination of waste products and the flow of nutrition to the tissues of the skin and muscles. There are several petrissage movements, e.g. kneading, pinching, pounding, friction, squeezing and pressing. Kneading and friction are the main movements used on the scalp. Only the lighter, milder movements should be used on the scalp, face and neck. (Fig. 13.2b).

(*c*) *Tapotement* is a stimulating movement which consists of tapping or patting, hacking and clapping. These are all quick beating movements applied with the hands or fingertips, and may be used for stimulating nerves, restoring muscle tone and breaking down fatty deposits in the skin.

(*d*) *Vibration* is a shaking movement usually applied with hands or fingertips. Light vibrations are soothing but heavier ones are stimulating. These hand movements may be imitated by vibratory machines, commonly called 'vibros', and are mainly used on the body. If lightly applied to the scalp they are useful for stimulating nerves, muscles, blood and nutrient supplies to the tissues. (Fig. 13.2c).

Massage is only beneficial when applied in a quiet, relaxed atmosphere. Noise and heated discussions will not afford the client or the operator the relaxation for the correct application of the massage movements. There should be no hard, jerky or painful movements applied, and the total duration of scalp or face massage should not exceed 15 minutes. To exceed this period could prove harmful and discomforting.

Massage should not be given if there are signs of inflammation, breaks or cuts in the skin, spots, rashes or signs of disease, or if the client is undergoing other

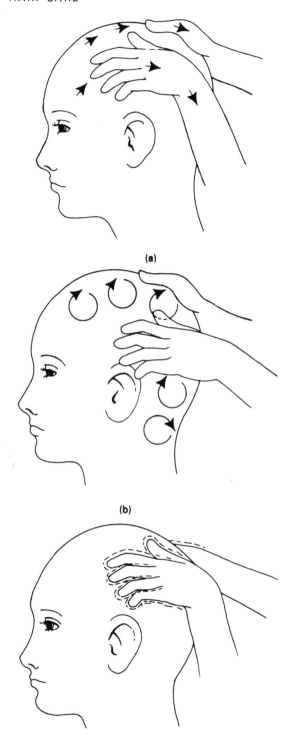

Fig. 13.2 Massage hand movements:
(a) effleurage; (b) petrissage; (c) vibration

medical treatment.

Scalp massage application stimulates grease, loosens skin scale and dirt from the pores, and is best given before shampooing. If the scalp is very dirty then shampoo before and after massage. Massage lotions may be used, e.g. spirit or specially prepared lotions, which help the fingers and hands to grip the surface of the skin.

Application of scalp massage should be made when the client is comfortably seated and suitably protected. The effleurage movement is first used and applied by drawing the fingertips firmly over the head from the front hairline down to the bottom of the neck and on to the shoulders. This should be repeated several times, making sure that the whole scalp is covered by the movements.

This should soothe the surface and underlying skin structure and relaxation of the client should soon become obvious. Discussion between client and operator results in muscle tension and loss of massage benefits.

Petrissage follows, which should be lightly applied; hard, fierce movements on the scalp may rupture small blood vessels and cause discomfort. The fingertips should be made to feel through the hair for the scalp, and when in close contact rotated so that the scalp moves over the skull.

If the fingers are clawed and moved towards the thumbs the correct balance, pressure and movement may be achieved and maintained. Slowly and gently cover the whole scalp without exerting too much pressure, particularly with the small fingers in the temple areas.

The scalp massage is completed by repeating the effleurage movements to remove excess blood brought to the scalp. Allow the client to remain seated for a few minutes to enable the effects and benefits to be enjoyed. Do not prolong the duration of massage, but this will depend on the tolerance of the client. Older clients may be more sensitive and unable to tolerate long periods.

Hot towels are an old-established method of applying heat to the hair and skin, and the newer face and scalp steamers are largely replacing their use. Hot towels may be heated in specially designed towel heaters, sterilizers, or urns, or soaked in hot water enclosed in a dry towel and wrung as dry as possible. When these are applied to the hair the moist heat softens the cuticle and the hair expands.

The towel should be neatly folded and applied to the scalp, outlining the hairline, and be removed as soon as it begins to cool. Several towels may be applied in succession, and if carefully carried out this becomes a soothing and relaxing part of the treatment. Very hot wet towels should never be applied; always make sure they are dry and that scalds or shocks do not occur.

Steamers are now commonly used to apply moist

heat to the skin and hair, before or during conditioning or other treatments. The scalp steamer consists of a hood, water reservoir and kettle with electric elements, fitted on an adjustable stand. The element heats the water, drawn from the reservoir, in the kettle to boiling point and steam passes through a tube or channel to the hood. When placed over the head, steam is able to flow around the hair which allows softening and expansion. An added advantage of the steamer is that medicaments and conditioners may be placed in the water reservoir and applied, with steam, to the hair. (Fig. 13.3).

The use of steamers is beneficial when colouring and bleaching since normal processing time is halved. Distilled water should be used to prevent tubes and kettles being corroded with salt deposits from some tap or hard water.

Accelerators, which operate with radiated light and dry heat, are useful for ensuring deeper penetration of conditioning agents. The accelerator consists of an adjustable hood, with strategically placed light bulbs which emit radiant heat and infra-red light, on an adjustable column. Like steamers they assist the hair to absorb and reduce the processing times of conditioners. (Fig. 13.4).

A system of switches, indicated by coloured lights, enables different parts of the head to be treated, i.e. speeded up or slowed down. The radiant heat or infra-red rays may be concentrated by suitable reflecting surfaces which evenly irradiate and eliminate hot spots in the hood and on the head. Some accelerators are designed with few bulbs and others are multi-bulb. These are used before or during, but usually during, conditioning treatments.

Radiant heat and infra-red light may be supplied from specially designed bulbs or lamps mounted on stands. These are used to irradiate the head in a similar way to an accelerator. The shorter rays of infra-red and those of radiant heat penetrate deep into the skin and are used in some treatments to activate chemical processes, or to heat the hair for conditioning. *Ultra-violet light* is used in some treatments of hair and skin but should never be used in the salon without the necessary protection, i.e. goggles are required to protect the eyes from the harmful effects of ultra-violet rays, together with a licence and qualified experienced operators.

Thermal caps are pliable plastic caps, fitted with heating elements, which fit over the head and apply heat direct to the hair. Several types are available and they must be used as directed by the manufacturers. They have largely been replaced by the use of accelerators and steamers. The principle of dry heat and the hair-softening action is used for many conditioning treatments.

The 'vibro' or vibratory machine is an electrically operated massager designed to produce vibratory movements similar to the petrissage friction movements of hand massage.

Effects produced by vibratory treatments are: hyperaemia, i.e. warmth produced by increased blood flow, and stimulation of skin and follicle appendages, nerves and muscles, due to the massage movements. A vibro massage may be used after an oil application or with other agents.

The vibratory machine is usually supplied with

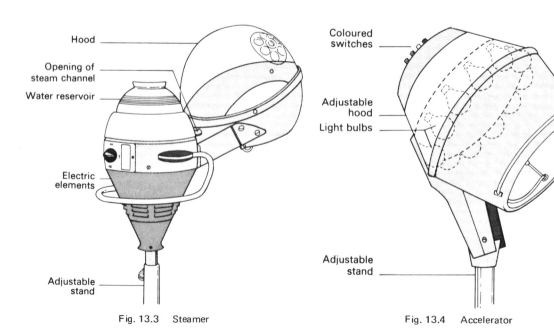

Hood

Opening of
steam channel

Water reservoir

Electric
elements

Adjustable
stand

Coloured
switches

Adjustable
hood

Light bulbs

Adjustable
stand

Fig. 13.3   Steamer   Fig. 13.4   Accelerator

three or more applicators, e.g. (a) the spiked, rubber-pronged applicator for use on the scalp; (b) the soft, rubber sponge applicator for use on the face areas of the head; (c) the harder, vulcanite or rubber applicator for use on nerve endings and stimulation. Various other applicators are made and used on different parts of the body, but in the salon only those designed for face and scalp are required. (Fig. 13.5).

Application of the vibratory machine should be light and firm, and used in circular movements on the scalp, or in straight movements from front to neck. By periodically lifting the vibrator, hair tangle may be prevented. The spiked applicator is mainly used for scalp treatments, sometimes followed by the harder applicator, preferably used over the fingers. Treatment is completed by effleurage stroking movements with the hands. (Fig. 13.6).

Treatment is applied before shampooing, unless the hair is dirty, since the movements will loosen scale and grease. It is important to exert little pressure; the machine weight is sufficient, and massage should not be prolonged for more than 15 minutes.

Cleaning applicators requires special care, particularly after use with oil. Oil may be removed by first dipping in soapless shampoo, then rinsing in warm water, sterilizing with a suitable disinfectant, e.g. dilute formaldehyde, 40 ml to 0·5 litre water, and the rubber preserved by powder.

Oil treatments, applications and shampoos are methods of hair conditioning particularly useful on very dry, overbleached or overprocessed hair.

An oil treatment or application is a method of conditioning which consists in the application of a vegetable oil, e.g. olive, almond, palm or coconut, to the scalp and hair. This may be done with a brush or swab, i.e. a piece of cotton wool, or cotton wool wrapped round the tail of a tailcomb. The method of application is similar to that of a tint except that larger sections are taken, e.g. 12—25 mm.

The oil should be pre-heated to a comfortable temperature; hot oil must never be applied, as this is dangerous and could cause severe burns and shock. Alternatively the oil may be applied cold, and heat added by means of hot towels, thermal caps, radiant

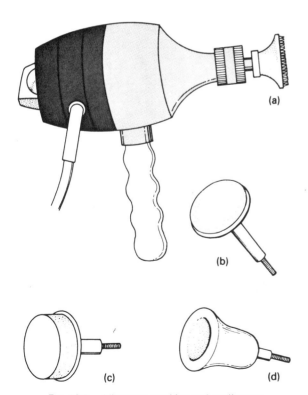

Fig. 13.5   Vibratory machine and applicators

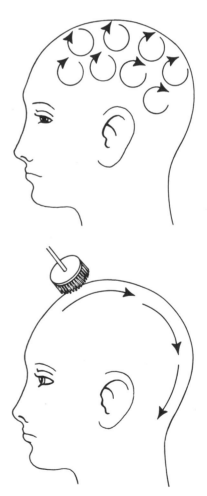

Fig. 13.6   Uses of vibratory machine

heat lamp, a steamer or accelerator, before or after the application. The oil should be allowed to remain on the hair for 5—15 minutes.

During this time a hand or vibro massage may be given. The oil should be removed by applying soapless shampoo direct to the oily hair, before rinsing with water. The shampoo will combine or emulsify the oil and both will be rinsed clear with water. If the water is applied first it will combine with the shampoo and on further rinsing will leave the oil still coating the hair.

Proprietary oil shampoos are made from carefully selected materials, mixed and adjusted to a suitable pH with conditioning additives and emollients, i.e. tissue softeners. These are applied and heated similarly to oil treatments, and a hand or vibro massage carried out. The oil shampoo is removed by adding water, lathering and shampooing in the usual way, and finally rinsing from the hair.

Massage, when oil is on the scalp, consists of gently stroking and moulding the hair, rather than deep petrissage. After the use of oil treatments and shampoos the hair should be pliable, easier to set and with added shine or gloss. Oil treatments should not be applied before chemical processes; to do so could interfere with the process.

High frequency is the term given to an electrical current, produced by a high-frequency generator, of high voltage and low current strength. An induction coil, i.e. two coils, one a primary which consists of wire wound round an iron core of rods, and a secondary which consists of insulated wire wound round the primary, produces an induced, alternating or intermittent current. This is used in high-frequency treatments and the current is applied by means of electrodes, i.e. applicators. The portable type of high-frequency generator or machine is commonly used in the beauty and hairdressing salon. (Fig. 13.7a)

Application of high frequency is twofold, direct and indirect. The *direct* method consists of applying glass electrodes to the skin. Various shapes and sizes are designed to fit different parts of the body, but those made for use on the scalp and face are: (a) the round glass bulb or surface electrode, for use on bare areas of the face and scalp; (Fig. 13.7b) (b) the glass comb or rake electrode, for use on the hairy parts of the head; (Fig. 13.7c) (c) the metal bar or saturator which is designed for the use of *indirect* methods of application. (Fig. 13.7d)

The saturator electrode is held in the hands of the client, and when the current is switched on it is directed to the areas to be treated by the operator's hands. As the fingers touch the client's skin, so the current flows from the machine, through the applicator holder, to the saturator bar and client, to the operator's point of contact, i.e. where the hands touch or massage the skin.

The bulb electrode is applied with a rotary action

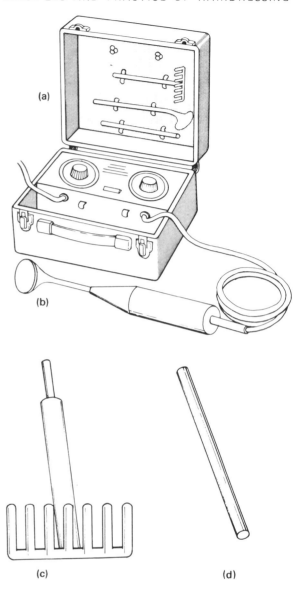

Fig. 13.7(a) — (d)   High-frequency machine — electrodes

and to bare areas of skin. If used over a thickness of hair, the current builds up and causes discomfort. The comb electrode is passed through the hair upwards towards the crown, being pushed rather than pulled (which could remove it from the holder and cause discomfort), and is designed for use on thick, hairy parts of the head.

Before applying the electrodes the operator should be in contact with them, touching them, until they are placed in position. This prevents sudden sparking of the current between the electrode and the skin. They may be used in succession, first the bulb if bare areas are to be treated, followed by the rake, and finally the saturator which is usually used in conjunction with hand massage of the scalp. The recommended maximum time for the use of electrodes is 3 minutes each.

Uses of high frequency. The treatments are used to stimulate skin and its appendages, and to increase blood flow in the areas treated, producing hyperaemia. Nerves, muscles and tissues are stimulated and secretion and diffusion of nutrients in the skin are assisted. Its psychological effects and the results of hand massage are probably the most important, and some clients find this treatment most satisfying and relaxing.

Contra-indications, i.e. symptoms or states present which make treatment inadvisable, of high-frequency applications are: signs of inflammation, evidence of disease, or if the client is receiving medical treatment.

Precautions as for other electrical equipment should be taken, e.g. broken plugs, sockets, flex or other parts of the apparatus should be reported or corrected, and the machine never used carelessly. Modern equipment should be internally earthed and periodically maintained by an electrician.

The current should be low for the first treatments and only increased when the client's tolerance increases, which may occur after the first two or three applications. Total treatment time may be increased but should not exceed 12 minutes.

Spirit, sometimes used as a massage lotion, should not be allowed to contact the electrodes or equipment when in use. Volatile spirit may be ignited by the sparking of the apparatus, and if used on skin could cause burns.

Contact with the mains electricity supply should not be made, by the client or the operator, when the machine is in use.

Do not use near water or water containers, e.g. water pipes, or there could be a sudden build-up of current causing shock.

Check all glass electrodes before use and never use cracked ones.

Loose metal, e.g. earrings, bracelets, zips, may become points of irritation through sparking of electricity where skin contact is made, and should be removed or covered before treatment commences.

Clean all electrodes and equipment after use and disinfect to prevent the growth of bacteria and the spread of infection.

8. Electrolysis, epilation, and depilatories are the terms for hair treatments which deal with its removal rather than its care. They are included here for convenience and whilst they may be dealt with in some salons, they should only be applied by operators qualified and able to do so.

Electrolysis is an electrical method of permanently removing superfluous hair. This is achieved by the passage of an electric current through a needle which is inserted in a hair follicle. An electrical discharge destroys the hair papilla which prevents the growth of hair in that particular follicle permanently.

Depilatories are physical and chemical agents used to remove surplus hair temporarily. The wax depilatory is softened by heating, applied and allowed to harden around the hair. It is then forcibly removed so that the hair is pulled out with it. Chemical depilatories dissolve the hair so that its removal is made easy. Epilation is the forcible and temporary method of hair removal, e.g. plucking with tweezers.

9. The science of hair care is largely based on the science of cosmetics. Blending of chemicals for beauty products is a complex and varied field, and the formulae, actions, applications and effects of them are interesting.

The cosmetic scientist or chemist is constantly producing new substances and products which aid the hairdresser and client appearance. The modern hairdresser as well as the cosmetician, i.e. beauty culturist or operator, requires training to understand and appreciate the effects and applications of these substances.

When dealing with such a range of products, ignorance of their simple effects could prove dangerous, e.g. hair-colouring cosmetics may cause skin reactions if carelessly used. Understanding of the body systems, various internal and external conditions, uses of electricity, and their effects on skin and hair, is of considerable help.

10. Aesthetics and hair care are good examples of the blending of art with science. One of the aims of cosmetology, i.e. cosmetic science, is to create beauty, in addition to beauty products, and directly concerned are methods and forms of presentation, lettering, colouring and packaging, etc.

The art of poise and communication with the application of beauty products, and hair care generally, requires attitudes and manner based on aesthetic understanding of social and general requirements both environmental and cultural.

11. Hair care and postiche. The hair used in boardwork and postiche does not have the benefit of natural secretions, e.g. sebum, for natural shine and gloss. After continued cleaning it becomes necessary to apply conditioners to improve its appearance and enable it to be comfortably managed. Those suitable for use on dry hair are those most suitable for postiche, e.g. reconditioning creams, oils, rehabilitating rinses, etc. Dressings, e.g. vegetable oils or other suitable cream or liquid dressings, are commonly used.

It helps to retain condition if the hair to be used for postiche is carefully stored in airtight containers to prevent contamination with dirt, dust and insects. The old boardworkers stored hair in silver sand which helps to retain a natural gloss and its supple flexibility. This is particularly useful for storing white and blonde hair, and also prevents discoloration.

Cleaning and disinfecting are important aspects of hair care and several products are made which enable this to be carried out easily. Most normal salon hair-conditioning treatments are applicable to postiche. Generally all hair of postiche should be inspected, well washed, disinfected and well stored before use, and all after-care treatments carefully carried out.

Revision test 1

Q. 1   How may the normal state or condition of hair be affected? List points and give reasons.
Q. 2   What are conditioners and what do they do?
Q. 3   What is massage and what are its uses?
Q. 4   What is high frequency, how is it applied to the scalp as a treatment, and what are its uses?
Q. 5   Describe suitable treatments for very dry and very greasy hair.
Q. 6   Describe treatments of superfluous hair.
Q. 7   How should a healthy head of hair be maintained?
Q. 8   Fully describe an oil treatment with massage.
Q. 9   Why is heat used in conditioning and how is it supplied?
Q.10   Briefly describe each of the following terms:
        (a) Hyperaemia. (b) Vibro. (c) Petrissage. (d) Contra-indications. (e) Rehabilitating rinses.

Revision test 2

Complete the following sentences:

1   Name three contra-indications of high frequency:
     (a) ...., (b) ...., (c) ....
2   Name three types of surface conditioners:
     (a) ...., (b) ...., (c) ....
3   Name three things achieved by penetrating conditioners:
     (a) ...., (b) ...., (c) ....
4   Dry hair may be corrected with ...., greasy hair may be helped by ....
     conditioners, and broken split hair corrected with ....
5   Name the active chemical ingredients in two surface conditioners: (a) ...., (b)
     ....; and two penetrating conditioners: (c) ...., (d) ....
6   Name five corrective conditioning treatments:
     (a) ...., (b) ...., (c) ...., (d) ...., (e) ....
7   The names of four massage movements are:
     (a) ...., (b) ...., (c) ...., (d) ....

Revision test 3

Complete the following sentences with the word or words listed below:

Effleurage. Contra-indications. Petrissage, Steamers. Tapotement. Accelerators. Soapless shampoo. Thermal cap or radiant heat. Disease. Hot towels.

1   Moist heat may be applied to the hair by means of .... and .... Dry heat is
     applied by means of .... and ....
2   Any signs of .... are .... of conditioning or other treatments.
3   A soothing, stroking surface massage movement is called .... The deeper, kneading, massage
     movement is called ...., and the plucking, tapping or patting movement is called
     ....
4   When removing oil from the hair .... should be added, before water, to emulsify the oil.

Vocabulary

Accelerator	Apparatus which supplies infra-red or radiant heat and aids or speeds processes.
Conditioners	Substances or methods of correcting or improving the state of the hair.
Reconditioners	
Conditioning	
Reconditioning	
Congestions	Accumulation of secretions, fat or waste products in the skin.
Fatty adhesions	
Contra-indications	Signs or reasons why treatments should not be given or applied.
Effleurage	⎫
Petrissage	⎬ Hand massage movements.
Tapotement	⎭
Electrodes	Term for high-frequency applicators.
Emollient	Substances that soften tissue.
Emulsify	Combination of oil and water or other substances.
High frequency	Electrical current used in treatments.
Hyperaemia	Warmth, heat or redness in the skin produced by massage and increased blood flow.
Infra-red rays	Invisible heat radiation from the red end of the spectrum, between visible light and wireless waves.
Irradiate	To treat with therapeutic rays.
Oil application or treatment	An application of oils, accompanied by massage or other stimulation.
Oil shampoo	Usually contains sulphonated castor oil, which conditions the hair.
Penetrating conditioners	Substances capable of entering the hair.
Radiant heat	Rays from the red end of the spectrum.
Rehabilitating rinses	Usually acid conditioners or rinses.
Resilience	Capable of returning to its original shape, elastic or elasticity.
Saturator	Terms used for high-frequency electrodes.
Surface bulb	
Rake	
Steamers, scalp and face	Apparatus which produces moist heat and aids and speeds processes.
Surface conditioners	Ones which do not penetrate the hair but act on the surface cuticle only.
Ultra-violet rays	From the violet end (beyond) the spectrum, used for treatments and disinfecting.
Vibro	Abbreviation for the electric vibratory machine.

Chapter Fourteen

Hair and Scalp Diseases

1. A normal, healthy skin and body resist the attack of many forms of bacteria present on the skin and hair. It is when the body organs and systems become sluggish or abnormal owing to over-tiredness and ill-health, that signs of disease soon become felt and seen. The skin may in these circumstances display the effects, and the hair, which is an integral part, may be directly or indirectly affected.

Prevention of disease is best achieved by maintaining normal healthy functions of the body, good health and habits, general and personal hygiene, and being able to recognize infectious and contagious conditions.

Often, clean, normal, healthy people become susceptible to bacterial infection because they do not have the necessary antibodies or resistance to it. Others, owing to the surrounding environment, may be subjected to constant infection without ill effect because they have been able to build resistance. Those who have not, unfortunately, in many countries, die or become severely crippled.

2. Cause of disease of the hair and scalp may be due to chemical or physical irritants, animal parasites, vegetable organisms or bacteria, which may produce dietary and metabolic deficiencies and other malfunctions of the body systems, e.g. dermatitis, pediculosis capitis, ringworm, acne and seborrhoea. Psychological and sociological effects and aspects of sex, age, heredity, climate and occupation all play their part.

Recognition of disease is made by assessing the signs and symptoms present, particularly in the early stages of skin reaction. The hairdresser is in a good position to note early stages of disease, and assist in preventing further infection, by recommending that the client visits her doctor.

It is important that hairdressers do not diagnose or treat diseases which should be left to the doctor, dermatologist or trichologist. Exception may be taken to inaccurate suggestions of infectious or contagious conditions present, and legal contingencies or loss of clientele could result. Tact and understanding are necessary when circumstances arise where advice has to be given.

Symptoms are the characteristic lesions, e.g. spots, pimples, sores, exhibited by many diseases. The first to appear are called primary lesions, and may be accompanied by other signs, e.g. inflammation, itching, tightness of skin, soreness. The skin may react in several ways, and further infection and complications may develop if the initial cause is not treated. These secondary signs and symptoms sometimes make it difficult to determine which condition is actually present and to what it may be attributable.

Diagnosis, the identification of the disease, is made from the signs and symptoms, examination of the history or background of the client, and the results of tests and culture growths, etc. This the trained and qualified specialist will do to confirm that what is apparent is actually so. Accurate diagnosis is important for the disease to be correctly treated and cured.

3. Hygiene. In the event of attending a client who has, or who one learns recently had, an infectious or contagious disease, it is important to ensure that it is not spread to the staff or other clients. This is achieved by washing and disinfecting, separately, all protective coverings used, cleaning hands and fingernails, spraying suitable disinfectant throughout the salon, and ensuring that ventilation and light is sufficient to kill any remaining bacteria. All tools used on the source of infection must be cleansed and sterilized. The chair, basin and area the client occupied should be similarly treated.

Resistance of most operators to disease is probably high, owing to the fact that they have been in contact with many people for long periods and exposed to various infections. Provided they are in good health, and good hygiene is practised, there is much less chance of contracting disease. Having been in contact with disease does not necessarily mean that it will be caught; there are many other factors involved.

4. Diseases of special interest to hairdressers are listed below. They may be commonly seen about the face, neck or scalp, and may be recognized by certain characteristics displayed. Some diseases are contagious, i.e. communicated by contact, and others are infectious, i.e. acquired without direct contact by air, water, etc., and others are neither contagious nor infectious. The causes of some are not clearly known,

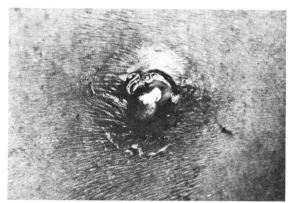

Fig. 14.1   A furuncle

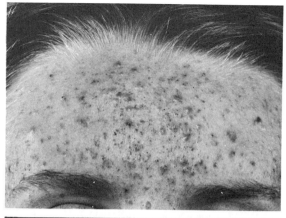

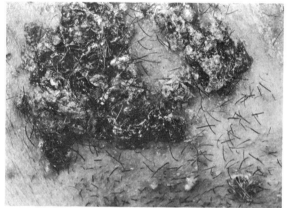

Fig. 14.3   Impetigo

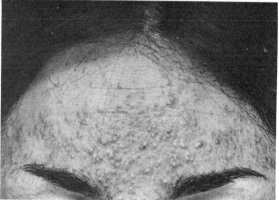

Fig. 14.2(a) — (b)   Acne

but aggravated conditions may arise due to further infection and contagion. Where there is doubt, preventative precautions should be taken as if they were infectious or contagious.

A *furuncle* is a boil or abscess. Where boils or abscesses are present the condition is known as *furunculosis.* It is *caused* by bacterial infection, and the skin reaction in an endeavour to rid itself of the invading bodies and collected waste matter. The *symptoms* are raised, pus-filled lesions, i.e. a spot or pimple filled with waste matter and poison from the infection, surrounded by inflammation. It is usually situated at the site of a hair or follicle, and irritation precedes or accompanies the early stages. If it becomes larger, pressure is exerted and it becomes painful. Boils are *infectious* and should not be picked, pinched or squeezed for risk of further infection. They should be covered with clean dressings and treated by the doctor, but never in the salon. (Fig. 14.1).

Acne vulgaris, or common acne, is an infection of the sebaceous glands by bacteria, which causes retention of the fluid sebum. The *symptoms* of this condition are the familiar pimples of adolescence,

greasy skin, and blackheads of *comedones,* i.e. small blackened plugs of oxidized sebum, which block the skin pores and follicles. These may contain harmless mites or parasites called *Demodex folliculorum.*

Acne is usually aggravated by lack of exercise or open-air activity, constipation, and too much carbohydrate or starchy food. Keeping the skin free from grease usually helps. The condition should be treated as *infectious,* and medical treatment may prevent further complications, but some states are easily and quickly cured. (Fig. 14.2 a & b)

Impetigo is a staphylococcal and streptococcal, i.e. bacterial, infection of the skin. The *symptoms* are very small, red spots, which soon break to form a thick yellow crust. The lesions join together to form large areas commonly seen on the face on which they quickly spread. There is usually intense irritation. It is *infectious* and easily spread by dirty towels. The condition may soon clear after medical treatment. (Fig. 14.3).

Sycosis is sometimes called sycosis barbae or barber's rash. The *cause* is bacterial infection of the hair follicle. *Symptoms* are red pustules, i.e. raised spots filled with pus, which appear yellow, and each

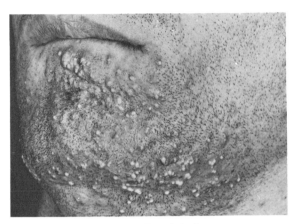

Fig. 14.4   Sycosis barbae

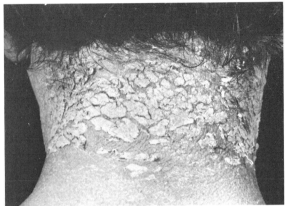

Fig. 14.5(*a*)   Seborrhoeic dermatitis

surrounds a follicle. The top lip and chin are usually first affected. The condition is *infectious* and should be treated by a doctor. (Fig. 14.4).

Pityriasis capitis is the term given to dry, small scales, or scaling conditions, of the scalp. It is sometimes referred to as pityriasis simplex or sicca. It is commonly called *dandruff*. The *cause* may be due to harsh physical treatments, the effects of chemicals, or infection by bacteria, which increases the normal skin shedding. It is often accompanied by itching which increases the scaling. The *symptoms* are very small, dry flakes of skin, greyish or whitish in colour.

If the condition is ignored a serum may exude from the skin, which makes it appear and feel greasy, and binds the small scales to the skin. This causes circular patches to occur and is given the name pityriasis circinata. If this stage is allowed to remain untreated, the scalp becomes more inflamed, the infection deeper-seated, and a condition called pityriasis steatoides develops. Further development, if untreated, results in dermatitis or skin breakdown.

Infection and inflammation of the eyelids and eyes, e.g. blepharitis and conjunctivitis, are often associated with pityroid conditions, i.e. dry, scaly states. Pityriasis capitis should be dealt with as *infectious* and treatment carried out by a doctor or trichologist.

Dermatitis is at its simplest an inflammation or reddening of the skin. The term is usually given to infected states of skin, often when skin function is near to complete breakdown. It is *caused* by irritation due to chemical or physical actions, e.g. scratching, or reaction of the blood and skin to various bacteria and organisms. The *symptoms* are inflammation, dry or moist skin, cracks in the skin, itching, and, in severe stages, pain.

There are several non-infectious types of dermatitis, which may develop into severe infectious ones if the initial cause is not dealt with. Dermatitis often accompanies other skin diseases, and preventative

Fig. 14.5(*b*)   Seborrhoeic eczema

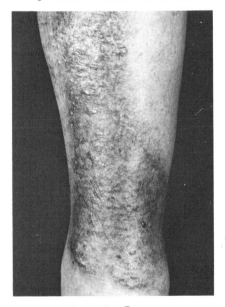

Fig. 14.6   Eczema

precautions should be taken as the conditions may be *infectious or contagious* and must receive medical attention.

Seborrhoea is the term given to the abnormal secretions of the sebaceous glands which produce excessive oil on the hair and skin. There are many other confusing terms given to seborrhoeic conditions, but it is commonly called seborrhoeic oleosa, and the term *scurf* is used to describe large, greasy skin scales.

The condition may be *caused* by ill-health, poor diet or physical traction, and may be aggravated by bacterial and fungal infections. *Symptoms* are oily, lank, greasy hair and skin, which if excessive and allowed to remain may become infected and the normal skin scale made to adhere to the scalp. This may produce large yellow or white skin scale, i.e. scurf, which if allowed to accumulate will produce skin conditions similar to advanced pityriasis states. If untreated the conditions become severe and the infection deep-seated, and *seborrhoeic steatoides, seborrhoeic eczema* and *seborrhoeic dermatitis* may result. These conditions require specialist medical treatment.

There are preventative measures that may be taken for 'normal' or 'natural' oiliness of the skin and hair, but where there are signs of inflammation, pustules, irritation or breaks in the skin, it should be treated as *infectious* and receive medical attention. Acne and comedones are associated with seborrhoeic conditions of the hair and skin. (Fig. 14.5 a & b).

Eczema is an inflammation of the upper part of the skin. It may be *caused* by external irritants, chemical, physical or bacterial, and there are various forms. The *symptoms* are inflammation, dry or moist skin, swelling and itching. Small spots filled with lymph or serum may form, and break; crust and patches or areas of them develop which become thickened. Water or washing usually aggravates the condition and oils are used to remove the thick skin scale, which must receive medical attention. (Fig. 14.6).

There are forms of this disease which are not infectious, although various stages are likely to become infected and the necessary precautions should be taken.

Scabies is a disease of the skin caused by an animal parasite called *Acarus scabiei,* i.e. itch mite. The *cause* is infection of the skin by mites which tunnel or burrow in the skin where their eggs are laid. The *symptoms* are red irritating spots and lines produced by the activities of the mites, often seen between the fingers and folds of the skin. There is intense irritation and the disease is highly *contagious* and must be treated by a doctor. (Fig. 14.7 a & b).

Pediculosis capitis is the infestation of the head by the animal parasite, *Pediculus capitis,* the scalp or head louse. The *cause* is the parasites attacking and

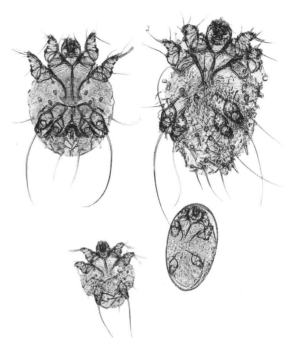

Fig. 14.7(*a*)   Scabies (mites)

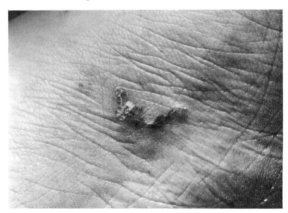

Fig. 14.7(*b*)   Scabies condition

feeding from the skin, and the females laying their eggs, nits or ova on the hair. The *symptoms* are the presence of closely adhering nits or eggs on the hair. These may be slid from roots to points and removed from the hair. Irritation and scratch marks may be seen, particularly above the ears, in the hairy parts of the scalp. Clients with this disease should not be attended in the salon, as it is *contagious.*

There are several preparations which may be used to kill these organisms, but the eggs or nits must be removed to clear the condition completely. Combing the hair with fine toothcombs, after loosening with acetic acid rinses, is useful for removing the nits from the hair. The disease may be present without the client being aware of it, and if treated it may be cleared almost as quickly as it is caught.

The disease is often associated with very dirty people, which accounts for the embarrassment caused to clean hygienic people, but the disease may attack any person. Because of these associations, tact and understanding need to be used when advising clients with this condition. Usually one application of a number of modern remedies, purchased by the client at the chemists or prescribed by the doctor, will kill the parasites concerned. (Fig. 14.8 a & b).

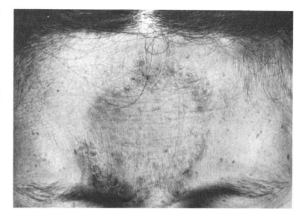

Fig. 14.8(a)   Pediculosis capitis (parasites)

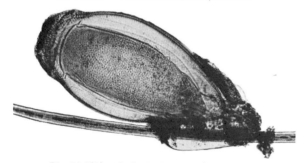

Fig. 14.8(b)   Pediculosis capitis (egg or nit)

Ringworm or *tinea capitis* is a fungal infection of the hair and scalp. The *cause* is the plant parasites attacking and feeding from the hair and skin. The *symptoms* include hair broken close to the scalp and circular areas of greyish skin surrounded by a red active ring. The denuded skin in the centre of the ring becomes roughened. The condition is very *contagious* and strict hygienic precautions must be taken to avoid the spread of this disease. It is commonly seen on children. Clients with this condition must not be attended in the salon and must be advised to visit their doctor. (Fig. 14.9 a & b).

Warts or verrucae are virus infections of the skin. The *cause* is the skin reacting to the infection by producing a variety of lesions differing in size and shape. The *symptoms* are raised, smooth or rough

Fig. 14.9(a) — (b)   Tinea capitis

areas of soft or hardened skin. They are commonly seen on the fingers and face; some are *infectious* and require medical attention. They should not be removed by picking, or cauterizing (i.e. the application of an agent to burn), in the salon. (Fig. 14.10).

Psoriasis is an abnormal thickening of the skin. The *cause* of this condition is not known and it does not appear to be due to any one organism. There is

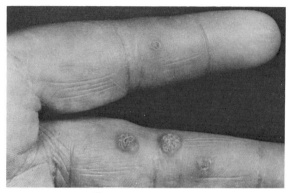

Fig. 14.10   Verrucae

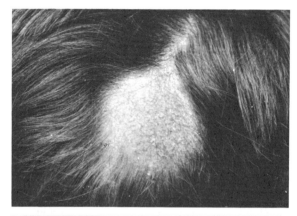

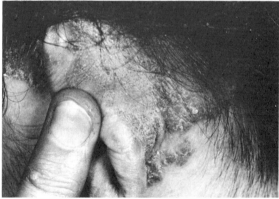

Fig. 14.11(a) — (b)   Psoriasis

usually a family history of the disease. The *symptoms* are thick, raised, dry, silvery lesions, often circular in shape, inflamed under and around the lesion, and formed separately or in clusters. There may be irritation, and the condition varies at different times of the year. Removal of a thickened lesion reveals a tiny bleeding point. Although the disease is *not infectious or contagious,* a neglected state may become infected and good hygiene should be applied.

The treatment of psoriasis is difficult and requires medical attention.

The unsightly nature of this condition causes a great deal of distress to the sufferer, who is often of a nervous disposition. The hairdresser is able to offer comfort by the application of tact and understanding. Provided the condition has been attended by a doctor there is no reason why normal hairdressing may not be applied. It should be explained to young hairdressers that the condition is not infectious and that though looks deceive, it is quite harmless. Unfortunately distaste is often expressed, which offends and embarrasses the client. (Fig. 14.11 a & b).

Alopecia is the term given to loss of hair or baldness. There are many reasons and *causes* of alopecia, with a variety of accompanying conditions. If the necessary nutrients and materials required for cellular growth in the hair papilla are not received, the hair cannot grow or the old hair be replaced, which results in one small area of baldness.

Alopecia areata is baldness in circular patches or areas. The *symptoms* are smooth skin, often paler or redder than the surrounding areas, which may be slightly depressed, and it may appear greasier or more moist than normal. There may be several hairs on the bald patch visibly thicker at the point end, i.e. so-called exclamation-mark shaped hairs. Occasionally there appears a fine, lanugo covering of hair. The *cause* is not clearly understood but is thought to have a nervous, not neurotic, origin. (Fig. 14.12).

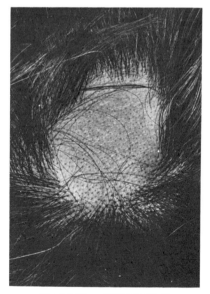

Fig. 14.12   Alopecia areata

If alopecia areata continues to develop, the round areas join, and eventually complete and total baldness of the head results. This is called *alopecia totalis,* i.e.

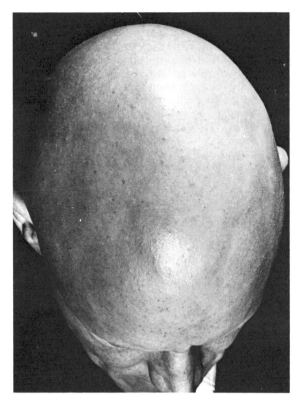

Fig. 14.13   Alopecia totalis

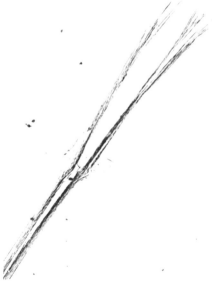

Fig. 14.14   Fragilitas crinium

baldness of the head. (Fig. 14.13) *Alopecia universalis* is the name given to the complete loss of hair of the whole body.

Alopecia conditions may appear and worsen rapidly; they may equally improve and regain normal growth, with or without treatment. Mild stimulation usually assists the scalp to function normally again and the conditions are *not infectious or contagious.* There are various patterns of baldness which may be due to different causes, and each requires specific treatment by the doctor or trichologist.

Cysts are fluid-filled sacs in the skin. The *cause* is a retention of fluid which causes the skin to rise and swell. *Sebaceous cysts* are due to the retention of sebum of the sebaceous glands. The *symptoms* are small or large bumps in the skin, which may appear anywhere on the scalp or head. They are usually treated by a doctor by the removal of their contents. They are *not infectious* or contagious.

Fragilitas crinium is a defect rather than a disease of the hair shaft. The *cause* is harsh chemical or physical treatment, which dries, splits, roughens or breaks the hair, and often leaves brushlike ends to the hair. It may be treated by cutting and conditioning. It is not infectious or contagious. (Fig. 14.14).

Trichorrhexis nodosa is a defect of the hair shaft. Its *cause* is similar to that of fragilitas crinium. The *symptoms* are characteristic swellings or nodules of the hair shaft which contain areas of splitting hair. The hair often breaks at these nodules to produce frayed, split ends which are very dry. It is not infectious and may be treated by cutting and conditioning. (Fig. 14.15).

Monilethrix or beaded hair is a condition of the hair shaft. The *symptom* is an alternately swollen and constricted hair, throughout its length. Unlike trichorrhexis nodosa there are no areas of split hair, and breakage of the hair often occurs level with or near the scalp.

The *cause* is irregular formation in the growing stage, or malfunction of the hair papilla. It is a hereditary condition which often disappears at the age of puberty. It is not infectious or contagious but must receive medical attention since it may be a symptom of other diseases. (Fig. 14.16).

Canities is the name given to grey, white or colourless hair and is a defect rather than a disease. The *causes* are obscure but the condition is brought about by the lack of colour pigment produced or distributed in hair during the growing stage. The hair structure does not appear to suffer; in many cases the hair becomes stiffer, bristly and often resistant. Synthetic colourings may be applied to match the white with the naturally coloured hair.

The condition is associated with the ageing process but is often seen in the young. It may appear after periods of stress or illness, but comes gradually. The change from coloured to white hair is as slow or fast

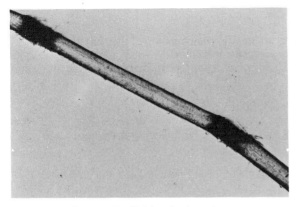

Fig. 14.15   Trichorrhexis nodosa

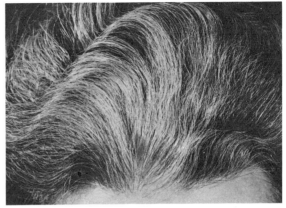

Fig. 14.17   Canities

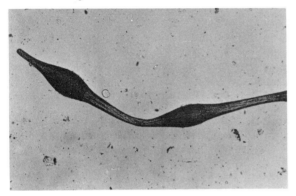

Fig. 14.16   Monilethrix

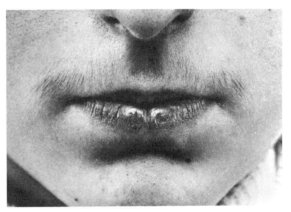

as hair growth during which the colour pigments, if present, enter the hair structure. (Fig. 14.17).

Ringed hair is a form of canities, a defect of the hair. It is caused by irregular colour formation which appears as white or coloured alternate rings or bands. The reason for this is not clear but occurs during the papilla activity of hair formation. It is not infectious or contagious.

Hypertrichosis or *hirsuties* are terms given to excessive hair in areas not usually covered, or all over the body, which is rare. The cause is probably due to a combination of abnormal body functions which affect hair growth formation. The type and amount varies from thin, fine hair to large amounts of thick, coarse hair. It may occur temporarily in women and girls, prior to the onset of menstruation and during the menopause. The few hairs on the top lips of some women, and the bearded lady of the circus, are extreme examples of this condition. Methods of permanent hair removal, e.g. electrolysis, may be used to treat minor forms of this condition. (Fig. 14.18 a & b).

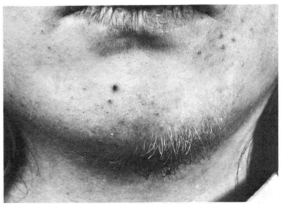

Fig. 14.18(a) — (b)   Hirsuties

Apart from the recognizable symptoms of disease, many individual characteristics make it difficult to 'name' the condition, and where there is doubt a visit to the doctor, trichologist or specialist is indicated.

Revision test 1

Q. 1   Describe the causes of disease and how, directly or indirectly, they may affect the hair and skin.
Q. 2   Briefly describe two skin diseases caused by animal parasitic infection.
Q. 3   Describe the disease, cause, symptoms and possible course, if untreated, due to excessive oily states.
Q. 4   What is diagnosis and how may it be carried out?
Q. 5   What is the difference between dandruff and scurf?
Q. 6   What effect has personal and general hygiene on hair and scalp diseases?
Q. 7   What are symptoms of skin diseases?
Q. 8   Name two defects of the hair shaft and how they may be treated by the hairdresser.
Q. 9   What is ringworm and how may it be recognized?
Q.10   Briefly describe each of the following terms:
       (a) Pustule. (b) Resistance. (c) Hair defect. (d) Skin scale. (e) Primary lesion.

Revision test 2

Complete the following sentences:

1   Healthy hair and skin may be maintained by:
    (a) ...., (b) ...., (c) ....
2   The cause of skin disease may be due to:
    (a) ...., (b) ...., (c) ....
3   Pediculosis capitis is due to infection by .... and is recognized by .... and ....
4   Pityroid conditions, e.g. ...., are recognized by ....
5   The name given to baldness is .... When it occurs in circular patches it is called .... Complete baldness of the head is called ...., and of the whole body ....
6   Dermatitis is .... and may be caused by ...., ... and ....
7   Dry, splitting hair in poor condition is called .... and may be treated with .... and ....
8   A skin disease caused by a virus is ...., by a vegetable parasite, ..., and by bacterial infection, ...

Revision test 3

Complete the following sentences with the word or words listed below:

Animal parasite. Vegetable parasite. Infectious. Fungal. Contagious. Hygiene. Cysts. Canities. Hirsuties. Alopecia.

1   Ringworm or tinea capitis is caused by a .... infection which is a ....
2   *Pediculus capitis* is an ....
3   Scabies is a .... disease.
4   The application of good .... helps to prevent the spread of .... diseases.
5   The condition of grey or white hair is called ....
6   A condition of baldness is called ....
7   Excessive hair growth is called ....
8   Fluid-filled sacs or swellings in the skin are called ....

Vocabulary

Alopecia	The term for baldness.
Blepharitis	Infections of the eyes and eyelids.
Conjunctivitis	
Comedones	Blackheads, plugs of hardened sebum.
Contagious	Communicated by direct contact.
Cysts	Fluid-filled sacs in the skin.
Dandruff	Name for very small, branlike skin scale.
Defect	Failure to become normal; abnormal formation.
Dermatologist	A specialist in skin diseases.
Diagnosis	Recognition of disease by its symptoms.
Disease	A condition of the body, or parts of it, due to pathological organisms or other causes, which disrupts normal functions or working.
Fragilitas crinium	Brittle, fragile hair, usually broken.
Infectious	Disease which can be acquired without direct contact.
Lesion	A change in tissue structure due to disease, e.g. spots, pimples, pustules.
Metabolism	Chemical processes in living organisms.
Mite	A very small parasitic insect.
Ovum	An egg.
Ova	Eggs.
Parasite	An organism living in or on another living organism. May be plant or animal.
Pediculosis capitis	A head of hair infested with lice.
Pediculus capitis	The head louse.
Pityroid	Resembling bran, fine dry scaly skin, e.g. pityriasis.
Pus	Waste matter produced by infection and cellular activity.
Scurf	Name given to greasy skin scale.
Seborrhoeic	Affected with seborrhoea; greasy states.
Serum	A fluid part of the blood, e.g. material with which blisters may be filled.
Symptom	A sign or indication of disease.
Wen	A sebaceous cyst.

Chapter Fifteen

Hairdressing and Related Subjects

This chapter is intended to be used as a summary of subjects related to a particular aspect of hairdressing. It is hoped that it will serve as a convenient list of 'points of contact' of the subjects concerned and as a progressive work guide.

It is important that the related subjects be integrated, wherever and as soon as possible, with practical hairdressing. It may not be possible for all the work of the related subjects to follow closely the natural progression of practical hairdressing all the way through, but the relation must be made for the

work to be meaningful.

Although the related studies included in the text have not been treated as a whole (the size of this volume would not permit this), they have been included to a fuller extent in the work summary.

English and liberal studies are of considerable importance to the whole field of hairdressing. These have not been included because of their far-reaching and wide coverage, and it should not be assumed that their exclusion in any way minimizes the valuable part they have to play.

Practical Hairdressing — Part One

1 and 2. Introduction. Client reception. Handling tools. Combs and combing. Brushes and brushing. Basic methods of hygiene and cleanliness. Preparation of the client and client's hair. General salon procedures.

3. Curls and curling. The tools. Basic formations, methods, uses, types and varieties. Methods of sectioning, exercises and practice. Setting and the basic pli.

4. Shampooing and shampoos. Equipment and layout. Methods and techniques. Positions and hand movements. Shampoos, variety, uses, types and effects.

5. Perming. Preparation. Sectioning. Winding. Processing. Normalizing. Cold, tepid and hot methods. Differences and applications. Hair straightening, modern methods. Effects, uses, varieties, faults and corrections of perming and straightening.

6. Finger waving. To ensure manipulation, control, practice and exercise with hair. Appreciation of shape. Basic method and application. Hair-moulding techniques. Effects, reasons, uses, methods and variations.

7. Waving with irons for practice and hand manipulation, to achieve wave and curl shapes, control and appreciation. Basic methods and practice on hair weft or blocks.

8. Cutting. The tools, use, practice and exercises. Tool maintenance, uses, techniques and control. Precautions, dangers, faults and corrections.

9. Dressing. Use of tools, hands and control products. Control of hair. Moulding of basic pli. Methods, techniques and applications of dressing to achieve modern and simple basic shapes.

Related Science — Part One

1 and 2. Introduction: science and hairdressing. Tools, materials and equipment. Hygiene, salon, general and personal. Dirt, removal and dangers. Antiseptics, disinfectants and sterilization.

3. Science, curls and curling. Anatomy and physiology, introduction — the body, skeleton, bones and joints. Basic properties of hair, elasticity. Wet and dry hair, and effects of heat. Dryers and drying.

4. Science, shampooing and shampoos. Basic chemistry. Units of measurement, metric system. Laboratory equipment — balances, weighing, volume. Solutions. Matter composition. Atoms, molecules and elements. Compounds, salts, acids, alkalis, gases, properties and uses. Water — rain cycle, sources, storage, disposal and waste removal. Hot and cold systems. Hardness and softening of water. States of matter.

5. Science and perming. Basic chemistry of perming. Physical effects. Hair structure. Effects of heat on hair and matter. Heat and expansion. Thermometers and temperature scales. Radiation, convection and conduction. Ventilation. The atmosphere, composition, moisture. Oxidation and reduction.

6. Science and finger waving. Applications of heat and hair-moulding techniques. Basic electricity. Hygroscopicity. Materials used.

7. Science and waving with irons. Heat and electricity. Conduction and resistance. Effects on the hair and body. Electric and heat-producing equipment.

8. Science and cutting. The hair and skin. Functions, growth, distribution, varieties. Measurements and angles. Digestion, metabolism and nutrition of hair and body.

9. Science and dressing. Cosmetic preparations. Setting agents, lotions and creams. Oil, fats, waxes, emulsions, gels, uses and effects. Technique effects.

Aesthetics and Hairdressing — Part One

1 and 2. Aesthetics and reception. Introduction to related art, materials and equipment. Use of art tools. Basic exercises with simple forms, patterns and media. Primary and secondary colours and combinations.

3. Aesthetics, curls and curling. Use of curl shape and form. Curl compositions. Line, and effects on curved and other lines and surfaces. Curling paper and paper waving. Curl collage.

4. Aesthetics, shampooing and shampoos. Water movements, shapes and colours as an art form. Simple drawing. Basic design of shampoo containers and equipment. Real and abstract shapes.

5. Aesthetics and perming. Design, shape and form of perming equipment. Diagrams, drawings and sketches of simple structures, tissue patterns and internal hair changes due to processes. Straight line, curves, proportion, head and face studies of shape.

6. Aesthetics of finger waving. Wave forms, shapes, movements and patterns. Use of wave and curl in design and texture. Shapes and textures of different media.

7. Aesthetics and waving with irons. Equipment design. Rhythm and movement, flow of line, straight and curved. Effect on head shapes. Contours, proportions and general shapes of head, face and neck.

8. Aesthetics and cutting. Vertical and horizontal lines. Diagonal line effects. Impressions and effects created by angled lines on balance and proportion. Angles and perspective. Cutting diagrams, drawings and sketches.

9. Aesthetics and dressing. Simple line exercises of geometric shapes. Abstract balance and design. Effects of colour on shape, bulk and mass. Head and face drawings and studies from various angles and views.

Boardwork and Hairdressing — Part One

1 and 2. Boardwork and reception. Introduction. Relation of boardwork and hairdressing. Boardwork tools, equipment and materials. Reception of client and postiche orders. Recording orders, and methods of work. Combings and cuttings, the weaving frame. Weaving practice and weft work. Making simple pin curls, waves and marteaux.

3. Boardwork, curls and curling. Varieties, methods and techniques of temporary curling of hair for postiche. Curling methods application. Curling and setting postiche. Making of weft work, marteaux, switches, double-loop clusters, diamond mesh or cache peigne.

4. Boardwork, shampooing and shampoos. Cleaning, preparing, mixing, turning and storing hair. Methods of making weft postiche. Methods of finishing, sewing and cleaning completed boardwork.

5. Boardwork and perming. Application of permanent curling methods to hair and postiche. Use of straight and curled hair. Traditional and modern curling methods.

6. Boardwork and finger waving. Application of traditional methods. Historical weft postiche. Application of modern hair-moulding techniques. Waved postiche or making postiche for waves with weft.

7. Boardwork and waving with irons. Application of modern and traditional methods and techniques. Introduction to foundational postiche. Foundation work, tools, materials and equipment. Knotting, various types, uses, applications. Differences between weft and knotted postiche.

8. Boardwork and cutting. The application of basic cutting shapes to full wigs and other postiche. Making and shaping eyelashes. Dangers and precautions of postiche cutting.

9. Boardwork and dressing. The application of basic dressing techniques to postiche. Dangers and precautions. Heating and drying postiche. Making and dressing theatrical beards, moustaches, eyebrows and other pieces. Partings, descriptions.

Practical Hairdressing – Part One *Continued*

10. Hairstyling. Design for suitability, practicability and variations. Ladies' and men's styles. Choice and selection. Methods and varieties. Basic face shapes.

11. Hair colouring. Varieties, types, uses, methods, applications, processing, results, effects, faults and corrections. Dangers and precautions. Recording.

12 and 13. Hair care. The hair and skin. Hair condition recognition. Conditioning methods, reasons, uses, and effects. Simple treatments. Applications, processing and results.

14. Hair and scalp diseases. Recognition of the basic stages. Abnormalities. Action to be taken and advice to the client.

Practical Hairdressing – Part Two

1 and 2. Building a clientele. Effects of client reception. Varieties of tools. Uses of tools and method varieties. Importance of salon, personal and general hygiene. Attention to client and salon management.

3. Curls and curling. Setting and the planned pli. Uses of curl direction, line, movement, foundation, varieties and combinations. Curls in setting and dressing.

4. Shampooing and shampoos. The chemical and physical effects on hair and skin, and in relation to other processes. Selection and choice of shampoo. Importance of correct procedures.

5. Perming. History and traditional techniques. Application of modern processes. The chemical and physical effects on hair. Fashion perming, techniques, methods. Faults and corrections. Dangers and precautions.

6. Finger waving. Modern aspects. Application to live heads. Modern methods and techniques of moulding and shaping. Historical and traditional aspects.

7. Waving with irons. Formation of modern pli, all types of iron. Modern aspects. Effects on hair. Dangers, faults, precautions and corrections.

8. Cutting. Application of method, variety and techniques to modern shapes. Fashion and style cutting. Selection, choice, application of cut shapes to face and head.

Related Science – Part One *Continued*

10. Science and hairstyling. Light, reflection and refraction, composition, effect on hair, mirrors. Basic colour chemistry. The spectrum and effects of light rays.

11. Science and hair colouring. Pigmentation. Chemical varieties and chemistry. Alkalinity and acidity, pH values and scales. Hair oxidation.

12 and 13. Science and hair care. Treatments and effects. The effects on blood, nerve and muscular systems of the head and body. Chemistry of conditioners and conditioning.

14. Hair and scalp diseases. Hair defects. Recognition of disease. The hair and body, in health and disease.

Related Science – Part Two

1 and 2. Science and the client. Hygiene. Bacteria, fungi, animal and plant parasites. Infection, contagion and prevention. The materials, actions and effects of combs and combing, brushes and brushing. Culture of growths of fungi, moulds, etc., from salon tools. Infestation. Diseases liable to spread.

3. Science, curls and curling. The effects of curling on the hair structure. Protein keratin and its importance in hair and skin. Capillarity, hygroscopicity, elasticity and the internal chemical structure of hair. Examination of cells, tissues, organs and systems.

4. Science, shampooing and shampoos. Effects on the blood, muscles, scalp, head and body. Soaps, soapless shampoos. Detergency, surface tension. Chemistry. Atomic and molecular properties of matter. Hairdressing chemicals, mixtures, compounds, setting agents. Water – heating, distillation, costing, uses, advantages and disadvantages of different systems and methods of water use.

5. Science and perming. The tools of perming. Machines. Exothermic chemicals. Chemistry. Actions, uses, effects, chemical and physical properties of new materials, systems and methods.

6. Science and finger waving. Materials and chemicals, their effect on hair. Hair-moulding techniques and equipment. Electricity, sources, types, mechanics, chemical, general and salon uses. Motors – hand and hood dryers, and other heat-producing machines.

7. Science and waving with irons. Equipment maintenance. Consideration of modern equipment. Physical and chemical effects on hair and skin. First aid in the salon. Effects on keratin. Differences between setting, perming and other forms of waving.

8. Science and cutting. The types, maintenance, operation of cutting tools. Dangers, faults, precautions and corrections. Effects on hair. Cutting angles and measurements. Psychological effects of cutting and hairdressing. Protective materials and fabrics. Hand and muscle movements, stance and effects on the body.

Aesthetics and Hairdressing — Part One *Continued*

10. Aesthetics and hairstyling. Balance, line, movement, rhythm, symmetry, asymmetrical exercises with all media. Hair shapes imposed on face and head shapes.

11. Aesthetics and hair colouring. Colour principles, theory and practice. Mixing and use of tones, pastels. Colour patterns, shapes and designs. Contrasting and complementary colours. Blending, shading and effects.

12 and 13. Aesthetics and hair. Structure and care. Three-dimensional head, face and hair shapes. Modelling hair textures. The patterns, shapes, colours, of mixtures and chemical materials. History of hair style, introduction.

14. Aesthetics and hair diseases. The shapes, pattern and textures of disease-causing organisms. Microscopic images, plant and animal life. Microscopic examples of various media in two and three dimensions. Textures, patterns and rhythms of plant and animal parasites, etc.

Aesthetics and Hairdressing — Part Two

1 and 2. Aesthetics and reception. Décor and salon layout. Display and design. Lettering and advertising. Curtain fabric and wallpaper, designs and patterns. Colour schemes. Window dressings and show displays.

3. Aesthetics, curls and curling. Modelling curls and head, various media. History of styles. Display of colour and curls. Drawings, design, collage of curl shapes and patterns.

4. Aesthetics, shampooing and shampoos. Design of shampoo equipment and areas. Abstracts from water movements. Advertising and display media. Fashion styles and clothes.

5. Aesthetics of perming. Design and shape of equipment. Modern and historical style patterns. Hair structure patterns and changes due to chemical and physical effects.

6. Aesthetics and finger waving. Modelling head, face and neck shapes in all media. Sketches, paintings, real and abstract designs, using wave and curl shapes. Interpretation of modern wave of fashion designs from historical dressings.

7. Aesthetics and waving with irons. Illustrations and sketches of techniques. Rhythm, flow, movement of line, shape and colour. Equipment design and shape.

8. Aesthetics and cutting. Patterns and shapes of cutting styles, using different media. Geometric line and shape. Drawings of cutting patterns, hair and other media. Angles and measurements. Painting, drawing and three-dimensional shapes for expression and effect.

Boardwork and Hairdressing — Part One *Continued*

10. Boardwork and hairstyling. Making and styling postiche for addition to various hair styles. Making fringes, fronts, chignons, knotted and wefted. Fashionable postiche. Variety of foundational work, e.g. galloon and galloonless edges, tension and positional springs. Partings, basic and preparatory work.

11. Boardwork and hair colouring. Traditional and modern colours and colouring. Bleaching and colouring bulk hair. Dangers and precautions of colouring processes and their effects on postiche foundations.

12 and 13. Boardwork and hair care. The sources, cleansing, conditioning and care of hair postiche. Dangers and precautions. Application of modern hair care methods to postiche.

14. Boardwork and hair diseases. Bulk hair as a disease carrier and sterilization of bulk hair. Recognition of parasitical hair infection. Use of postiche on bald or scarred areas. Differences between synthetic and hair postiche.

Boardwork and Hairdressing — Part Two

1 and 2. Boardwork and reception. Presentation and display of postiche. Complete details and measurements for workroom orders, costing, matching and making. Variations of combs, combing, brushes and brushing.

3. Boardwork, curls and curling. The making and addition of all types of curl, weft and foundational. Paper patterns and measurements for wig mounts.

4. Boardwork, shampooing and shampoos. Chemical and physical effects of shampoos and shampooing on postiche, synthetic materials and hair. Wig-making methods.

5. Boardwork and perming. Types and variations of permanent waving in boardwork. Modern aspects. Dangers and precautions. Patterns for semi-transformations, and transformations.

6. Boardwork and finger waving. Details of modern and historical techniques. Modern designs for waved and curled postiche and methods of making.

7. Boardwork and waving with irons. Reproducing replicas of historical iron-waved dressings, in miniature. Preparation and making model display heads for waved postiche. Applications of modern processes and techniques and the effects of hair and foundations.

8. Boardwork and cutting. Fashion and style cutting for modern postiche. The production and making of various postiche of varying lengths.

Practical Hairdressing – Part Two *Continued*

9. Dressing. Uses and application of modern techniques to achieve basic, fashion, modern, historical styles. Use of hands, tools, equipment. Dressing long and short hair. Variations of dressing methods. Overdressing. All comb and brush techniques.

10. Hairstyling. Style variety. Modern day, cocktail and evening dressings. Competition and display styling. Ladies', men's and children's styling. Suitability. Choice, Designing, creating and completing a variety of hair styles.

11. Hair colouring. The chemical and physical effects on the hair. Appreciation of colour choice, selection and application of all varieties. *Bleaching* and *toning,* the effects, techniques, application, processing and results. *Decolouring,* techniques, varieties and applications. Dangers and precautions. Faults and corrections.

12 and 13. Hair care. General study of the hair and skin. Corrective treatments. Application of conditioning products, reasons, choice, effects and results. Hand massage. Vibratory massage. High frequency, treatments and applications. Appreciation of hair structure, growth and distribution. Dangers and precautions. Modern conditioners, conditioning, rehabilitating treatments and related processes.

14. Hair and scalp diseases. Recognition of the common conditions. Understanding of diagnosis, and the symptoms and causes of conditions. Dealing with infection and contagion.

Related Science – Part Two *Continued*

9. Science and dressing. Effects on hair, skin and body. Chemical and physical properties of tools and materials used. Cosmetic chemistry. Ventilation, lighting, salon systems and conditions.

10. Science and hairstyling. Uses of scientific products. Physiology, reasons for face shapes, wrinkles and other features considered when styling. Light reflection and refraction, and appearance of style shapes. Looking, seeing, and physical and psychological effects of hairstyling.

11. Science and hair colouring. Chemistry of colour, and colourings. Hair and skin reactions and tests. Chemical and physical properties of bleaches, bleaching, toners, toning and decolouring. Dangers and precautions. Faults and corrections. Glandular systems, blood and skin reactions to all colouring processes. Mixing, measuring, applications. Compatibility and incompatibility.

12 and 13. Science and hair care. Chemicals and materials of conditioning products. Chemical and physical actions. Reactions to further processing. Differences between hair care treatments and treatment of disease.

14. Science, hair and scalp diseases. Recognition of diseases and defects of the hair and skin. Common diseases and defects. Diagnosis. Microscopes and microscopical investigations, simple laboratory techniques used in diagnosis. Infestation.

Aesthetics and Hairdressing – Part Two *Continued*

9. Aesthetics and dressing. Proportions of head and body. Pli patterns and designs. Designing and displaying. General fashion studies. Application of colour and art techniques to dressing.

10. Aesthetics and hairstyling. Modern interpretations from historical designs. Hair proportions on head, neck and body. Hair displays and shows, both hair and general fashion.

11. Aesthetics and hair colouring. Art colours and mixing. Light, lighting and the effects on hair colours. Colour and colouring effects on shape. Colour exercises, all media. The selection and suitability of colour for particular effects.

12 and 13. Aesthetics and hair. The design, shape and effect on hair care products, equipment and client, Packaging, display and design of products. Advertising, graphics, presentation of products and materials.

14. Aesthetics and hair diseases. Further study of hair and skin patterns and shapes. Effects on hair in health and disease. The use of art techniques and media to display hair diseases and defects for recognition. Art patterns and shapes from media culture and microscopic studies. Further development of artistic and aesthetic skills and appreciation.

Boardwork and Hairdressing – Part Two *Continued*

9. Boardwork and dressing. Fashionable and modern dressing techniques and methods for postiche, to be worn and displayed, in addition to basic dressings. Preparation of demonstration and competition postiche. Partings, drawn through and methods of making.

10. Boardwork and hairstyling. Reproduction of fashion, display, competition, demonstration postiche, all styles. Study of historical and modern styles. Considerations and applications of modern styled postiche.

11. Boardwork and hair colouring. Comparisons of boardwork and hair colourings, dangers and precautions. Reactions and incompatibility of colourings. Tests. Fashion postiche colouring. Fantasy and display colourings and postiche.

12 and 13. Boardwork and hair care. The effects, dangers and precautions of chemical and physical processing of hair and postiche. Hygiene.

14. Boardwork and hair diseases. Recognition of disease and defects, and precautions to be taken, when dealing with hair and postiche. Preparation and making of foundational postiche for use after hair loss through disease. Semi-transformations and transformations, and other knotted foundational pieces. Further development of the skills and practice of boardwork in the light of modern developments. The modern workroom and boutique.

Appendix I

Metric Units, Symbols, Examples and Equivalents

Length

1 millimetre	(mm)		=	0·03937 in.
1 centimetre	(cm)	= 10 mm	=	0·3937 in.
1 metre	(m)	= 100 cm	=	39·370 in.
		= 1000 mm		
1 kilometre	(km)	= 1000 m	=	0·6214 mile
25·4 mm		= 2·54 cm	=	1 inch
0·3048 m		= 12 in.	=	1 foot
0·9144 m		= 3 ft	=	1 yard
1·6093 km		= 1760 yds	=	1 mile
8 km		= 5 miles (approx.)		

Hair grows approx. 12·7 mm (½ in.) each month.
Haircutting scissors may be 140—190 mm (5½—7½ in.) long.
Approx. head measurements used in boardwork are:

(a)	Circumference	558 mm	(22 in.)
(b)	Forehead to nape	345 mm	(13½ in.)
(c)	Temple to temple round back	355 mm	(14 in.)
(d)	Ear to ear over top	292 mm	(11½ in.)
(e)	Ear to ear round front hairline	279 mm	(11 in.)
(f)	Nape (side to side at neck)	101 mm	(4 in.)

Area

1 square millimetre	(mm^2)		=	0·00155 sq. in.
1 square centimetre	(cm^2)	= $100\ mm^2$	=	0·155 sq. in.
1 square metre	(m^2)	= $10\ 000\ cm^2$	=	10·764 sq. ft
		$1\ 000\ 000\ mm^2$		
1 hectare	(ha)	= $10\ 000\ m^2$	=	2·471 acres
1 square kilometre	(km^2)	= 1000 ha	=	2471·05 acres

A salon size could be approximately:

length	by	breadth	=	area
10 m	x	5 m	=	$50\ m^2$
(33 ft	x	16½ ft	=	544½ sq. ft)

The salon area required for working on a client could be $1·6—1·9\ m^2$ (17—20 sq. ft) approx.

Volume

1 millilitre (ml)	=	1 cubic millimetre (mm^3)	
1 litre (litre)	=	1000 ml	= 1·7598 pints
1 cubic metre (m^3)	=	1000 litres	= 1·3080 cubic yds
28·4 ml or 0·0284 litre	=	1 fluid ounce	= 1/20 pint
568 ml or 0·568 litre	=	20 fluid ounces	= 1 pint
4·546 litres	=	8 pints	= 1 gallon

Approximately 14—28 ml (½—1 oz.) of liquid shampoo is required for the average head.
Approximately 56 ml (2 oz.) of perm lotion is required for the average perm.
A 113 ml (4 oz.) measure may be used for mixing small quantities of liquids.
9 litres equals approximately 2 gallons.
1 litre of 20 vol. 'peroxide' produces 20 litres of oxygen.

Mass (Weight)

1 gramme (g)		= 0·0353 oz.	
1 kilogramme (kg)	= 1000 g	= 2·2046 lb.	
1 tonne	= 1000 kg	= 0·9842 ton	
28·350 g	= 1 oz.		
453 g or 0·453 kg	= 16 oz.	= 1 pound	
6·3503 kg	= 14 lb.	= 1 stone	
1·0161 tonnes	= 20 cwt.	= 1 ton	

A tube of cream tint may contain 71 g (2½ oz.) approx.
A switch of hair should contain hair weighing not more than 21—28 g (¾—1 oz.) in each stem.
226 g or 0·226 kg equals the weight of ½ lb. of reconditioning cream.

Temperature

		ice	steam
degree Celcius (°C.)	scale range	0°C.	— 100°C.
degree Centigrade (°C.)	scale range	0°C.	— 100°C.
degree Kelvin (K.)	scale range	273·15K.	— 373·15K.
degree Fahrenheit (°F.)	scale range	32°F.	— 212°F.

1°C. = 1°K.   32°F. = 0°C.
Normal body temperature is 37°C. (98·4°F.)
Rules for converting thermometer scales:
F. to C. = minus 32, multiply by 5, and divide by 9
C. to F. = multiply by 9, divide by 5, and add 32.

Electrical terms

Unit of electrical current	= ampere (A)
Unit of electric force	= volt (V)
Unit of electric power	= watt (W)
Unit of electrical resistance	= ohm
1 kilowatt = 1000 watts	= 1 kW
1 kilowatt hour (kWh)	= work done by 1 kW maintained for 1 hour.

The relationship between electrical current amperage, electric force or voltage, and electric power or wattage may be expressed as follows:

$$\text{Watts} = \text{volts} \times \text{amps} \qquad \text{Amps} = \frac{\text{watts}}{\text{volts}} \qquad \text{Volts} = \frac{\text{watts}}{\text{amps}}$$

A hair dryer of 750 W on a supply of 250 V will require a fuse of 3 A $\left(A = \frac{W}{V} \text{ or } \frac{750\ W}{250\ V} = 3 \text{ amps}\right)$.

Costing the amount of power consumed consists of dividing the total wattage by 1000 to arrive at the number of kW, multiplied by the number of hours used to determine the number of kWh, the unit of electricity costing, and finally multiplied by the rate per unit.

e.g. Six dryers of 750 watts each are run for 2 days, eight hours a day. Total consumption =

$$750 \times 6 = \frac{4500}{1000} = 4{\cdot}5 \text{ kW} \times 2 \times 8 - 72 \text{ kWh or units. 72 units at 3p per } 4{\cdot}5 \text{ unit} = £2{\cdot}16.$$

Metric divisions

Length

$$1 \textit{ millimetre (mm)}$$
10 mm = 1 centimetre (cm)
10 cm = 1 decimetre (dm)
10 dm = 1 *metre* (m)
1000 m = 1 *kilometre* (km)

Square measure

$$1 \textit{ square millimetre } (mm^2)$$
100 mm^2 = 1 *square centimetre* (cm^2)
100 cm^2 = 1 square decimetre (dm^2)
100 dm^2 = 1 *square metre* (m^2)

Large square measure

100 m^2 = 1 are (a)
100 a = 1 *hectare* (ha)
100 ha = 1 square kilometre (km^2)

Cubic measure

1000 *cubic millimetres* (mm^3) = 1 cubic centimetre (cm^3)
1000 cm^3 = 1 cubic decimetre (dm^3)
1000 dm^3 = 1 *cubic metre*

Dry and liquid measure

$$1 \text{ cubic } \textit{millilitre } (ml^3)$$
10 millilitres (ml^3) = 1 centilitre
10 centilitres = 1 decilitre
10 decilitres = 1 *litre*
100 litres   = 1 hectolitre

Weight

$$1 \text{ milligramme (mg)}$$
10 milligrammes (mg) = 1 centigramme (cg)
10 cg = 1 decigramme (dg)
10 dg = 1 *gramme* (g)
1000 g = 1 *kilogramme* (kg)
1000 kg = 1 tonne

Italicized units are those recommended by the Système International d'Unités, known as S.I. units.

Safety Factors in the Salon

Generally precautions must be taken with chemicals, equipment, tools, personal and general hygiene to safeguard the public, and those who work in close contact, from dangers and abuses.

Chemicals in any form, e.g. perm lotions, tint creams, or raw chemicals used to make salon preparations, e.g. acids, alkalis, detergents, etc., must be correctly stored and clearly labelled.

They should all be treated as caustic, corrosive or poisonous and stored well away from children and juniors.

Never use containers which may be used for eating or drinking, e.g. cups, dishes, milk bottles, to store or dispense them.

Many substances and products lose strength and become ineffective after a while, and should be date-stamped when stored.

Do not be tempted to use products which have lost their labels or whose labels have been disfigured.

When mixing chemicals or products do not allow them to drip or splash, and do not bend over them to breathe in or expose the eyes, nose or throat to any dangerous fumes.

Make the correct dilutions and mixtures of substances according to the manufacturer's instructions. Do not allow these to remain in contact with a person longer than necessary.

Always make the necessary skin tests before the application of chemical products, e.g. tints.

Many chemicals and products are inflammable and must be kept away from naked flames or excessive heat. Good ventilation is necessary when they are being mixed or used.

Care and common sense must be exercised when dealing with any chemical product. If in doubt, check with someone who knows and understands what might happen through mishandling.

A good hairdresser will know her products, their effects and results, and will always use them safely.

Electrical equipment must be correctly installed, checked and passed fit for use, and periodically examined by qualified electricians.

Always check the plug, flex and sockets for signs of wear which must be repaired or reported.

Do not overload the supply by plugging too many pieces of equipment into one socket; this can cause overheating and fusing.

Avoid using equipment with wet hands, on a wet floor, or near water pipes and containers, as this may cause shock.

Never leave clients alone when they are under any electrical machine.

Do not allow wires or flex to trail dangerously over other equipment or loosely over the floor; this can cause accidents.

In the event of equipment breaking down, switch off the electricity supply at once, and disconnect the machine before examining and reconnecting the supply.

Use all electrical equipment as recommended by the manufacturers, e.g. high-frequency machines, massage and beauty equipment.

Unplug all electrical equipment, or disconnect from the mains supply, and store portable apparatus in dry clean cupboards.

Steamers and accelerators must be checked before applying to clients; they must not be too hot and they must be clean, particularly after using with tints.

Tools must always be clean and never placed in overall pockets. This is unhygienic and dangerous, e.g. scissors can fall on to feet or stab the body when bending.

Broken tools must not be used; they are a source of infection and dangerous, e.g. broken teeth on clippers may cause bad skin cuts if used.

Professional tools, specially made for hairdressers' use, are to be recommended, e.g. poor-finished combs can scratch and tear skin badly and break the hair.

Always protect the edges of sharp tools, i.e. razors, by placing in suitable cases or covers, and do not attempt to use them unless capable of applying them correctly.

Personal and general hygiene plays an important part in the safety and health of all concerned in the salon.

It is pleasant, and hygienic, for body freshness to be maintained by regular bathing and change of clothes.

Teeth should be regularly maintained by brushing and being checked by the dentist to prevent decay and bad breath. Eyestrain can be the cause of headaches and should be checked by an optician.

Shoes must be comfortable and regularly changed. Do not make a habit of wearing high heels outside the salon and very low ones when working; the strain on leg muscles can be too much. Change socks, tights or stockings regularly.

Hands and fingernails must always be clean. Wash them before and after attending a client. Do not scrub them but dry them gently by patting with a soft towel. Use skin and protective barrier creams or rubber gloves where possible. Nail varnish should be unchipped and maintained regularly.

The body must be free of disease or infection, and where there is any doubt a visit to the doctor is indicated.

Protect open wounds with suitable coverings and never expose others to infection.

The hair and skin must be clean. Hair must not be allowed to fall over the face and eyes, and never on to a client. This is both unhygienic and dangerous. Long hair must be suitably dressed or secured. Make-up must always be unimpaired and tastefully applied.

Loose, dangling or jingling ornaments or jewellery should be avoided for wear in the salon, e.g. pendants, bangles, etc., as they may cause accidents and irritate clients.

The salon should be well decorated, ventilated and lit. It should not be too steamy, hot, cold or draughty.

There should be no loose floor covers, or a too highly polished floor, on which it may be possible to slip and fall.

Loose hair or other material should not be allowed to accumulate on the floor or in corners of the salon. It should be moved to covered bins, then emptied in the dustbins outside, as soon as possible.

Stairways and passages to and from the salon must be well lit and uncluttered.

Suitable fire extinguishers should be available, e.g. fire blankets and carbon dioxide extinguishers, for use in the event of fire. If fire breaks out, vacate the salon immediately and warn others nearby. The fire brigade should be called at once.

A first-aid kit should be available and regularly maintained and replenished. In the event of serious accident the hospital or doctor should be informed immediately.

Thoroughly examine the hair and scalp before the application of any hairdressing treatment. If there are signs of infection, or if there is anything doubtful present, the manager or senior should be immediately informed, and hairdressing should not be carried out.

The ability to recognize common infections of the hair and skin is a valuable means of preventing the spread of infection. Infectious conditions must not be treated in the salon or by anyone other than a doctor.

Hydrogen Peroxide Percentage Strengths

A. Dilution of 30% (100 vol) hydrogen peroxide

30% H_2O_2	+	H_2O	=	100 ml H_2O_2		
10 ml	+	90 ml	=	3%	or	(10 vol)
20 ml	+	90 ml	=	6%	or	(20 vol)
30 ml	+	70 ml	=	9%	or	(30 vol)
40 ml	+	60 ml	=	12%	or	(40 vol)
50 ml	+	50 ml	=	15%	or	(50 vol)
60 ml	+	40 ml	=	18%	or	(60 vol)
70 ml	+	30 ml	=	21%	or	(70 vol)
80 ml	+	20 ml	=	24%	or	(80 vol)
90 ml	+	10 ml	=	27%	or	(90 vol)
100 ml	+	0 ml	=	30%	or	(100 vol)

B. Hydrogen peroxide dilution table

% strength (H_2O_2)	Parts H_2O_2		Parts H_2O		% strengths produced
30%	3	+	2	=	18%
30%	2	+	3	=	12%
30%	3	+	7	=	9%
30%	1	+	4	=	6%
30%	1	+	9	=	3%
18%	2	+	1	=	12%
18%	1	+	1	=	9%
18%	1	+	2	=	6%
18%	1	+	5	=	3%
12%	3	+	1	=	9%
12%	1	+	1	=	6%
12%	1	+	3	=	3%
9%	2	+	1	=	6%
9%	1	+	2	=	3%
6%	1	+	1	=	3%
3%	1	+	2	=	1%

C. Examples

30 ml of 12% (40 vol) H_2O_2 + 10 ml H_2O = 40 ml 9% (30 vol) H_2O_2

20 ml of 9% (30 vol) H_2O_2 + 10 ml H_2O = 30 ml 6% (20 vol) H_2O_2

20 ml of 12% (40 vol) H_2O_2 + 20 ml H_2O = 40 ml 6% (20 vol) H_2O_2

Index